HOW DANTE

CAN SAVE

YOUR LIFE

HOW DANTE CAN SAVE YOUR LIFE

The Life-Changing Wisdom of
History's Greatest Poem

———

ROD DREHER

Regan Arts.

To Julie, my Beatrice

DANTE ALICHIERI

It is well that endless be his grief
who, for love of things that do not last,
casts off a love that never dies.

—*Paradiso* XV:10–12

**Regan
Arts.**

65 Bleecker Street
New York, NY 10012

First Regan Arts hardcover edition, April 2015.

Interior illustrations by Gustave Doré

Library of Congress Control Number: 2014955527
ISBN 978-1-941393-32-1

Interior design by Daniel Lagin
Jacket design by Richard Ljoenes

Printed in the United States of America

10   9   8   7   6   5   4   3   2   1

CONTENTS

INTRODUCTION

WHY DANTE?

——

*A Fourteenth-Century Poem
for a Twenty-First-Century Life*

I don't much like poetry. Never have. Which makes what happened to me when I stumbled into Dante Alighieri's *Divine Comedy* all the more miraculous.

Dante's epic saved my life.

This medieval masterpiece, perhaps the greatest poem ever written, reached me when I thought I was unreachable, and lit the way out of a dark wood of depression, confusion, and a stress-related autoimmune disease that, had it persisted, would have dangerously degraded my health.

Dante helped me understand the mistakes and mistaken beliefs that brought me to this dead end. He showed me that I had the power to change, and revealed to me how to do so. Most important of all, the poet gave me a renewed vision of life.

Maybe you think about the *Divine Comedy*—if you think of it at all—as one of those great books you ought to have read but never got around to. Or maybe you did read it in high school or college and didn't really understand what the big deal was. This was me in the summer of 2013: a middle-aged man, lost and struggling, who never imagined a fourteenth-century poem would have anything to do with his twenty-first-century life.

Little did I know that Dante Alighieri, the failed Tuscan politician beggared by exile, knew me better than I knew myself. *La Divina Commedia*, as his poem is called in the original Italian, is radical stuff. You will not be the same after reading it. How could you be? All of life is in there.

Dante's tale is a fantasy about a lost man who finds his way back to life after walking through the pits of hell, climbing up the mountain of purgatory, and ascending to the heights of heaven. But it's really a story about real life and the incredible journey of our lives, yours and mine.

The *Commedia* is a seven-hundred-year-old poem honored as a pinnacle of Western civilization. But it's also a practical guide to living, one that promises rescue, restoration, and freedom. This book, *How Dante Can Save Your Life*, tells the story of how the treasures of wisdom buried in the *Commedia*'s 14,233 lines gave me a rich new life.

Though the *Commedia* was written by a faithful Catholic, its message is universal. You don't have to be a Catholic, or any sort of believer, to love it and to be changed by it. And though mine is a book that's ultimately about learning to live with God, it is not a book of religious apologetics; it is a book about finding our own true path. Like the *Commedia* it celebrates, this book is for believers who struggle to hold on to their faith when religious institutions have lost credibility. It's a book for people who have lost faith in love, in other people, in the family, in politics, in their careers, and in the possibility of worldly success. Dante has been there too. He gets it.

This is a book about sin, but not sin in the clichéd, pop-culture sense of rule breaking and naughtiness. In Dante, sin is the kind of thing that keeps us from flourishing and living up to our fullest potential, and it's also the kind of thing that savages marriages, turns neighbor against neighbor, destroys families, and ruins lives. And sin is not, at heart, a violation of a legalistic code, but rather a distortion of love. In Dante, sinners—and we are all sinners—are those who love the wrong things, or who love the right things in the wrong way. I had never thought about sin like that. This concept unlocked the door to a prison in which I had been living all my life. The cell opened from the inside, but I had not been able to see it.

This is a book about exile. What does it mean to know you can never go home? This was Dante's dilemma—and in a different sense, it was mine. Three years ago, when I returned after nearly three decades to live in my Louisiana hometown, I thought I had ended a restless journey that had taken me all over America, searching for a place where I could be settled and content. To my shock and heartbreak, I was wrong. The most difficult journey lay ahead of me: the journey within myself. Dante showed me the way through. He can do the same for you.

Until a few years back, I had never read the *Odyssey* and never thought to do so, except in the eat-your-broccoli sense that all cultured Westerners must eventually read Homer. When my young son Matthew's class took up the ancient Greek epic, I read along with him. It turned out to be one of the most thrilling intellectual adventures of my life, one that was even more pleasurable because it was a voyage I made with my son.

Matt and I talked constantly about how the challenges the hero, Odysseus, faced are like those we contend with in our own lives. When Matt and I were deep in conversation, the world of the *Odyssey* seemed more real than our own. Reading the *Commedia* was like that too. Great art speaks with wisdom and authority to what is eternal in the human condition. If we can learn to see these artworks with fresh eyes, they can help us to understand our own lives and worlds in new ways.

The *Commedia* is a work of awesome complexity, a labyrinth of spiritual, moral, philosophical, and psychological insight. It has inspired poets, clergy, and scholars for seven centuries. But it is also meant for common readers. Dante wrote his masterpiece not in Latin but in the language of the people, because he wanted ordinary folks to follow him on the pilgrimage out of the dark wood and into the light of the starry heavens. The *Commedia* is a work of the highest art, and it is also immensely practical.

For the poem to work its magic on the reader, it has to be taken up into the moral imagination in a personal way. You have to engage in dialogue with our Florentine guide along the pilgrim's path. When I gave myself over to him, I found that Dante is not a remote figure from an alien world but a warm companion with whom I had far more in common than

I could have imagined. He is simply a fellow wayfarer who has seen great things, both terrifying and glorious, along life's way, and wants to tell you all about it.

A caution: if you are looking for a scholarly book introducing Dante and the *Commedia* as a work of literature, *How Dante Can Save Your Life* is not for you. This is not a literary analysis, it is a personal view. It's a self-help book for people who may not read self-help books, but who are curious and delight in journeys of self-discovery along roads not often taken. Nothing would make me happier than for you to finish this book and take up the *Commedia*—but it's not strictly necessary.

I must warn you about something else before we continue. Many people lost in their own dark wood may convince themselves that the dark wood is all there is, that the journey of life is without direction, and that it can best be endured by taking one's pleasures where one can. The world is full of those willing to dissuade you from this arduous pilgrimage to liberty, love, and happiness. And it is true: there is no easy way out.

Some people, though, know in their hearts that staying put is to surrender to slavery. They have eyes to see the sunlight through the forbidding canopy and ears to hear the voice of a trustworthy guide calling them to take the hard road to true freedom. The *Commedia* invites you to stand up, get moving, and become the hero of your own life. Go into the deep, find out who you are, discover who you can be, and return to your everyday life changed—maybe even saved.

It happened to me. It can happen to you too. If you want to be a hero, I say to you, as Virgil said to the pilgrim Dante, "Let us go. The long road urges us."

Onward!

HOW DANTE
CAN SAVE
YOUR LIFE

PART I

FROM THE GARDEN
TO THE DARK WOOD

1

THE CHILD IS FATHER
TO THE MAN

My lady, therefore, who saw that I was freed
from staring upward, said: "Cast your sight below
and see how wide a circle you have traveled."

—*Paradiso* XXVII:76–78

How Family and Place Shape a Life

Florence has the Arno; Starhill has the Mississippi. Aside from that, the fields and orchards of the rural Louisiana settlement where my family has lived for five generations is about as far from the Tuscan capital as any place in the Western world.

This is the story of that place, and of two men who grew up there and whose lives have been defined by its traditions: my father and me.

Ours is a southern family, and that means one steeped in history and tradition, especially among the men. My father, Ray Oliver Dreher, named his only son after himself; he and my mother, Dorothy, called me "Rod," after my initials. Daddy wanted nothing more in this world than a son, a vessel into which he could pour all his considerable knowledge.

If there was something about the parish of West Feliciana—in Louisiana, counties are called parishes—that Ray Dreher did not know, it was probably not worth knowing. He had grown up in Starhill during the Depression in a cabin he shared with his mother, grandmother, and older brother, Murphy junior. Their father, Murphy senior, was on the road for much of Daddy's childhood, working on highway construction crews throughout the state to send what he could back home to his young family. The Dreher boys raised livestock to keep the family fed, but some lean nights, if they hadn't shot squirrels with their air rifles that afternoon, there was no meat in the pot.

My father never told these stories to me as a recollection of misery. To the contrary, these memories were dear to him. Daddy learned about his world through his family and through the land—woods and ponds, swamps and fields, bayous and rivers. And he loved that land. Even before he was old enough to drive, he bought a patch of Starhill farmland and a tractor and began to till the soil. This was Ray Dreher's land, and the land was Ray Dreher. He was a high school football star, a raiser of 4-H Club champion steers, an accomplished deer hunter, and a self-taught mechanic who applied his powerful intelligence to fixing anything. He believed there was nothing he could not conquer with sufficient force of will.

Perhaps he learned that from his mother. Raising two boys and caring for a mother-in-law in rural poverty, without a husband at home, was not easy for Lorena. The Dreher boys fought constantly. Ray was younger, but barrel-chested and strong. Murphy was skinny and clever. Unable to stop their backyard scrapping, Lorena gave her boys boxing gloves one Christmas in the hope that they wouldn't hurt each other too severely.

Murphy junior almost always started the fights; he teased the combustible Ray constantly. Ray came to think of his brother as a wily trickster who lived by his wits. But in the schoolyard, whenever Murphy junior got in a fight, even though he usually started them himself, Ray always joined the scrum in defense of his brother.

When he would tell me these stories as a boy, I couldn't make sense of them. "Why did you fight for him?" I would ask. "He started it. And he was mean to you at home."

"Honey, that's what family does," he would respond, as if I had wanted to know why water ran downhill. No matter how they treat you or you treat them, loyalty to family is the natural law.

Ray Dreher was intelligent, but he was not a scholar. He hated books, and hated to be indoors at all. He preferred to work with his hands. In the 1950s he went to Louisiana State University on the GI Bill because his mother wanted him to be the first in their family to earn a college degree. Every weekend he made the thirty-mile journey north from Baton Rouge to get back to Starhill and his land.

When he graduated, Ray came home to Starhill and began working as a state health inspector. In a rural parish like West Feliciana, that meant that he had the opportunity to help a number of poor country people bring running water into their houses. He knew all the back roads of the parish, and most of the people who lived on them. During deer season, he would take his rifle and head with his buddies into the Fancy Point swamp, along the banks of the Mississippi. When he married my mother, Dorothy, in 1964, she, like many West Feliciana women of her generation, had to accept that for weekends in the late fall and early winter, she would lose her husband to the hunting camp. That was just the way it was; the idea that anything could or should be different was scarcely conceivable.

I tell you all this because Ray Dreher brought into this world a lone son, an heir to his kingdom who was ambivalent at best about the role tradition assigned to him. I was a bookish child who preferred to get lost in my storybooks instead of the swamp. My father has said many times that he did not know how to deal with me. Most boys in the rural South could only dream of having a father like mine, one who loved sports, hunting, and fishing, who knew how to build anything, and who was loving. His father had been on the road for much of his childhood and emotionally distant when he was at home. Daddy was determined to give his son the paternal love and attention he had been denied.

When I was a boy, very little mattered as much to me as making Daddy proud. I loved my mother, but I worshiped my father. He was the center of our family's life, and for my sister and me, he was the center of the universe. He was the sun around which Mama, my sister, Ruthie, and I orbited, and this too was a natural law of our family.

This was much easier for my sister to accept than for me. She was just like Daddy. Alas, I was a weird little kid, and Ray Dreher was not built for weird.

Before I started kindergarten, I had a habit of naming myself after characters in my favorite books. For the longest time, I would only answer to "Pedro," the name of a burro in one of those books. My father finally had enough of this nonsense and asked me where he could find the little boy Rod that he and Mama had brought home from the hospital.

"He's in the top of the sweet olive tree at Loisie and Mossie's," I said.

Daddy marched me through the pecan orchard to the antebellum cottage where Aunt Lois Simmons and her widowed sister, Aunt Hilda Moss, lived in retirement. They were ancient, wise, and well traveled: both had been born in Starhill in the final decade of the nineteenth century but had served as Red Cross nurses in France during the Great War and had lived cosmopolitan lives before returning to the country for their final years. I loved them both.

Neither woman had children, but they were revered as matriarchs of the clan. Daddy had a special affection for Loisie, who had financed his boyhood 4-H Club trips and shown him something of the world outside West Feliciana.

I adored them because they doted on their eccentric great-grand-nephew and taught me about art, books, and European travel. I would sit on their red leather couch under three framed first-edition Audubon prints, reading the daily newspaper and listening to them explain far-away places—Paris, Dijon, Moscow, Tegucigalpa, New Orleans—and people with strange names like Brezhnev and Kissinger.

Daddy, on the other hand, would stand in the woods and try to teach me how to recognize the presence of a whitetail buck by antler rubbings on a sapling. But my mind was perpetually lost on the Western Front, on Esplanade Avenue in New Orleans, or in any number of magical places I visited every time I walked through the door of the old aunts' tin-roofed cottage, nestled under the protecting canopy of a pink-blossomed Chinese rain tree. Daddy thought they were making a sissified book-worm out of me, and he fretted greatly over this.

On the afternoon Pedro was to meet his doom, Loisie and Mossie watched from their front porch as Ray stood under the sweet olive tree with me, trying to make the four-year-old kid see reality. Daddy pointed to the crown of the fragrant tree and told me to observe that no one was there.

"Rod!" I called out. "Ro-o-o-d! Come down!" Finally I said, "Daddy, he's not coming."

"Keep calling."

I kept calling. At last I walked over to the base of the tree and started shaking it, trying to loosen Rod's grip on the upper branches. My father's face turned as fiery red as his hair. The old aunts tittered. He grabbed me by the arm and said gruffly, "Come on, we're going home."

In my family, that story became a legendary example of how vexing it was for Ray to deal with me. I laughed at it too for many years. And then decades later, from the bottom of my depression, I saw it in a different light. It appeared to me as a story in which my father tried with disproportionate vigor to compel me to see the world his way.

There has never been a time in my life when I have not acutely felt that I was disappointing my father. Something mysterious was turning in my depths during the Pedro era. I did a finger painting titled "For My Daddy" and signed it "Pedro." It is dark and turbulent. My father pinned it to his bulletin board at work, where his boss, a physician with the state health department, spotted it on one of his periodic visits.

"It looks like someone lost in the woods at night, trying to find the light," he told Daddy, and suggested taking me to a child psychiatrist. My parents did as they were told, but the visit was inconclusive. When he asked, I told the shrink that the painting was so dark because I had run out of bright colors. That's the story my parents tell, and maybe it is true, but when I look at the painting today, I find that explanation implausible.

Fortunately for my father, Ruthie, who was born two years after me, was the son he never had. She was a strawberry-blond tomboy, a country girl who loved all the country things and, more than anything, being with her daddy. Before she was out of diapers, Ruthie would go with Daddy to mend fences in the pastures behind our place; I would stay home with my head in a book, or hide out talking with Loisie and Mossie. Ruthie excelled at sports; I floundered. Ruthie loved being with the men skinning buck deer after the hunt and poking through an animal's guts to learn how its digestive system worked; I, with my queasy stomach and tender heart toward animals, couldn't take it.

We were both straight-A students, but Ruthie earned her grades through hard work and grit; academics came much more easily for me. Ruthie was socially at ease and friends with everyone; I was anxious and insecure. When we were teenagers, Ruthie was all about cowboy boots and Hank Williams Jr., while I was into thrift-store paisley shirts and the Talking Heads. You see where this is going.

Despite those fault lines, ours was a close family. Mama, ever the conciliator, never played favorites. Daddy tried not to, though his personality was so strong he could not easily conceal his preferences. Our family had peace whenever our wills were aligned with Daddy's. This was fairly easy to do, because he showered Ruthie and me with so much love and care that we wanted to do as he expected.

When I'm working till late in the evening on a deadline and hear myself telling my children no, I can't play a game with them because I'm busy, I think of how Ruthie and I never heard that kind of thing from our dad. He built a pond on our place, and on the weekends he took us fishing there. There wasn't a ball game of ours he missed (often he was coaching). "Hey, podna, get your glove," he would say to me, and we would go into the backyard and toss the baseball for an hour or so.

Cooking, cleaning, and managing the household were Mama's realm; Daddy took care of everything outside the house and on the farm. Mama drove a school bus, and no matter how cold or rainy it was outside, Daddy was awake early to get the bus warmed up, and on some mornings he'd heat buttered honey buns for Ruthie and me to eat when we padded into the kitchen.

We had wood in our fireplace because Daddy chopped it. When things broke around the house, Daddy fixed them, and he did repair work for other family members too. One gray winter day, he hung on a ladder out over the bayou, fixing a cracked water pipe for his mother and father. Daddy had told them to drip the line, but they forgot. It didn't matter; Ray would fix it. There didn't seem to be anything my father could not do, or would not do to help others.

When I think of the greatest gift he gave to my sister and me, I remember the many nights we would clamber into his lap as he sat in his Naugahyde-covered recliner just before bedtime. We would each claim a shoulder and snuggle close, the aroma of black coffee and tobacco and sweat from the labors of the day strong on him. He would ask us about our days, tell us about his, and talk to us about right and wrong. There was no worry we could not bring to him and no dilemma he could not resolve.

I swear Ruthie and I thought he held the world up on his big, broad shoulders. In Daddy's arms, Ruthie and I felt safe, loved, and at home in the world.

Unsurprisingly, Ruthie and I fought a lot, and like Murphy junior a generation earlier, I was almost always the instigator. Ruthie had a sweet nature but a hot temper, and I knew exactly which buttons to push to get a reaction. She was a smart girl, but her gifts were in mathematics and science, not the language arts. I was a clever rascal and could tie Ruthie up in knots with my teasing. The goal was to make her so mad she balled up her fat little fists and lit into me. I was bigger than she was and would curl up on the ground and absorb her blows, laughing the whole time—which only made her angrier.

These incidents brought forth from my father the Murphy-and-him fight stories, the telling of which always ended with a warning that we ought to show each other more love than that. He was right, of course, but our sibling rivalry didn't break our family's unity; the tumult of my teenage years did that.

I was not a bad kid, just a peculiar one by the narrow standards of my outdoorsy family. To my father, that was a distinction without a difference. The world of books and the imagination was more important to me than the mundane world I actually inhabited. On Sunday afternoons in

the late fall, Daddy would load the family in the car and cruise the country back roads looking for deer. "Get your head out of that book," he
would inevitably bark at me in the back seat.

To him, preferring the world of ideas to the natural world was no
mere aberration on my part. It was personal, and constituted a failure to
love. If I loved as I ought to love, I would desire the things he desired.

I cannot recall what issues began the cold war between my father and
me, but these clashes were always fundamentally about the same thing:
that I was not like him. We had intense arguments in which I would dis-
agree with him about something—usually matters of politics, history,
culture, or religion—and he would accuse me of calling him a liar.

"I'm not calling you a liar," I would say. "I'm just disagreeing with
you. This is not a matter of factual truth; it's a matter of opinion."

He couldn't grasp this concept. I remember standing in the living
room during one angry exchange, his face as tight as a fist, his eyes scan-
ning me, as if he were waiting for my skin to pull back and reveal the alien
underneath. "I don't know how I got a son like you," he spat.

Well, I thought, *neither do I.* It frightened me to see him like this.
Aside from a handful of spankings in childhood, my father never hit me,
or even threatened to. Yet he stood ten feet from me in the living room,
looking like he wanted to fight or run away. I didn't understand how calm
disagreement about intellectual matters could undo him like that. His
temper scared me in the moment, and later it made me furious.

It genuinely wounded Daddy to have his son question his opinion.
During one of our exchanges, he eyed me uncomprehendingly and said
with deep sadness in his voice, "Son, I'm your daddy. Why would I lie to
you?"

The door closed firmly on my childhood one late autumn day in 1981,
when I was fourteen. Daddy asked Ruthie and me to go squirrel hunting
with him in the nearby fields. As usual, I did not want to go; as usual,
I went. Shotgun in hand, I walked off into one field, a small and heavily
wooded enclosure that resembled an enclosed garden. He and Ruthie
ambled into another over the ridge. Walking the forested fencerow scan-
ning the treetops for gray and red squirrels, I spotted a big one all but

flying through the crowns of pin oaks. I raised my gun, fired, and watched not one but two bodies fall from the height of the tree.

I ran to them, and immediately saw that these were two young squirrels, not much more than babies, who had been running so close together in the treetop that they looked like a single adult. One was dead, but the other was still alive, its eyes clouding, a mist of blood spraying out its nose with each wheezing breath.

I froze in horror. I had killed many squirrels before, and some were not fully dead when they fell from the tree. I would pick them up by their tails and bash their skulls against a tree to put them out of their misery. It was unpleasant but no big thing.

This time was different. For some reason, I looked into the black beads framing the animal's bloody nose, and I saw suffering. It was scared and in pain—and I had caused this to happen. And for what?

If I had never let my gaze meet the dying squirrel's, I don't know what the trajectory of my life would have been. I might have beaten the creature's brains in as a mercy killing and would have grimaced, but only that. I did look, though, and when I grabbed the squirrel's tail and brought its head down on my gunstock with a sickening crack, I felt something break inside me.

I threw my shotgun on the ground where the two squirrels' bodies lay and sat down in a slough of self-loathing. Those animals had died because I lacked the courage to tell my father that I did not want to hunt. I couldn't do this anymore. I had no moral qualms about hunting itself, but I had no stomach for it—and this filled me with shame. Daddy wanted me to be a hunter, but I was no hunter. I was a fraud. I put my head on my knees and began to cry.

Suddenly Daddy and Ruthie were standing over me. "What's wrong?" Daddy asked. "Are you okay? Are you hurt?"

"I'm fine," I said, looking up with a face swollen from crying. "I shot those baby squirrels. They were just babies."

I looked up from the ground at my father and my sister. Ruthie burst into laughter. Daddy screwed his face up in disgust and growled, "You *sissy.*"

A thick iron gate slammed shut within me, and from behind it I regarded my father with cold contempt. He had struck me where he could do the most damage: my sense of manhood. I followed him and my sister out of the field, my face on fire, this time not with shame but with wrath. And from that moment on, I saw him not as my champion. I saw him as my adversary.

In school that fall semester, bullies had begun pushing me around; it would continue nonstop for two years. My folks were sympathetic at first, but after a while my father, who had been elected the most popular boy in his high school, began chastising me for being so weird that I surely must be setting myself up as a target for others.

Many years later, Daddy told me that he and Mama were worried at the time that I was going to kill myself. Yet he behaved as if there was nothing wrong with me that couldn't be mended by pressing me harder with his formidable will.

Mama saved me. Desperate for escape, I applied to a new public boarding school in north Louisiana, an academy for gifted kids. The academics interested me, but above all I wanted to run away. Neither one of my parents wanted their firstborn to leave home at sixteen. Daddy was afraid he would lose control of me, but Mama fought him.

"If we don't let him go, we're going to lose him," I overheard her say to him once. I don't know what my mother said behind closed doors, but she must have taken a strong, brave stand, for while Ray Dreher did not lose arguments in his house, he lost this one.

In those days, a car ferry took motorists across the Mississippi from West Feliciana to the next parish over. On a scorching day in August 1983, I stood on the deck of the ferry with my parents, who were driving me to the school, and I watched the banks of my home parish recede in the distance. *Goodbye,* I thought, and for the first time in ages I was happy.

Thirty years later, after spending most of my life living away from Louisiana, but having recently moved back for good, I sat in a rheumatologist's office in Baton Rouge, and received his verdict: if I didn't leave this place, the anxiety churning within me, a force I could not conquer, was going to destroy my health.

I would not leave, not this time. I was through running away. Now, if I was going to be saved, I would have to go within. It had taken me three decades of moving all over the country to see this.

HOW TO STOP RUNNING AWAY

Every part of yourself—what you love, what you hate, your sense of right and wrong, your self-esteem, and all that is great and base within your character—has its beginning in the people and the places of your youth. In your childhood, you learn the stories that explain the world and how to live in it.

As you grow older, you lose that sense of primal unity and order. It's common for people to spend the rest of their lives, one way or another, trying to return to its certainties, or to find new certainties to replace the old ones. It can't be done. Face it: the story that made sense for you as a child no longer does, nor does any equally simple, naïve story. Stop wasting your life trying to find a state of perfection that does not exist.

You can take the geographical cure, moving far away from home as an adult in hope of putting the problems of childhood behind you, but it's not going to work. Until you successfully complete the interior journey toward maturity, you will find that wherever you go—and whoever you marry, whatever your salary, however great your fame, whatever you drink or snort, and whatever you truly worship—there you are. The same miserable, maimed man or woman. It's time to stop running away. The answers and the peace you seek are within you. Go there, with eyes wide open.

2

THERE AND BACK
AGAIN — TWICE

You shall leave behind all you most dearly love,
and that shall be the arrow
first loosed from exile's bow.

—Paradiso XVII:55–57

North Toward Home—and Rome

Though I would stay at my parents' house for holidays and during summer vacations, I never really lived at home again. The resentment between Daddy and me grew as I gained independence. After I left, Ruthie became her class valedictorian and the homecoming queen. She fell in love with a local boy named Mike Leming, whom she would eventually marry. Ruthie spent all her free time with Mike, fishing and hunting and doing things that made sense to our dad.

I was rarely around, and when I was, I was even more of an enigma than before I had left for boarding school. Truth to tell, I can easily imagine that I was an arrogant jerk to my family back then. With my hair hanging over my eyes, my earring, and my New Wave music, I thought I was so much cooler than them, and repaid their harsh judgment of me with plenty of scorn of my own. I'm not proud of that, but I have to own it.

Ruthie and I ended up at Louisiana State University together. We lived in neighboring dorms, but we rarely saw each other. True to form, she was the diligent student who went to all her classes, worked hard, and kept a high GPA. I was the party-hearty college journalist and philosophy geek who favored late nights at the *Daily Reveille* followed by drinks at the bar. I made A's in the classes I loved, and barely passed in those I did not.

Around the same time, Daddy had tried to interest me in becoming a Freemason, as generations of men in my family had been. *Sorry,* I said, *it's not my thing,* and then I forgot about it. I'm sure he did not, and that he took it to heart as another instance of his ungrateful son turning his back on tradition.

In college, I rejected his conservative politics and became a campus liberal activist. When my photo appeared on the front page of the Baton Rouge newspaper carrying a sign protesting U.S. policy in Central America, Daddy called and demanded that I come home to talk to him. We argued hotly, not about the merits of the issue but (once again) about how, for God's sake, a man like him had gotten a son like me. To my dad, I wasn't rejecting Ronald Reagan. I was rejecting Ray Dreher.

After I graduated in 1989, the Baton Rouge newspaper offered me a job, and I took it. Two years later, Ruthie, who by then had married Mike, graduated and returned to West Feliciana to teach sixth grade in the same school where we had studied as children. We knew very little about each other's lives.

As a newly minted journalist with a paycheck that allowed me to buy imported beer for once, I was having a blast—writing by day, drinking and carousing by night. Eventually I bottomed out in my personal life and realized that if I didn't find God, I was going to ruin my own life and maybe even the lives of others.

I had been feeling a slow, steady pull back toward the Christian faith, which as a young teenager I had set aside as something that was hard to believe and incompatible with the freedom I wanted to have. I had lost the mild, neighborly Methodism in which I was raised, and though not hostile to religion, I didn't see it as important. However on a coach trip through Europe as a seventeen-year-old (Mama had won the vacation in a church raffle and given it to me), a visit to Chartres cathedral struck down my callow concept of faith.

I was going through an intense Hemingway phase at the time and was focused on getting to Paris. The guide annoyed me by scheduling a two-hour stop at Chartres, just outside Paris, to see its medieval cathedral.

Resentful, I followed the tour group inside. The soaring towers anchoring the façade instantly dispelled my air of sullen impiety.

I saw—no, I think the word is *beheld*—the most wondrous thing in the world. This church was indescribably complex and harmonious; it was like stepping into the mind of God. I was overcome by the desire to worship—a feeling I would not see as adequately articulated until many years later, when I would read Dante Alighieri's description, in his first book, *Vita nuova*, of the first time he, as a child, saw Beatrice:

> At that very moment, and I speak the truth, the vital spirit, the one that dwells in the most secret chamber of the heart, began to tremble so violently that even the most minute veins of my body were strangely affected; and trembling, it spoke these words: "Here is a god stronger than I who is coming to rule over me."
>
> (Trans. Andrew Frisardi)

I left the building eager to know more about the kind of religion that created temples like this, works of art that could connect people so profoundly with the transcendent that it was like taking hold of a live wire. Our group motored on to Paris, and to this day I cannot remember a single thing about that part of the trip.

The beauty of Chartres haunted me. I did not understand this at the time, but God set the hook in me inside that cathedral. It was there that I began an ambivalent quest for him, not really wanting to find him, but also unable to deny the power of that revelation. I could not explain how I knew that he existed—I saw him and felt him and was overawed by him at Chartres.

The presence of God radiated from the Chartres cathedral so powerfully that it even pierced the dark wood into which I had retreated to escape my father, whom I loved and hated and could not quit. I knew God

was there; I had experienced him in that old church. As long as I held
Chartres in my imagination, there was hope.

This was the first time God rescued me from despair through a work
of art. As I discovered in the middle of the journey of my life, when I
ambled into the medieval cathedral in a verse called the *Commedia*, it
was the last. What's more, as I would learn much later, after walking with
Dante along a sorrowful way of repentance, the price he and I both paid for
misunderstanding what had been revealed to us in those life-changing
moments of our youth would be severe.

But all that would happen decades into the future. Eight years after
Chartres shook me to the core, I reached out in prayer to the God who had
spoken to me through the carved stone and stained glass of the cathedral.
Eventually I found a Catholic priest in Baton Rouge to instruct me.

Shortly after we began our lessons, I received a job offer from the
Washington Times newspaper in D.C. My big break, at last! Now I was
truly leaving home. In the summer of 1992, I said goodbye to Mama,
Daddy, and Ruthie and drove away in a U-Haul truck, headed northeast.
I knew that in my father's eyes, I wasn't embracing Washington and a
promising career as a journalist, I was rejecting Starhill, the family, and,
most of all, him.

Washington was everything I hoped it would be. I had great new
friends and a job I loved, and I was received into the Catholic Church. After
a year of my being away, though, Ruthie and Mike had their first child, a
daughter, Hannah. I thought about that kid and Starhill all the time.

Since I'd moved away, Daddy and I had quit arguing. Maybe now that
was all in the past. I handed in my resignation, packed another U-Haul,
and headed back south.

Slamming into the Glass Door

One Friday night, after I had been there for about six weeks, Daddy and
I were out driving down a country lane. "I'm so glad you came home,
son," he said. "You finally realized that I was right."

I didn't say a word, afraid of what might come out. I thought about what I had given up to come home. A journalism job in the capital. Good friends. Bookstores, coffee shops, movie houses, a city life I had long dreamed of. I hid my panic for the rest of the evening, but that night in bed I tossed until I could no longer stand it. I arose, dressed, and drove my old blue Chevy pickup into Baton Rouge, where I sat in an all-night coffee shop near the LSU campus and pondered my future.

The sun came up on the Feast of the Immaculate Conception. I was the first one in the church of St. Agnes downtown for the morning mass. I knelt at the communion rail and prayed for deliverance from this mistake. After mass, I drove back to Starhill and went to Ruthie's house, which she and Mike had recently completed in a grove across the yard from our folks' place. I found her and baby Hannah still under the covers on that chilly morning. I sat on the edge of their bed.

"What's wrong?" Ruthie said.

I told her, and broke down over the mess I had made of my life, trying to do right by my family. I told her I now knew I could never live around Daddy, because he could not keep himself from trying to control me.

"Why can't he just accept me like I am?" I said.

Ruthie just shook her head and cried. She and Daddy were quite close, but she was aware of how strong-willed and demanding he was. She knew that my situation was impossible.

Two months later, I was back at my desk in Washington, grateful for a second chance. Four years later, I was newly married and a film critic at the *New York Post*. My wife, Julie, and I were discovering the joy of married life and falling head over heels for New York: film screenings, picnics in Central Park, the Union Square Greenmarket, mass at St. Patrick's Cathedral, our favorite French café on Madison Avenue. This was my life now, and I thought I must be in a kind of paradise.

In retrospect, I think this is when I began to lose my sister. She was teaching math now to middle schoolers; I was going to movies for a living, interviewing Hollywood stars, and turning up on cable TV shows. When Julie and I visited Starhill, Ruthie would be polite, but she was increasingly on edge the longer we lingered. "How much did you pay for that fancy haircut?" she might say snippily. Or "I guess y'all aren't worried at all about buying a house"—as if renting were no better than throwing our money on the sidewalk and setting it on fire.

On the first Christmas after Julie and I were married, we returned from Manhattan to spend it with my Starhill family. I phoned in advance to ask if Julie and I could make a bouillabaisse for them one night. I explained that it was a fish and shellfish stew with tomato, garlic, and onion, just like they're used to in Louisiana. It was the first fancy dish Julie and I had learned to cook together, and we were eager to make a pot of it for them if they were game.

My folks said yes. Julie brought special stock from New York on the plane; and once down in Louisiana, we drove into Baton Rouge and spent an entire morning buying the fish, shrimp, and crabs. We cooked all afternoon, and even made the traditional roasted red pepper mayonnaise the French serve with it.

And then it was dinnertime. We set down the black iron cauldron on a trivet in the middle of the table, aromatic steam rising from the rich, saffron-tinted broth. Nobody would eat it. My father tried a couple of spoonfuls, but he was the only one who would go that far. Ruthie took the opportunity to praise a family friend for being "a good cook—a good *country* cook." Mama sat quietly.

They saw this gift of love my wife and I had prepared for them as nothing more than uppity Rod inflicting his snooty cosmopolitan tastes on them.

Julie was taken aback. Within me, confusion turned into humiliation, and then to anger. I held it in. It was Christmastime, and I did not want to fight with my family. All I wanted was to get back to New York as soon as I could.

Despite occasional incidents like that, we had a good relationship with the family back in Louisiana. It was much easier to love each other if we didn't have to be in one another's company more than two or three times a year. Distance made it possible for all of us to believe the stories we wanted to tell ourselves about our family, and not test them against reality.

Ruthie and Mike had another daughter, Claire, and a third, Rebekah.

Julie and I had our first child, Matthew—Daddy's first grandson. I thought about how much Matt would miss by growing up far from his grandfather. That old familiar longing came over me again, but there was no moving to Starhill now, not with a wife and a child to take care of.

Although we loved New York, we knew we couldn't afford to raise a growing family there. A year after 9/11, I landed a job at the *Dallas Morning News*, and we moved to Julie's hometown. This delighted my folks, who would be seeing a lot more of us now that we were within driving distance.

Over the next six years, we had two more children, Lucas and Nora, and spent a lot more time in Starhill. Still, an uncanny distance persisted between Ruthie and me.

In the fall of 2009, not long before we were to move to Philadelphia for my new job, we were in Starhill sitting down to Sunday dinner. "Rod, you say the blessing," Ruthie announced. "You're so holier-than-thou."

I chose not to respond, but after lunch I asked Daddy, with whom I was getting along well now, what Ruthie's problem was. "I don't know, son," he said, "but there's something there."

Maybe she was feeling bad; she had developed a persistent cough. Still, I hated moving far away again with this unacknowledged hostility between us.

"Sister's Got Cancer!"

Shortly after we arrived in Philly, we received word from my mother that doctors had discovered spots on Ruthie's lungs. They scheduled exploratory surgery for Mardi Gras day. My mobile phone rang just past nine that morning. It was my mother. "It's cancer!" she sobbed. "Sister's got cancer!"

I caught the next flight out, and made it to her hospital bedside that night. Ruthie had inoperable stage IV lung cancer. It had spread to her hip and to her brain. She had never smoked. She was otherwise healthy. And she was a good person—one of the most beloved people in our town. She had done everything right. But now, at the age of forty, she had been handed what, barring a miracle, was a death sentence.

And yet that horrible week in the hospital was a triumph for her. Her hope and strength of character astonished everyone who came to see her. I know; I was there, and I saw it.

One of the young nurses who cared for Ruthie wrote her a letter saying that she had been struggling in her faith because of all the suffering she had seen in her job, but the grace with which Ruthie accepted her diagnosis had given her new hope. Over and over, things like that happened because of my sister being the same steady, sweet Ruthie she always was.

Days after her diagnosis, before I returned to Philly, I sat with her on the front porch of her home in Starhill. Through tears, I told her how sorry I was for every bad thing I had ever done to her. I asked her forgiveness and told her I wanted everything to be clear between us.

It had been well over half a lifetime ago that I had teased her so unkindly, but I knew that she harbored resentment against me still. Whatever it was, I wanted it in the past. We needed to be a strong family in the face of this cancer, and I wanted no painful memories or hard feeling to exist between us.

Ruthie hated moments like this. She burst into tears, flicked something unseen away with her right hand, and embraced me. She said nothing. I thought with that gesture she was offering me both forgiveness and her own apology for her bitter sniping at me.

Two months later, her friends threw a fund-raising concert to help cover her medical bills. In her humility, Ruthie asked them not to make a fuss over her, but they refused to listen. I flew down from Philadelphia to be a part of the event, which was held at the 4-H Club Fair Barn north of town.

David Morgan, a Starhill neighbor, and his country band performed for free that night. Well over a thousand people came, filling the big barn with dancing and merry-making. People paid for hot dogs with hundred-dollar bills, all out of love for Ruthie, who was by then bald and badly swollen from chemotherapy. I spoke to a woman who had driven six hours from Houston for the show. She and her family used to live in nearby St. Francisville, and Ruthie had taught her children.

"We love her so much," the woman said. "She has given so much to our family. We couldn't *not* be here."

At the concert that night, Mama pointed out to me a family who were poor but who still came to give what they had to my sister, out of love. It reminded me of Daddy's story about Calvin McKnight, the old black man who was his farmhand in the 1960s. Calvin lived in a dilapidated former slave cabin and had few worldly goods. On the day before my father was scheduled for back surgery, Calvin brought his savings, a shiny silver dollar, to my mom, a newlywed who faced the prospect that her new husband might suffer permanent paralysis.

"I want to give this here to pay for Little Boss's operation," Calvin said, tears running down his cheeks as he pressed the coin into my mother's hand. In that moment, black and white mattered not, nor did social class or anything else. Only love and solidarity.

Ruthie lived for nineteen months after her diagnosis. One of the only comforts my family had was in a line Ruthie would say to buck up our faith as we saw her decline: "We just don't know what God is going to do with this." She was an unfussy Methodist who found peace in trusting God's will. "I hope and pray that I make it," she would say, "but if I don't, I know God is in whatever happens."

She carried that hope in her heart until the morning of her sudden death, from an embolism. She died at home in Starhill, in the arms of her beloved husband. On the night before her funeral, I sat up late writing my sister's eulogy. I chose to open with a memory that, for me, captured the grace and mystery of Ruthie Leming. On one occasion early in our childhood together, I had done something awfully mean to Ruthie, God only knows what, but it was so bad that Daddy told me to go lie down on my bed and prepare for a spanking. That was rare, and I recall that I felt quite sure that I deserved it. Before he took off his belt, Ruthie, the victim of my nasty teasing, threw herself across my back and begged Daddy to spank her instead. He spanked no one that day. Forty years later, that was the story I told to a standing-room-only congregation of mourners so that they would know what kind of person my sister had been.

They didn't need telling. These were the people of our town, the people who had watched her grow up and seen her marry her high school sweetheart and return home from college to teach in the town's public school. Ruthie had taught many of their children, and because of her skill, patience, and tenderness with her students, she had become one of the most beloved teachers in the parish. I had always known my sister was good, but I didn't know that she was also great until I began hearing stories from students and the parents of students, telling what she had meant to them.

Following Ruthie's Little Way

Watching events in Starhill from our Philadelphia vantage point, the enormous outpouring of love, support, and community solidarity that had engulfed my Louisiana family after Ruthie's cancer diagnosis moved Julie and me deeply. Standing under a live oak tree in front of Ruthie's church on the night of her wake, I had an epiphany: the same tight familial and community bonds that felt so constricting to me as a teenager had held Ruthie and the others in my Louisiana family together through this terrible trial.

We buried Ruthie the next morning and afterward went to a big party thrown by her Starhill friends. It was typical of this place, and typical of my sister, that they would send one of their own off with cold beer, barbecue, and shared memories.

"No matter who you were, Ruthie made you feel like you were *it*," her best friend, Abby Cochran, mused. "You were her family, you were always comfortable—'Come in, sit down, let me fix you something to eat.' Everybody was welcome in her house. You knew you were at home there, and everything was good."

I thought of my life with Julie. It had been twelve years since our newlywed idyll in Manhattan. Three kids, two moves, and a Ford minivan later, this was the kind of paradise I longed for now. The family in which we argued over things like fish stew seemed to be a relic from the distant past. After the party, Julie and I gathered the kids and went back to my mom and dad's house for a nap. As we lay in my old bedroom, I made a confession.

"I can't believe I'm actually going to say this, but I really think we should consider moving here," I said, cringing in anticipation of my wife's reaction.

"That's so funny," she said. "I've been thinking the same thing. I think we need to be here."

We wanted to be a help to Ruthie's widower, Mike, and their three girls, and we wanted to be a support for Daddy and Mama. Whatever we had to give up in Philly, we happily would. My heart had been changed by seeing what a difference Ruthie's lifetime of giving to and serving her school and town had accomplished. And my wife and I both understood that what had happened to Ruthie—terminal illness striking like a bolt from the clear blue sky—could happen to us too; unlike Ruthie, though, we had moved so many times for my work that we did not have deep roots to keep us anchored on solid ground amid the flood of suffering and grief we were experiencing.

The day before we were set to return to Philly, I shared the news with Mama and Daddy that we were planning to move back. They were overjoyed. It meant the world to me to be able to give them that amid their grief. They sat on their front porch beaming and telling the visiting friends gathered around them how thrilled they were.

I felt like such a good boy. But a friend of my parents motioned for me to follow him out to his pickup truck.

"I'm not sure this is a good idea," he said. "You need to give this some time. Think it over. Y'all are in an emotional state right now. This is not the time to make big decisions."

But the decision had already been made, and having told Mama and Daddy of our intentions, we couldn't back out now. Nor did we want to. Not only were we going to be doing our duty by our family in their time of need, we wanted to be part of their lives. We *needed* to, in fact, and we needed to be part of a community like the one that had walked with

Ruthie and her family on their long and grueling cancer pilgrimage. Now we were going to step out on faith.

And so love built a bridge back home for me. In late 2011, three months after Ruthie died, my family and I rolled into town in a Penske truck and a minivan, just in time for Christmas. I was so glad to be home at last. My father had written me a letter telling me how grateful he was that his only son was coming back—the thing for which he had prayed year after year.

The explosion of grace from Ruthie's passing blasted open the vault of my heart and revealed a path to a new life for our family. The promise of healing that I had mistakenly thought would come with Hannah's birth repeated itself with Ruthie's death. Things would be different now. How could they not be, after what we had all lived through?

We rented a lovely old house in the historic district of St. Francisville, the parish's only town, which is six miles north of the Starhill community. We arrived in town just in time for our cousins' annual family Christmas Eve party, a gumbo-and-caroling extravaganza that lit up the Starhill sky with fireworks. My kids were ecstatic. They hadn't known there were so many kids in the extended family. And they'd had no idea that you could shoot off fireworks on Christmas.

Mama gave us rocking chairs for our front porch, and before long we acquired chickens for the backyard. Lucas quickly made friends in the neighborhood and rode his bike up and down the town's main street. Matt volunteered at the library. Outgoing and funny in that sassy way Texas women have, Julie had no trouble finding friends everywhere she turned. Before long, she was serving on the Friends of the Library board, had the kids involved in 4-H, and ran the roads to and from the sports park, where Lucas and Nora took tennis lessons.

I went down to the town's coffee shop for grits and eggs one morning shortly after we returned. Listening to the chatter of the town—*my* town now—waking up made me feel like I had stepped into a southern version of a Garrison Keillor monologue. I began writing a memoir, *The Little Way of Ruthie Leming*, to tell the full story of my amazing sister, the gift she was to the world, and how her life and death had taught me the importance to a good life of love, and home, and family.

Telling the Family Secret

As I reported the book, I learned from questioning my sister's friends, her husband, and my parents more about why Ruthie held me in such disdain. It had to do with my moving away to the city; Mike said that she always felt that I belonged in Starhill, and that she took my leaving as a personal rejection. It had to do with my having tastes and beliefs she didn't understand; for Ruthie, as for Daddy, "different" was a bad word. It had to do with her believing that I was getting away with something, being paid to write for a living instead of doing honest work. And it had to do with, well, me; even her best friend, Abby, said that she couldn't fathom why Ruthie's patience with everyone else was endless, but she could barely tolerate me for a moment.

This was all illuminating, but it made me thankful that my sister and I had had that moment of reconciliation on the front porch. It showed what could be accomplished with apology and forgiveness. Now I was home, living in harmony with the family, and had, in the poet T. S. Eliot's words, found my end in my beginning.

As I penned the final chapter, I took Hannah, then nineteen, to Paris for her college spring break. She had been taking her mother's death particularly hard. Hannah couldn't bear to see her mother dying and had stayed away from home as often as she could manage during Ruthie's cancer journey. And Ruthie wouldn't force her to be with her. Now she was tortured by guilt. Over the past few years, I had shared my love of France with Hannah and had promised to take her to Paris one day. So even though Ruthie would have hated it, I was making good on that promise and hoping that the City of Light at Easter could scatter the dark cloud that had settled over niece's life.

Over platters of raw oysters on our last night in the city, I told Hannah that she must not live her life running away from painful and difficult truths. It is always better to live in truth than to live in falsehood, I said, no matter how comforting the lie may be. We finished our oysters, drank the last of the Muscadet, and wandered out into the night.

We were standing at the corner of the Boulevard St-Germain and the Rue du Four when Hannah told me the family secret that changed everything. We had spoken earlier about how standoffish her sisters had been to Julie and me, no matter how hard we tried to reach out to them. Now, emboldened by my speech about living in truth, Hannah dropped a bombshell.

"Uncle Rod, I need to tell you something," Hannah said. "I really think you and Aunt Julie should stop trying so hard to get close to Claire and Rebekah. It's not going to work."

"Why not?"

"Because we were raised in a house where our mama a lot of times had a bad opinion of you," she said. "She never talked bad about you to us, but we could tell that she didn't like the way you lived. We could hear the things she said, and Paw too. I had a bad opinion of you myself until I started coming to visit y'all and I saw how wrong they were.

"I was fifteen the first time I did that," she continued. "My sisters are still young. They don't know any different. All they know is how we were raised. It makes me sad to see you and Aunt Julie trying so hard, me knowing you're not going to get anywhere. I don't want y'all to be hurt."

Hannah said she and her sisters had grown up with Ruthie and Daddy disparaging me as a "user"—my father's word for the most contemptible sort of person, one who gets things done craftily, usually by taking advantage of others. I asked her to give me an example of why her mother considered me a user.

"You remember that time you and Aunt Julie took me to that fancy French restaurant after my high school graduation?" she said.

I did. It had been a great weekend. None of us had thought that Ruthie would live to see Hannah graduate, but she made it. She would be dead less than four months later.

"When y'all dropped me off at home, Mama was waiting up for me," she continued. "I told her all about the evening, and then I told her that you talked to the manager, and that he gave you a recommendation for a restaurant in Paris."

"That was the restaurant we ate at the first night we were here," I said.

"Mama said, 'Isn't that just like Rod, only talking to people if he can get something out of them.'"

My stomach clenched, and I thought I might throw up. I jammed my hands into my pockets, looked up and down the boulevard, and swallowed hard. I did not know what to say. I did not know if I could say anything. It was over now. Once again I had been a fool about my family—but this time I had dragged Julie and the children into my folly.

As we continued walking up the boulevard talking, me roiling with emotion and spitting fire, Hannah finally had enough.

"Mama wasn't a bad person! She loved you."

"I know!" I said. "I think she was a saint. It makes no sense. That's why this is driving me so crazy. I *know* she loved me. It would be a lot easier to figure out if I believed she didn't."

Seeing how stricken I was, Hannah nearly burst into tears of regret, but I told her she had done the right thing. It is always better to live in truth.

However, I was very nearly destroyed. I now knew that I would never be able to return home. The alienation and rejection that I thought grace had reversed were, to my shock, deeply rooted within the culture of my family. I wrote about Hannah's prediction in *Little Way*, but ended the book on a note of hope, of the possibility of redemption.

Falling Down a Hole

Hannah was right: no matter how hard Julie and I tried, there was absolutely nothing we could do about the situation with our nieces. We didn't blame them; they were only doing as they had been taught. I learned too that the front porch embrace had not meant apology, as I had thought, and any forgiveness it conveyed had dissipated long before Ruthie's passing.

Mama and Daddy tried to be understanding, but they could not bear the weight of anything that contradicted Ruthie's goodness. Nor would they entertain the idea that anything her children thought, felt, or did was wrong or might need gentle correcting. I tried to master my resentment; after all, our family had recently sustained a devastating loss, and it seemed selfish and cheap to judge them for not paying more attention to us. But I failed. The sense of hurt and betrayal reverberated through me like the echo of a bell struck ages ago in that field in the far corner of Daddy's land. All this defeated me. Home from Paris, I began to slide into depression. And what I thought were allergy attacks started again.

In the spring of 2010, a month or so after Ruthie's diagnosis, I had begun to have episodes in which I would feel swelling in my sinuses and have to lie down and sleep, sometimes for hours. Allergies had never been a problem for me, but then, I had never lived in Philadelphia before. My doctor prescribed allergy medicine, but it did no good. It was a frustrating condition, but it faded in time.

Now it was back, and much more severe than before. After nearly collapsing while mowing the yard one day, I made an appointment with my local doctor. It took a month of testing to determine what I had: chronic mononucleosis, which is caused by the Epstein-Barr virus. Most people carry the virus dormant in their system. Intense and prolonged stress can compromise the immune system so severely that EBV goes active.

With my health in free fall, I spent hours every afternoon sleeping. When I wasn't asleep, I was constantly thirsty, frequently felt exhausted, and often didn't leave the house. To what extent this was depression and to what extent mono, I couldn't say. It didn't matter; I was slammed hard.

Fortunately, I wrote for a living, the one job I could do from my armchair in the den or my bed. Most of my life was lived inside and online. While I was by no means an invalid—twice a week I drove Matt to classes in Baton Rouge, I ran errands around town when I was up to it, sometimes we had dinner parties, and sometimes we went to them—mostly I was a mess. With me largely out of commission, Julie had to keep the house going and take care of the kids—including home-schooling them—almost entirely on her own.

"I'm sorry," I told her one day, and meant it. "I can't help this. I feel so guilty about all that's on you."

"I know, Rodgie," she would say, using her pet name for me. "It's not your fault, but it's scary when you see your husband so sick and you don't know if he's ever going to get better. Is this going to be our life from now on?"

I'd try to sound reassuring, but I didn't know; maybe this *would* be our life. Chronic EBV is very rare, and we were not sure why I wasn't getting better. I kept from Julie and everybody else this fact: those unlucky few with chronic EBV are 33 to 100 percent more likely than others to contract cancer of the lymphatic system. After having just seen Ruthie die young from cancer, this terrified me.

Things only got worse between my Starhill family and me. I showed Mike the manuscript of *Little Way* before I turned it in, and asked him to let me know if he wanted me to make any changes. He did not ask for changes, but as I learned much later, the book displeased him greatly. He thought I had used his wife's death to tell a story about myself.

Family relations turned chilly. I took my kids to see their grandparents a good bit, and spoke to my folks by phone daily, as was our longstanding habit. We rarely saw the Lemings, though, and the distance between us grew. My mom and dad made it clear that they blamed Julie and me for the breach.

When I landed the *Little Way* book deal, Julie and I set aside some of the money to fulfill a lifelong dream of mine: to live in Paris for a time, however brief. In early 2012, we had reserved an apartment near the Panthéon and bought plane tickets. And then I'd gotten sick.

Everything was nonrefundable, so off we went with the children, hoping for the best. Astonishingly, within a week of being in the city, and despite a busy schedule of museum-going and sightseeing, most of my symptoms, especially the chronic fatigue, cleared up. They returned shortly after our plane landed in Louisiana.

By Thanksgiving, I was once again sick and depressed, and had grown so estranged from the Starhill clan that I defied my folks by taking Julie and the kids to a restaurant in New Orleans for the holiday meal. I did not feel physically or emotionally capable of sitting at my father's table, pretending everything was fine. *They can't treat us like this and expect us to act like all is well,* I thought. Of course, my protest gesture only made things worse.

"Are y'all coming for Christmas?" my mother phoned to ask me a couple of weeks later.

The tone of her voice indicated that to her, our absence at Thanksgiving was utterly inexplicable. But I had explained to both her and my father why we were not coming to Thanksgiving. Still, none of it made sense to them. Their attitude was that no matter what your kin do to you, family is family, and you don't break that bond. Being family means never having to say you're sorry.

"Yes, Mama," I said, "we will be there for Christmas." I could practically hear her sigh of relief.

A Light in the Darkness

In the midst of all this darkness, a bright spot appeared. Not long after we moved to town, we had helped to start a church in Starhill. It was an Eastern Orthodox mission called St. John the Theologian. In 2006, after thirteen years of living devoutly as a Catholic, the last five reporting on the sex abuse scandal, I lost my ability to believe in the Catholic Church. So did Julie.

At sea and drifting, we washed ashore in the ancient Orthodox Church, which had parted ways with Rome in 1054. We were humbled and we were broken, and they took us in.

Amazingly, there were a few other Orthodox converts in West Feliciana when we arrived. We all put our resources together and called a young priest, Father Matthew Harrington, and his family from the Pacific Northwest. That is how the Divine Liturgy of St. John Chrysostom, completed in Constantinople in the fifth century, came to be chanted every Sunday in a tiny rented space in Louisiana plantation country. The church and its fledgling congregation comforted and sheltered me during this difficult time.

Aliens Among Them

Little Way was released in the spring of 2013, and early reviews were stellar. But a week before publication, I was standing in my mother and father's living room, having a screaming match with them over the family's fate.

"You and Julie aren't reaching out enough to those girls!" my father barked.

"That's not true," I shot back. We had invited them over many times, but they usually declined politely. On the few occasions they did come, they were visibly uncomfortable.

Julie had offered to take them shopping; they'd found someone else to do it. We had shared some of the money from the book advance with them and had set up college funds for the girls. Still nothing. In exasperation, we'd finally given up.

"They just don't want to be with us," I said. "Hannah told me that's how Ruthie and y'all raised those kids."

"Well, can you blame them?" my father said. "Y'all are so damn weird."

And there it was. We would be held responsible for doing more and more to win the Leming children's love, though it would be impossible to do so because of our original sin: being unlike my father, my sister, and the rest.

There is no exile quite like being a stranger in the midst of your own family. My dream was dead, and I struggled mightily. I pushed myself through the *Little Way* book tour but felt like a fraud at every stop. Once I was back home, I slipped back into the bog of malaise.

That summer, I consulted a rheumatologist for extensive testing to see if there was any underlying physiological condition responsible for my chronic mono. The answer: no, nothing. When tests turn up no apparent cause, the doctor said, the source of chronic autoimmune disease is almost always deep and constant stress.

"What are you stressed over?" he asked.

I told him. And I told him that the only time the disease had gone into remission was during the month I was away with my wife and children in Paris.

"Well, you have a choice," he said. "Leave Louisiana, or resign yourself to destroying your health."

I told him I couldn't do either one. My wife and kids are happy here, and none of us have the emotional strength to uproot ourselves again. Besides, however hard the situation might be, I couldn't leave my elderly parents. And my kids loved going out to the country to see their grandparents; I couldn't take that away from them.

The doctor shrugged. "All I can tell you is that you had better find some way to get inner peace," he said.

Inner peace? The phrase made me recoil. Anytime I heard someone speak of "inner peace," the instinct to snark was irresistible.

Julie had no patience with my reaction. "Look at you," she said. "You're a wreck. You're sick, you're depressed, you sleep all the time. You've got to get out of this hole. We can't live this way."

She insisted that I start seeing a therapist. Under protest, I agreed to set aside my pride and go talk to someone. There was no other way out. I couldn't carry on slogging through the mud. I couldn't keep putting Julie and the kids through this.

Around the same time, I found support from Father Matthew at our church.

And then I found Dante.

A Message in a Bottle

Shortly after I saw the rheumatologist, I found myself in a Barnes & Noble bookstore in Baton Rouge, killing time. I am not much of a poetry reader, but there I was in the poetry section, browsing. I pulled a copy of Dante's *Inferno* off the shelf and began thumbing through it. I don't know whose translation it was; here are the opening lines from Robert and Jean Hollander's (which I will use throughout this book):

Midway in the journey of our life
I came to myself in a dark wood,
for the straight way was lost.

That struck me: he's talking about what we would call a midlife crisis. Was I having a midlife crisis? Well, I was forty-six, and I was certainly in a crisis. I had always considered midlife crisis to be a vulgar episode in a man's life in which he is prone to take up with a mistress or buy a convertible. Neither appealed to me in the slightest, but if a sense of disorientation and disappointment bordering on despair counted as a midlife crisis, then, to my embarrassment, I was smack in the middle of one.

I read on, through the first two cantos, and was instantly caught up in the drama. Here was a man who was trapped in a thicket of fear and confusion, powerless to escape. Dante's verse captured the feeling of my own depression and anxiety precisely. Wild animals blocked the man's path at every turn. Suddenly the shade of a great poet of antiquity, Virgil, appears before the man and promises to show him the hard road to a good place—but first the man has to trust him.

I put the book back on the shelf, but I kept thinking about it, unable to get Dante and his journey off my mind. I am a great believer in synchronicity, in meaningful coincidences. This was hard to ignore, especially considering the sheer unlikeliness that I would have opened the *Commedia* in the first place. A week later, in July 2013, I bought a copy and began my own Dantean pilgrimage.

KNOWING IF WHAT GLITTERS IS GOLD

It is hard to perceive the truth of a situation when you are emotionally invested in seeing it a certain way. If you refuse to consider the possibility that something disturbing might be true, you don't make it go away, but only disarm yourself in the face of danger.

It is even more difficult to see reality when the lines between good and bad are so tangled and blurred. Everyone has a shadow side, but sometimes the light burns so brightly within them that the shadow cannot be easily seen. As C. S. Lewis said, "Brass is mistaken for gold more easily than clay is." Don't let the virtues in others prevent you from facing their faults.

It is better to choose to know the painful truth rather than settle on a comforting lie. Resolve to look for and to accept the truth, no matter how much it hurts. Nothing built on lies lasts.

Your rescue may come in an unimagined way. Be watchful and open.

3

THE SUPER TUSCAN

If you [Florence] recall your past and think
upon it clearly,
you will see that you are like a woman, ill in bed,
who on the softest down cannot find rest
but twisting, turning, seeks to ease her pain.

—Purgatorio VI:148–151

The World That Made Dante

The world of Dante Alighieri was one of passion, beauty, and creativity, but also one of violence, cruelty, and chaos. Thirteenth-century Florence was one of the richest, most sophisticated, most dangerous cities in the world.

We know surprisingly little about Dante's life, aside from what he tells us, but as one of the most prominent intellectuals of the High Middle Ages, he was undoubtedly at the hub of Florence's artistic and civic life. As an ambitious and talented seventeen-year-old, Dante wrote his way into Florence's brotherhood of poets, who dedicated themselves to hymning the god of romantic love, and he quickly became a star among them. Through the medieval guild system, he embedded himself in city life, and served as one of the six priors who governed Florence.

To be one of the Florentine elite meant power and status that extended far beyond the city's borders. In the decades before Dante's birth, the

Tuscan city on the river Arno became a boomtown, owing to its success in banking and manufacturing, which in turn fueled a trade boom that attracted thousands of immigrants from the countryside. But the peace that made Florence's prosperity possible came under threat from two feuding political factions: the Guelphs and the Ghibellines.

The Guelphs supported the power of the pope (who was also a secular ruler of some Italian territories) against Frederick II, the Holy Roman Emperor; the Ghibellines took up the imperial cause. Florentine families aligned with one side or the other. Their rivalry eventually turned violent, sparking an episodic civil war that lasted more than a century. These warring families were neighbors, sometimes even living on the same block. For the thirteenth-century Florentines, there was no such thing as the common good. There was just Us versus Them. Depending on which side ruled, loyalty to family and faction meant riches or ruin, and sometimes even life or death.

Dante Alighieri was born into a politically mixed marriage. His father, a minor businessman named Alaghiero di Bellincione, was a Guelph; his mother, Bella, who died when Dante was eight, was a Ghibelline. In 1274, a year after Bella's passing, young Dante accompanied his father to a May Day party at the nearby home of the prominent Portinari family of bankers. There he saw a little girl named Beatrice, a year younger than he, a vision that changed both his life and the course of literary history. In his early memoir *Vita Nuova*, "New Life," compiled when he was thirty, Dante recalls the first time he laid eyes on Beatrice.

Dante never forgot her. Though he and Beatrice lived in the same neighborhood, it was nine years before they met again, at a chance encounter on the street, in which she disdained him. By this point, Dante was a rising poet and still madly at love with Beatrice. In medieval Florence, marriages between people of means were typically not affairs of the heart but business and political arrangements negotiated by their fathers. Beatrice's father married her off to a young man from a prominent banking family. She died at the age of twenty-five.

Dante, meanwhile, married Gemma Donati, a daughter of the leading Guelph clan in the city. Though she bore him at least three children,

Dante never mentions Gemma in his poetry. His true love, the woman he could not have, remained Beatrice. The mystical experience of wonder at that childhood party had seized Dante's imagination and set him on a journey to explore the meaning of love and its power to build up and to destroy.

Love and the Lady

For Dante, Beatrice—her name means "the blessed one"—was the embodiment of Love. In his early poetry, Dante followed the conventional thinking of his Tuscan counterparts, penning fulsome tributes to women and to Love, which he described as his "lord." In the verses of Dante and the poets of what would be called the "sweet new style," erotic attraction would become spiritualized and the search for love treated as an ennobling quest. Yet mistaking his exalting youthful passion for Beatrice for true love, and Beatrice for a kind of deity, led Dante astray, into the dead end symbolized by the dark wood at the *Commedia*'s beginning.

Years later, with Dante in exile, it was through Beatrice's memory that God spoke to the mature Dante's broken heart. The poet came to see that he had made an idol of Beatrice and of Love instead of seeing them as icons through which the Divine shines and God calls us back to himself. This is how Dante found his way back—or, rather, was led back—to faith, truth, and wholeness.

Rethinking Everything You Thought You Knew

As a young man Dante excelled in poetry and gained fame. Building on his reputation, he entered politics, ascending to power in 1301 as one of the priors of the Guelph-led city-state, which faced nearly constant subterfuge from the machinations of the elite families. When the Guelphs split into violent rival factions called the Blacks and the Whites, Dante, a White, was forced to send leading political figures, including his best friend, a poet named Guido Cavalcanti, into exile. The peace of the city depended on it.

But the tide turned when the Blacks, who had the support of the conniving Pope Boniface VIII, took control of the city in 1302. They stripped Dante of his money, his property, his status, his family, and his home, sent him into exile, and told him that if he ever showed his face in Florence again, they would kill him.

It wasn't the death penalty, but for a medieval Italian, to be sent permanently away from one's city was close to it. For Dante, though, the loss of nearly everything he held dear saved his life. How? Because it forced him to rethink everything he thought he knew.

Why did Italians who loved their communities fight constantly among themselves? Why did those who professed undying love for their families end by destroying them? Why was the Church, which was supposed to guide the people in holiness, so corrupt? Why did everybody talk about love but act out of spite? Was the meaning of life to be found in the pursuit of desire, or was there something greater? Whom, and what, could he trust? And where had he himself gone wrong?

The trauma of exile compelled Dante to take stock of the mess his own life had become, and the mess his world had become. He began writing *Inferno*, the first book of the *Commedia*, around 1306, when he entered his forties. *Inferno* is a diagnosis of what's wrong with the world—and what's wrong with the soul of its author—as seen through the eyes of a character named Dante, who is a pilgrim in the afterlife.

The Journey Within

The character Dante is thirty-five years old—by medieval reckoning, midway through life's journey—when the *Commedia* begins on Holy Thursday in the year 1300, a year when tens of thousands of Christians made the Jubilee pilgrimage to Rome. The pilgrim plunges into the maw of the inferno, crawls up the rocky crags of purgatory, and soars to the pinnacle of paradise.

The pilgrim Dante's journey teaches him that the source of all the chaos and misery is disordered desire. If everyone, including himself, loved as they should love, they would love God more than they loved themselves and their passions. To harmonize with the will of God requires us to overcome our passions and our ego, to make room for the transforming love of God. Out of the ashes of his destruction, Dante the poet erected a monument to redemption—his own and everyone else's; he could not have done it any other way. To clear the pathway to paradise, Dante had to heave his own considerable ego out of the way.

The poet's personal story does not have a conventional happy ending. Dante died in exile, never returning to his hometown. But as we will discover on the road ahead, Dante's story ends not with happiness in the ordinary sense but with something much better: joy.

If it had not been for the catastrophe that took everything he had from him—his power, his wealth, his family, his sense of place—Dante probably never would have found his way to his true and only home, and never would have given the world the priceless gift of the *Commedia*. Near the end of his journey, the pilgrim Dante says:

I now see clearly that our intellect
cannot be satisfied until that truth enlighten it
beyond whose boundary no further truth extends.

In that truth, like a wild beast in its den, it rests
once it has made its way there—and it can do that,
or else its every wish would be in vain.

—*Paradiso* IV:124–129

Dante's Exile—and My Own

I am not Dante. Circumstances did not destroy my reputation, reduce me to a wandering beggar, or threaten my life. In my case, I had moved back to my hometown after a lifetime of exploration, believing I was returning to a family that wanted me there. I thought that, like me, they had seen in the bright sadness of Ruthie's passion and death the worth of the bonds of family and of setting aside old grudges and harsh memories for the sake of love and togetherness. In fact, I had never imagined the degree to which my Louisiana family, despite their undeniable (if complicated) love, saw me as a prodigal, as someone whose personal happiness and professional success in the world outside West Feliciana Parish marked him as a selfish squanderer of the family's inheritance.

There are far worse tragedies—like, say, losing your beloved daughter, wife, or mother to cancer. But if you find yourself in a dark wood, telling yourself that you have no right to your pain and confusion because others have it so much worse does not get you very far.

Had I taken the rheumatologist's advice, packed up my family, and left, shaking the dust off my feet, I could have temporarily solved the problem, as I had done before. But at what cost? I could not run away this time. I had to face down, call out, and defeat whatever dragons were hiding in the recesses of my heart, or I would never really be free.

So when I stood in the bookstore that summer day in 2013, reading the opening lines of a seven-hundred-year-old poem by a medieval Italian telling me that he woke up in the middle of his life and felt lost, I understood. And when he said that he "forsook the one true way," implying that he had some guilt in the matter, I wondered if I too was responsible for my own exile.

Dante said in those early lines that he ultimately came out of the dark wood. What had he learned on his journey that brought him from despair to joy? What had he learned that set him free? What did this wayfaring Florentine, the disgraced castoff who became the greatest of all Tuscans—indeed, possibly the greatest poet in the world—have to say to me? I was not coming to Dante for pleasure, for Great Books–type edification, or because my professor told me to. I came to him as a beggar. A lost soul. A drowning man.

The *Commedia* was a most unlikely rescue vessel, especially for a reader like me, who vastly prefers nonfiction. But when you are drowning and someone throws you what looks like a lifeline, you seize it, hoping someone at the other end will pull you aboard to safety.

And so I seized it.

HOW TO REFUSE DEFEAT

Life is fragile and uncertain. Sooner or later, you will experience a great loss in life, when suffering reveals that the world is not the place you think it is, and that your dreams will not come true after all. What then?

Don't blame others for what happened to you, even if it might well be their fault. This is a dead end. And don't settle for stoic acceptance of your fate. Merely bearing up under strain is noble, but it's wasting an opportunity for transformation. You have the power to turn your burden into a blessing.

What if this pain, this heartbreak, this failure, was given to you to help you find your true self? Make adversity work for you by launching a quest inside your own heart. Find the dragons hiding there, slay them, and bring back the treasure that will help you live well.

4

RULES OF THE ROAD

---

*The aim of the whole and of the part is to remove
those living in this life from a state of misery and
to guide them to a state of happiness.*

—From Dante's letter to his patron Cangrande
della Scala, on the meaning of the *Commedia*
(trans. Charles Sterrett Latham)

A Short Tour Guide for the New Pilgrim

I f you're like me, the idea of taking up the *Commedia* is intimidating. Don't panic. I am a journalist, not a scholar. What I know about art and literature could barely fill a pamphlet. But if I can read Dante, absorb his words and ideas, and be changed by his verse, so can you.

Just as it is helpful to know something about Dante's life to get the most out of the *Commedia*, it is also helpful to understand a little about the ideas that inform the poem. I'm not going to bore you with theology or literary theory, but there are a few things you need to know at the start of this journey.

You do not have to accept Dante's theological or moral beliefs to learn from the *Commedia*, but you do have to know basically what they are. The *Commedia* is an unsurpassed expression of the Christian imagination, and most importantly of the Roman Catholic vision, as Dante was a devout Roman Catholic.

The Mind of the Middle Ages

The poem assumes a universe created by a loving God who desired to live in unbroken communion with humankind, the pinnacle of creation. Adam, the first man, broke that communion through disobedience, committing the first sin, which greatly impaired, but did not wholly sever, all of humanity's relationship with its Creator.

In Dante's vision, God became incarnate as Jesus Christ, who suffered, died, and rose again to defeat sin and death. Through faith in him fallen man can receive the grace to be healed of his sinful condition and after death be fully united with God for eternity. Those who reject Christ with their hearts thereby choose themselves over God and after death spend eternity separated from him.

Catholics coming to Dante for the first time are often startled by Dante's ferocious criticism of the Church. Note, however, that the poet does so in the mode of a biblical prophet, as an act of love. He believes that Jesus Christ established the Roman Catholic Church as the ordinary means of salvation and that no degree of clerical corruption can alter that fact. As much as he loathed the despotic Pope Boniface VIII, an archvillain in the *Commedia*, Dante affirmed that he was a legitimate pope and that the papacy was a divinely instituted office.

For non-Catholic Christians, the realm of purgatory—traversed in the second of the *Commedia*'s three books—is theologically problematic. In Catholic theology, purgatory, which is a middle passage between the mortal life and paradise, is a place where the souls of the saved whose repentance was incomplete dwell temporarily, to be purged of the sinful tendencies that render them unready to withstand the brilliant glory of God.

You don't have to accept the doctrine of purgatory to appreciate its symbolic meaning here. In Dante, purgatory represents the earthly life, which requires a constant struggle against our sinful nature in order to open our souls up ever more to God's grace.

Atheist or agnostic readers might find it a challenge to work through the religious language and symbolism, but Dante's conceptual grammar conveys truths about human nature that are universally applicable. Hell is a dark and loveless place of absolute egotism. Heaven is filled with love, light, and the complete absence of ego. Purgatory is life as we experience it: a never-ending contest between love and hate, altruism and selfishness, good and evil—and the way we elect to respond to these challenges matters.

The philosopher Jean-Paul Sartre taught that because free will is part of the human condition, we are responsible for the choices we make. There was no heaven or hell at the end of life, as far as the atheist and existentialist thinker was concerned, but he shared Dante's belief in the ultimate meaning of moral choice.

The best strategy for all contemporary readers is the one suggested by Dante translator Charles Singleton: to adopt "a willing suspension of disbelief and an imaginative and sympathetic surrender to the experience of the Poem."

For medieval people, everything was a sign pregnant with meaning. "Dante's universe did not simply exist; it *meant*, and it meant intensely," writes Louis Markos. "The universe was less a thing to be studied than a poem to be loved and enjoyed." For the medievals, the whole world was an icon of the divine, a manifestation of God. That is, God wasn't a distant, absentee figure but as close as the sun in the sky, the wind in the trees, the cry of a baby, and the sigh of a lover.

What's more, people in the Middle Ages believed that the earth was the center of the created universe and that it existed at the heart of a series of spheres, like a Russian nesting doll. On the outside of these heavenly spheres lies the Primum Mobile, or "first movable," which is the border with the Empyrean, an endless, eternal realm of light where God dwells with the angels and saints. The energy of divine love passes from the Empyrean through the Primum Mobile and moves everything in creation. To unite yourself to God is to increase the flow of love—the energy of God—through yourself and into the world.

That divine energy was a thread that bound all souls together in this life, as they would be bound eternally in the afterlife. Medieval people did not think of society as we do, as a vast collection of individuals, but rather saw it as a single organism rooted in the transcendent realm. To see your life as wholly your own, free from obligations to God, family, and neighbor, is to live in illusion. Your own fate is inextricably bound to the fate of the community. *How, w/ Puli*

Change From Within

The *Commedia* is about avoiding hell and gaining heaven, but salvation is not about being a respectable citizen, believing the right things, going to church on Sunday, and thereby earning a pass into paradise. To be saved is not to be saved from the consequences of sin but to be freed from the desire to sin—that is, from the desire for our own will over God's.

What's more, salvation does not begin after you die but starts right here, right now. At every moment, through the choices we make, we are either being saved or losing our salvation. This is because God's grace works on us the way a stovetop fire works to warm the soup in the pot. By its steady application, over time, the soup can be brought to boiling. But if the fire keeps going out, the soup is slow to boil. If the fire goes out permanently, the soup turns cold.

The more we allow God's grace to work within us to change us, the closer we come to boiling. The key concept here is that *the change happens from within*. The greater the action of grace, the more we are transformed by it into the likeness of God.

As we will see, the souls in hell have lost forever their lifeline to God and therefore to transforming grace. They cannot change. The penitents climbing up the mountain of purgatory are saved by God's mercy, but they are not yet ready to bear the brilliant intensity of his love. By the end of their journey, they have fully set aside their own wills. This makes them strong enough to dwell in paradise, in the overwhelming light and love of God, which fills their souls.

A Symbolic Journey

The *Commedia* is written as an allegory of the soul's journey through life. It is a religious poem, but it should not be read as theology. Dante's architecture of hell as a series of concentric circles, each one reserved for a particular kind of sinner, is entirely the poet's own creation. So too is the rendering of purgatory as a mountain. To read Dante literally is to misunderstand him.

One way to read the *Commedia* is as an elaborate retelling of the Exodus story from the Hebrew Bible. Dante's *Inferno* is like the Israelites' slavery in Egypt. The *Purgatorio* represents the chosen people wandering in the desert, having the corrupt ways of thinking and behaving adopted in their Egyptian captivity worn away through asceticism. The *Paradiso* stands for their entry into the promised land of God's abundance and blessing.

Another way to read the poem—one that meant a lot to me—is as an allegory of the story of the prodigal son from the Gospel of Luke. In the parable, the prodigal son demands and receives his inheritance early from his father. He takes it to the city and blows it in fast living. Hungry and destitute, he returns home, begging to be taken in. His overjoyed father opens his arms to the lost son, showering him with affection. In Dante's *Commedia*, *Inferno* represents the prodigal son wasting his inheritance and destroying his life; *Purgatorio* represents him gathering himself in humility, admitting his errors, and throwing himself on his father's mercy; *Paradiso* represents the welcome-home party for the penitent, fully restored to his father's household.

The journey we will take through the *Commedia*, then, is an allegory of the soul's journey to perfection. We start by taking an honest accounting of our own sins and failings. We continue by learning how to turn away from those tendencies within ourselves that cause us to fail. And we end with learning how to live a life filled with love and grace. After our death, we hope for *theosis*, or full unity with God, in which we will know and enjoy complete harmony among ourselves, God, and the universe.

Three Is the Magic Number

The architecture of Dante's universe is enormously significant. Nothing is left to chance. Numbers meant the world to the medievals, who believed that a rationally ordered universe, as measured by numbers, revealed the mind of God.

In the universe he created in the *Commedia*, Dante enshrined three, the number of the Holy Trinity. There are one hundred cantos, or chapters, in the *Commedia*, thirty-three in each book, plus one extra (in *Inferno*) to symbolize the three-in-one unity of God.

Dante invented a poetic form called *terza rima* for the sake of constructing this cathedral in verse. He built the poem on tercets, or three-line verses, each one linked in rhyme to the next, like a golden chain binding his creation. Each tercet contains exactly thirty-three Italian syllables, eleven in each line. In making his universe, Dante sought to imitate God, whose rationality pervades all that is, who leaves nothing to chance, and through whom all things are united.

The Architecture of the Afterlife

As we set out on this journey, notice that the path through the inferno spirals down toward the pit of hell, while the path through purgatory spirals upward in the direction of heaven. There is no spiral in paradise, because all is perfect and timeless there. In heaven, God gives the pilgrim Dante the illusion of progress through concentric spheres so that he, within his human limitations, can better understand the lessons being taught to him.

The spiral design symbolizes how we fall into the depths of sin and how we may ascend out of them. Few of us lose our soul in a single moment. To become captive to sin typically requires slowly circling around vice, descending a bit more each time, barely perceiving our descent, until finally we arrive at the bottom: circling only around ourselves, prisoners to the ego.

Similarly, few are immediately delivered from the habits of sin. To be made holy requires a similar journey, slowly circling away from ourselves, ascending to God, purging ourselves of devotion to our passions and our egos, allowing ourselves to be filled with healing grace. The circles become smaller as they spiral upward, culminating in the soul circling in a concentrated way around God—a progression perfected in paradise. The Dante scholar Andrew Frisardi writes that medieval labyrinths, which are in spiral form, are meant to symbolize how complex the descent into and out of sin is, and how difficult it is to find our way out of the maze without God's help. The poet builds the logic of the labyrinth into the *Commedia*.

It is endlessly fascinating to tease out the patterns, number symbolisms, and layers of meaning embedded in the *Commedia*. In this book, though, we will keep our eyes on the *Commedia* at its most basic, which is most useful to the general reader. Dante didn't write the poem for scholars; he wrote it to help the lost find their way home.

The road to heaven leads first through hell. In order to find his way out of the dark wood, Dante has to be shown how he got there.

HOW TO THINK MEDIEVALLY

Knowing something about the medieval mind is key to understanding Dante. It was a radically different time from our own. For the medievals, God was not distant and separate from the material world. To the mind of the Middle Ages, everything that exists has meaning, everything is a sign pointing to God, and everything is mystically connected. The point of life—the only way to be human—is to let go of one's ego and live in harmony with God and the cosmos.

Keeping this in mind will help you read the pilgrimage map Dante unscrolls in the *Commedia* as he searches for the meaning of life, and how to live. That said, the *Commedia* is not a puzzle to be deciphered as an experience to be embraced. Dante scholar Charles Singleton says the best way for the modern reader to approach it for the first time is through "an imaginative and sympathetic *surrender* to the experience of the Poem." Suspend your disbelief. Let down your defenses. Disarm your critical faculties. The *Commedia* is so vast and complex that it is impossible to say definitively what it "means." For the new reader, it's better to let the poem pass through your heart, and reveal what it means to *you*.

PART II

—

INFERNO, OR WHY YOU ARE BROKEN

5

THE STORIES OF OUR LIVES

To a truth that bears the face of falsehood
a man should seal his lips if he is able,
for it might shame him, through no fault of his,
but here I cannot be silent.

[*Inferno* XVI:124–127]

Myth, Memories, and the Meaning of Our Lives

A man wakes up in a dark forest. He doesn't know where he is or how he got there. He is frightened and alone, and he wants to run away, but he can't get out. His name is Dante, and this is how his story begins.

Something happened in your brain just now when you read that description of the setting for the *Commedia*'s opening scene.

Neuroscientists have found that the telling of a story, no matter how simple, lights up parts of our brains that lie dormant when we process language. In fact, research has shown that the brain reacts to stories in the same way it responds to actual events. When a story fully enters into your imagination, it is as if you experience it yourself. The more vivid and sensual the descriptions within a story, the more powerfully its lessons, moral and otherwise, lodge in the brain.

Annie Murphy Paul, writing about these discoveries in *The New York Times*, observed: "Reading great literature, it has long been averred, enlarges and improves us as human beings. Brain science shows this claim is truer than we imagined."

Stories tell us how to think and what to do. They teach us what to love, what to fear, what to hope for, and whom to trust. Stories reveal to us how we differ from others and how we are the same. They tell us where we came from, where we stand, and where we are going. Stories impose order on chaos. From grand cosmic myths to intimate family tales, it is in stories that we find meaning, purpose, and the truths by which we live—or, if we are unlucky, the lies that lead us astray.

Our choices often emerge from how we feel about the information we take in and how the stories we have accepted as truthful accounts of reality train our emotions to engage and to interpret the world.

The Anglican bishop N. T. Wright observed, "Tell someone to do something, and you change their life—for a day. Tell someone a story, and you change their life."

If we don't understand ourselves as part of a greater story, or tradition, we will have no idea what we are supposed to do with our lives. In our modern world, we have lost the story that for centuries gave most people in our culture a way to make sense of their lives: the biblical narrative.

Losing the Plot of Our Own Stories

In our secular age, we no longer believe we are part of any universal story. We are free to choose our own narratives, which means we can follow our hearts. If there is no story except the one we write for ourselves, we are liberated to do whatever we like.

The trouble with this is that to be free from the imposition of someone else's story means we become slaves to our own passions. If there is no story that is objectively true, how can we know when we've chosen correctly? *If it feels good, do it; if it feels right, believe it,* may strike you as the only sensible guide to conduct. This is how many people think today.

When you are the captain of your own soul, though, and have cast aside all the maritime charts showing you the safe route through dark waters, navigating only by your own stars, it's easy to make a shipwreck of your life. You wake up one day and wonder, *Where am I? How did I get here? How do I get home?* This is where Dante, the pilgrim, finds himself in the opening lines of the *Inferno*:

> *Midway in the journey of our life*
> *I came to myself in a dark wood,*
> *For the straight way was lost.*

> [*Inferno* I:1–3]

He has been sleepwalking through life when suddenly he awakens and realizes that he is lost. He once was on the "straight way" through life, but somehow he strayed off the path and now finds himself in unfamiliar territory.

Dante Alighieri had done all the right things, according to the story of his culture. He had written beautiful poems that won him fame and respect. He married and had children, and he was a man of the Church, faithful to his God. Later he took up political leadership in his city and tried to govern justly, even when it meant sending his troublemaking best friend into exile.

And what had that gotten him? He lost everything: his wealth, his power, and his family. If he hadn't fled into exile, Dante would have lost his life.

Few of us will suffer a fall from grace quite like Dante's, but our day will assuredly come. It could be in the form of a betrayal by someone we love. It could be divorce, bankruptcy, or professional failure. Maybe it will be a loss of faith in religion or a cherished ideal—including the ideal that we will become successful and secure because we are good and play by the rules. Possibly it will be an accident that robs us of our health, or the serial humiliations of an aging body. It might even be the untimely death of someone we love.

Whatever it is, it will provoke a crisis within us. It will be a moment of reckoning in which we know that something went wrong for us. And we will discover that we took a wrong turn in our lives and now are wandering in circles, in the darkness of a forest, where there are no paths.

> *Ah, how hard it is to tell*
> *the nature of that wood, savage, dense and harsh—*
> *the very thought of it renews my fear!*

> [*Inferno* I:4–6]

This is how I felt after returning to Louisiana. The story I had lived by all my life told me that coming home would make everything right. I had tried this once before and failed, but I was a much younger man then. Since that time, I had married, had three children, and achieved much as a professional journalist. I had done everything correctly according to the conventional American narrative, but something still didn't feel right.

Ruthie's death showed me what it was, or so I thought. I needed to reclaim my roots. The story with which I was raised taught that uniting once and for all with family and place would create harmony within me. And the parable of the prodigal son, a key story in the narrative of my faith, primed me to expect welcome. While Dante left home in exile, I came home to exile. Things were not supposed to turn out this way.

A New Hope

As he stumbles around the dark wood, Dante comes to the end of the valley, and there he sees the rising sun, which he calls:

> *. . . the planet*
> *that leads men straight, no matter what their road.*

> [*Inferno* I:17–18]

In the *Commedia*, the sun symbolizes God, the Light of the World, the One who illuminates all paths, and the beacon calling us to our true home. Here, in the first lines of *Inferno*, are the conditions that make the journey out of the dark wood possible.

To save yourself from the dark wood, you have to first believe that you are lost. And you cannot find your way back to your destination if you don't believe your life is a journey that is taking you somewhere. *AMEN*

For Dante, all journeys, however varied, must end in a return to God. Only if we make unity with God the end point of our pilgrimage can we find the straight path and discern between the right way and the wrong way. The important thing is that Dante's awakening teaches him two things he needs to save his life: that *he is lost*, and that *there is a way out*.

He can't prove either. But he knows, somehow, that they are true. These are acts of faith. And there is another act of faith the pilgrim makes in this canto: that despite fear, confusion, and evil, *God created the universe as an act of love*, and that divine love is responsible for everything that happens in the world.

In my own crisis, the one thing that gave me hope was the conviction that God was there and that he did not will me to be miserable. I was sure that there was a right way out of this dark wood, that I wouldn't spend all my days shrouded with fatigue and sidelined by anxiety and depression. Many afternoons I would retreat into the dark guest bedroom, which was outfitted with two cavelike sleeping alcoves concealed behind thin curtains. I would draw the curtain, lie down on one of the beds, and stare at the ceiling until I could close my eyes and sleep for hours.

There had to be light in this darkness. The confidence that I would not be abandoned there may have been the only thing that kept me from total despair.

As soon as Dante makes a move toward the light, a leopard, a lion, and a she-wolf block all his paths out. The she-wolf is the last of the three to advance on the woebegone traveler.

> *And like one who rejoices in his gains*
> *but when the time comes and he loses,*
> *turns all his thought to sadness and lament,*

such did the restless beast make me—
coming against me, step by step,
it drove me down to where the sun is silent.

[*Inferno* I: 55-60]

Sin as a Failure of Love

The wild beasts symbolize sin. Let's dwell on that word for a moment: *sin.* The novelist Francis Spufford says that nowadays everybody knows that "sin" refers to indulgence, or naughty pleasure, but that's about it. For Christians, though, sin refers not to what Spufford calls "yummy transgression"—a chocolate sundae, getting drunk at a party, a roll in the hay with one's lover—but rather, to paraphrase his pungent expression, to the human propensity to screw things up.

When you think about sin this way, you cannot help recognizing that you—yes, you—are a sinner. No matter how hard we try to do right and how sincerely we want to do good, we fail. That's how we are. It's like a sickness that we can't quite shake. If you cannot admit that you too have a propensity to screw things up despite yourself, then you are probably suffering from the sin of pride.

Not long ago I was complaining to my wife about a certain man in our town who has a reputation for self-righteousness. "How can he think so highly of himself?" I said. "Is he really so blind?"

No sooner had the words left my mouth than I thought about my own high opinion of myself. I never set out to hurt anybody or to do the wrong thing. But I do. Every single day. Maybe I don't do it as much as I used to, but scarcely an hour goes by when I don't pass harsh judgment on someone else, or bark at my kids for their misbehavior, or blog something clever but cruel, or miss an easy opportunity to comfort and encourage someone who is struggling and in need of healing. There are people in my town who are sick and who could use a visit from me, or at least a phone call. But I don't go see them and I don't call them. There is always an excuse, and sometimes they're good excuses.

This is a failure of love on my part. It's screwing things up. It is sin. Sure, the world is full of drug dealers and thieves and adulterers and warmongers, all of whom no doubt do more active harm than a small-town writer with a sense of humor and a potbelly and a weakness for rich food. I mean, look, I go to church regularly, I give to charity, I'm a good husband and father, and I scratch my dog under his chin when he asks. I never do anything seriously wrong in my life, right?

Wrong. That's not good enough. I'm not responsible for the sins of the drug dealers, thieves, adulterers, and warmongers. I am responsible for myself. Every time I do the things I shouldn't do or fail to do the things I should do, I sin. The weight of our sins can seem overwhelming, so much so that we feel trapped by them in a dark wood of our own making.

What makes it worse is the sense in contemporary culture that sin is either not real or no big deal. Unfortunately, this attitude is common in contemporary churches, many of which preach that it's more important to affirm the faithful in their okayness than to lead them away from sin.

Soft Patriarchs, Squishy Christianity

This was my primary experience of Christianity. It reached its nadir on Ash Wednesday when the priest at my Dallas Catholic parish preached that Lent is a season in which we are to come to love ourselves more. I came to despise this rubbish. My sins and failings were clear to me, and I knew how much I needed God's help in overcoming them. I craved guidance, direction, and the kind of loving, firm hand my father had provided when I was a boy. Though Daddy could be too rigid in his moralism, one of the greatest gifts he gave me was a strong sense of right and wrong and of the importance of fighting for what's right, both in the world and inside yourself.

Our breach in my teenage years had left me adrift, bereft of the kind of masculine wisdom I craved. It was the fatherly strength of Pope John Paul II that helped draw me into Catholicism. Here was a man who had the same qualities I admired in Daddy—the paternal compassion, the conviction, the strength of character—without the stridency and narrowness.

The Catholic Church I found, though, often lacked the moral clarity and courage of its pope. Its teachings were clear, but I often felt that its clergy abdicated their role as credible spiritual leaders. To a surprising degree, I learned, this was also true in Dante Alighieri's time.

Dante translator Anthony Esolen points out that Dante, in his treatise *Convivio*, says that a young man who lacks guidance from his elders will lose himself in the woods of life. "Such a forest is made all the rougher for corruption in papacy and the empire," Esolen adds, referring to the Europe of Dante's time, "for then there are no reliable spiritual guides to direct us on the right path and no temporal authorities to check us when we wander from it."

This is what happened to Dante, who had believed in the Church and the state and sought to serve them faithfully but was betrayed by both. Now he is trapped in the woods, with wild animals—symbols for Dante's paralyzing tendencies to screw up his life. Though he did not directly cause his downfall, Dante is to some degree responsible for it, and he is too weak, frightened, and confused to deliver himself from his torment.

A Light in the Darkness

Just when all seems hopeless, a stranger appears. He is a messenger.

"Have mercy on me, whatever you are," Dante pleads, "whether shade or living man." It is in fact the shade of Virgil, the august poet of Roman antiquity. He asks the pilgrim why he's stuck in this desolate place.

Dante is stunned. "You are my teacher and my author," he says, praising Virgil—who lived thirteen hundred years before our man—as the artist whose verses taught him how to write. The pilgrim tells Virgil that he's lost and that the beasts won't let him leave the dark wood. Dante is so overcome with fear that he weeps.

"It is another path that you must follow," says Virgil, "if you would flee this wild and savage place." The Roman offers to be his guide "through an eternal place" of torment and pain.

The shade of an ancient poet appears and promises to deliver you from your misery but says that the road ahead is going to be arduous, even horrible. A reasonable man would have said to the ghost, "Wait a minute, you died ages ago. I must be having a hallucination. How do I know you are who you say you are? I have to think about this." But the pilgrim did not say that.

Nor did he say, "Thanks, but I'll wait here; things might get better." He didn't say, "How can I trust that you know the way out? Maybe you are wrong. Maybe you will lead me to ruin." And Dante didn't say, "Show me the whole picture, the entire map ahead, and then I will follow you."

He said none of those things. He simply said, "I trust you, and I will follow you." That was a leap of faith.

Though Virgil had been sent by God, via his messenger Beatrice, on a mission to save Dante, the master didn't lay it all out for the lost pilgrim in their first meeting. Dante was in no condition to see the whole picture. All Dante knew in that moment was that if he stayed where he was, he would suffer and die—and that before him stood an authority figure he trusted would lead him to safety.

Reading those opening lines, it struck me: I am the pilgrim Dante, and the poet Dante is offering to be my Virgil.

Those opening cantos dazzled me. They lit up my brain and kindled my curiosity. It was as if the Tuscan poet himself stood in front of me, in the Florentine red tunic and matching hooded cap, inviting me to follow him, telling me he knew the way out.

I believe in epiphanies and revelations. That is, I believe that there are moments in life in which the heavens part, a sunbeam descends, and you know intuitively that you are standing at a crossroads. They come when we are open to them, when we believe by faith that there is someone out there who sees us, loves us, and wants to help us. And they especially come when life humbles us to the point where the illusion of self-sufficiency is no longer tenable, where the idea that we can figure out everything and handle it without help is shown to be a lie.

As my priest Father Matthew has reminded me often, in a moment like that, you have no choice but to open your eyes, fall to your knees, and say, one way or another, "You are God. I am not. Please help."

I was in that desperate spot in the summer of 2013, and it was from that place of brokenness that I prayed that prayer. God sent me a guide; his name was Dante Alighieri. He appeared to me not in a desert or a dark wood but in a bookstore, arising from the pages of his poem. I hesitated, but because I knew that if I stayed mired in fear, anxiety, and illness I would perish, I suspended my skepticism and cynicism and chose to give Dante a chance.

I needed a new story. Maybe his story could help me rewrite my own. In any case, it would be nice to quit thinking about my own problems for a while.

"Why, why do you delay?" Virgil says to Dante when he quails. "Why do you let such cowardice rule your heart?"

Why, indeed? I thought. *I will be brave. I will see where this road and this poet take me. I will follow. I will.*

HOW TO SEE THE VALUE OF FAITH

If you want to find God, or at least a way out of the trap you are in, you have to open yourself to faith. I'm not talking about religious faith, necessarily; I mean faith that someone else can see more clearly than you, knows better than you what you need, and can be trusted to show you the way to freedom.

To save yourself from your own dark wood, you must first make three acts of faith: affirm that you are lost, affirm that there is a way out, and affirm that there is a God, or Higher Power, that loves you and will not abandon you in the shadowlands.

The good news is that you have the power to do something about it. The road to illumination and healing is before you, but you have to humble yourself to follow an experienced guide. The guide can be a pastor, a teacher, or a wise elder. It can also be the author of a book whose wisdom has stood the test of time. This is your final act of faith before the journey: to be willing to trust your guide and submit to his authority. After all, if you knew the way out, you wouldn't need him.

6

INTO THE BLACK HOLE

THROUGH ME THE WAY TO THE CITY OF WOE,
THROUGH ME THE WAY TO EVERLASTING PAIN,
THROUGH ME THE WAY AMONG THE LOST.

[*Inferno* III:1–3]

How We Fall In, How We Climb Out

Though Dante tried to pass off his second thoughts about the journey as humility ("Neither I nor any other think me fit for this. And if I commit myself to come, I fear it may be madness"), Virgil knows self-deception and rationalization when he sees them. Dante's double-mindedness was awfully familiar to me. It's how I avoided getting serious about God for years.

For some time, when I was in high school, college, and shortly thereafter, I kept God at a distance. I was unsure that Christianity was true, or so I told myself. Some of my concerns were exactly that: reasonable uncertainty over the truth of the faith. But my position of inquiring skepticism was the virtuous gloss covering my fear and sloth. Deep down, I was afraid that Christianity *might really be true*—and of what the consequences for me would be if that were the case. I would have to change my life. And that was something I was not prepared to do. St. Augustine's prayer might have been my own: "Lord, give me chastity and continence, but not just yet."

All of us have something like that from our past (or maybe our present) that we can point to, a situation in which we masked our fear of acting behind a veil of virtue. This is a moment for the pilgrim Dante to be honest with himself, to take unsparing stock of his real motivations, and to conquer his fear. That is an incredibly hard thing to do.

After the rheumatologist's report, our family doctor and my wife told me that it was time to start seeing a therapist. I did not want to do this. I intellectualized my fear by telling myself that therapy was nothing more than navel-gazing and narcissism.

"You need help with this situation," Julie said. "You are letting your pride keep you from getting it."

"Am not," I said, petulance rising in my voice. "I just don't see the point in sitting around talking to a stranger for an hour every week about my problems. I know why things are messed up. I don't need somebody to explain that to me."

She wasn't letting me get away with that.

"You know what? You don't know everything," she sassed. "What you need is someone outside of the family system to take an objective look at it and help you figure out what to do. And you are going to do it because the kids and I are tired of you being absent from our lives because you're always sleeping."

The doctor texted me the name of a licensed Baton Rouge therapist he trusted, a guy named Mike Holmes, who happened to be an ordained Southern Baptist minister as well.

"I don't know about this guy," I said to my wife. "Do I really want a preacher doing my therapy? It seems weird to me."

Standing next to my leather armchair, Julie crossed her arms and fired a don't-mess-with-me look my way.

"Humble yourself and call him," she said with buckshot in her voice.

Humility as the First Step to Recovery

A week later, I found myself in a bland, cream-colored room in a south Baton Rouge office park, sitting on a puffy couch, facing Mike Holmes.

He was not what I had expected. Though he was nearly bald, he was younger than I. His shirt was untucked. He wore jeans, and he talked like a friend you would meet for coffee. I liked him instantly.

Mike listened to my story, asking few questions. As our hour came to a close, I concluded, "My wife says that I'm going to do the typical man thing and expect you to tell me what to do to fix it. And she said therapists don't do that. I wish you would. It would save us both a lot of time and trouble."

Mike smiled. "No, I'm not going to tell you how to fix it," he said. "But what I am going to do is this. We are going to explore all these stories you've told me, and look at them to see where you might be misreading the situation, and where there might be room for positive change.

"Here's what I want you to focus on," he continued. "You cannot control other people, but you can control your reaction to them."

"What do you mean?"

"I mean that your parents are old, and they've lived this way all their lives. They're not going to change," he said. "And your brother-in-law and nieces, they've thought of you in a negative way for as long as they've known you, and they've just suffered the worst thing that can happen to a family. They're just trying to put one foot in front of the other right now, and it's taking all they have."

"Yeah, I guess that's fair."

"So what you and I are going to do is figure out how to separate what you can't change from what you can, and work on the stuff you do have power over," Mike said. "You have a lot more control here than you think you do."

"Okay, let's do this," I nodded.

Where Hope Goes to Die

The pilgrim Dante and his Roman guide enter into the inferno on Good Friday in the year 1300. Good Friday is the day Christians mark the death of Jesus and on which, Christian tradition tells us, he descended into hell to rescue souls. Perhaps the most famous line from the book *Inferno* is

the last line of the inscription over its gate: ABANDON ALL HOPE, YOU WHO
ENTER HERE.

The lesser-known parts of the inscription explain the reason for hell's
existence: justice, wisdom, and love. How did those good things motivate
God to create a place of eternal torment? And what does it mean when
Virgil tells Dante that the shades he will encounter in this place have "lost
the good of the intellect"?

The damned have no hope, because their eternal fates have already
been decided. To have "lost the good of the intellect" implies that they are
no longer reasoning creatures but articulate zombies who have become
one with their sinfulness, forever.

God's love made the inferno because love will not force itself upon a
man. Life is a time for choosing; God loves us so much that he will give
us what we choose, for eternity. As we will see later on this journey, all it
takes to avoid hell is to say a single word asking for God's mercy, even in
your dying breath. Hell is for those who will not have God, those who
made a final, remorseless choice for their own passions over unity with
and submission to their Creator. Satan's sin was to rebel against God. The
root of all sin is this fundamental pride, a pride that prefers the self, with
all its disordered passions, to God.

The reason Dante must first go down before he can ascend is that he
has to become reawakened to the true horror of sin—that is, to be scared
straight. The torments he will observe all have meaning; they are not
random acts of cruelty. They represent the aspects of your self that you
loved more than God. The journey downward, then, is in truth a journey
of introspection for Dante. It symbolizes his personal pilgrimage into the
dark recesses of his own heart.

Sitting in my armchair, I felt a flutter of anticipation. I sensed that my
idea of hell, like my idea of sin, was about to be shaken up. I had always
thought of hell as a cosmic version of a medieval dungeon: a place where
bad people go when they die, to live forever in suffering. Despite surface
appearances, that's not how Dante sees it. Think of the inferno as a black
hole of the spirit.

The Soul-Killing Gravity of Sin

In astronomy, a black hole is a star whose gravity has become so strong it has collapsed in on itself. Nothing can escape it, not even light. At the center of the funnel-shaped black hole is a singularity, a point of infinite density and infinite gravity, which allows nothing, not even time, to escape its death grip. The outer rim of the black hole, called the event horizon, is the border of eternity: anything that crosses it will never be seen or heard from again. Eventually the object will reach the singularity and be annihilated.

Obviously Dante knew nothing of black holes. But the black hole model gave me a handle on the way Dante constructs his afterlife. Standing at the gates of hell, Virgil and the pilgrim are at the inferno's event horizon. There is no escape from this hole, which spirals to the center of the earth. At the bottom, at the point of the universe that in medieval cosmology is farthest away from God, dwells Satan, whose angelic name, Lucifer, means "light-bearer."

The Bible calls Lucifer the "morning star" and tells of his rebellion against God, his fall from heaven, and exile into hell. Think of pride as a spiritual form of gravity. With Lucifer, the first rebel—that is, the first created being to choose his own will over God's—his immense pride collapsed on itself and formed the black hole we call hell. All the souls in hell are small versions of black holes: they were so given over to gratifying themselves that love—symbolized by light—could barely escape the gravity of their egos.

When death carries them across the event horizon into the afterlife, they fall into the Luciferian abyss and are spiritually annihilated. To lose "the good of the intellect" means to lose the ability to perceive God and share in his love, which is what ultimately makes us human. Their personal gravity, so to speak, is so great that here in their eternity, blinded by the absence of divine light, they cannot see beyond themselves.

I closed the book and sat in my darkened living room in the pool of light cast by the reading lamp. The house was quiet; Julie and the children had gone to bed. I thought about my sins—not in my customary guilt-ridden way but as a force of gravity that distorts the light of love.

Preoccupation with my failed homecoming and the sense of anger, shame, and betrayal it engendered within me had darkened my perception. It colored everything I saw, and drained the joy from everyday life. It sapped my physical strength and weakened my immune system. These physical and spiritual effects came from sin, both my own sin and the sins of others against me. A bitter line from an old Randy Newman song characterized my attitude toward my Starhill family: "I want you to hurt like I do."

And I did. I was so overwhelmed by my own pain that I could not see that my Starhill family was also trapped by their relentless grief—a grief for which they stoically refused counseling.

The only counter to this alienating darkness was to make space for light and love, but I did not feel capable of it then. Still, I sensed that I had learned an important strategic clue: to think of sin not as a concept but as a malign force that bends love, brings the darkness, and blinds us to reality so profoundly that we lose our way.

Too Wicked for Heaven, Too Boring for Hell

The second clue came when I returned to *Inferno* and read about the first wretched souls Dante saw in hell—or rather, on its outskirts. These are the neutrals, those lukewarm souls who in life would not take a side, either for good or for evil. Neither good enough for heaven nor bad enough for hell proper, the neutrals dwell in no-man's-land, running this way and that after a flapping banner, naked, worms beneath their feet, and swarmed by stinging wasps who leave their faces bloodied.

Those who had no passion in life and who were dead to the world suffer punishment by having nothing but mindless passion and constant pain. This is how the poet Dante distributes justice in *Inferno*: either by giving the damned in full measure what they wanted as mortals or by forcing on them the opposite of what they chose in life.

They "never were alive," says the pilgrim. To live means to love, which is to desire either good or evil. To have no desire at all, or to remain indifferent to desire, is to stand outside of the drama of our existence, hedging your bets, hoping God will not notice. You cannot be both good and neutral, because to refuse desire is to refuse life. The goal is not to remove desire but to purify it.

As I lay in bed that night thinking of the cowardice of the neutrals, I remembered a conversation I had once had with Father Matthew. "There are times when I want to pack up and leave here," I told him, "and just be done with it once and for all.

"The thing that holds me back, aside from my commitments to Julie and the kids, and to my parents, is the sense that there's something I have to conquer within myself," I told him. "It's like there's a dragon down there that I have to slay. I can run away again, but I'm not going to know peace until I kill it."

"Any idea what that might be?" the priest asked.

"Kind of," I answered. "It has to do with my relationship to my family—most of all my dad. But I'm not sure what, exactly."

Lying under the covers, drifting off to sleep, I realized that if I left home now to get away from the pain and frustration, I would be no better than the neutrals. I would spend the rest of my life chasing banners, dragging my wife and children behind me, trying to find some substitute for what I longed to find in Louisiana: the end of exile.

I had to stay and fight this thing. But who was the enemy? And what was the nature of the battle?

HOW TO ESCAPE THE BLACK HOLE

You cannot control other people, but you can control your reaction to them. That is a key principle to your healing.

Sin is not the breaking of moral rules, but a failure of love. We love the wrong things, or we love the right things in the wrong way. All of us do this; it is the human condition. Nevertheless, you are responsible for your own sin. It's why you are in crisis.

Thinking of sin as law-breaking, as many of us do, disguises the way it works on our hearts and minds, and keeps us from dealing with it effectively. Here's a better model: Think of love as light, and sin as gravity, a force that bends light. The stronger the gravitational field, the farther love will fall from its mark. Hell is a black hole, where the light of love goes to die. Your goal in life: to put as much distance between your heart and the black hole's deadly gravity field as you can. Passing too close to it will make even your most sincere acts of love land far from their intended destination.

Don't worry about the hearts of others; you are captain of your own.

7

THE TEMPEST

The hellish squall, which never rests,
sweeps spirits in its headlong rush,
tormenting, whirls and strikes them.

. . . I understood that to such torment
the carnal sinners are condemned,
they who make reason subject to desire.

[*Inferno* V:31–33; 37–39]

Lust Is a Dark and Stormy Night

Because Dante's *Inferno* is an expansive catalogue of sin, I passed through circles of hell in which the sin punished was not one that afflicted me, though there was still plenty to learn there. However, early in the journey, I passed through the circle of a sin that was once a problem for me. This is how I discovered how deeply Dante Alighieri's vision penetrated the human heart.

Crossing into the Circle of Lust, Dante and Virgil pass into a dark place where "a hellish squall, which never rests," blows the damned around like lawn chairs in a hurricane. Because the lustful gave themselves over to turbulent, uncontrollable passion, the tempest is their eternal punishment.

We can't be certain of the role lust played in young Dante's life, but he would have been a very strange fellow had he remained chaste until marriage, and even within marriage. Italy of the Middle Ages was a place of robust sensuality, and the casual verses Dante exchanged with the men of his poetry circle—as distinct from his formal poems idealizing love— suggests that he partook with gusto of the pleasures of the flesh. In fact, his poetic mentor Guido Cavalcanti—himself no clean-living ascetic— once rebuked young Dante for blowing his talent through partying too hard.

You wouldn't know this from Dante's love poetry. One of his most famous of those poems appears in *Vita Nuova*, which appeared in 1295. That poem begins like this:

Women who understand the truth of love,
I want to talk with you a while about
My lady—not because I could run out
Of words and ways to praise her, but to set
my mind at ease. Her worth is so above
the rest, I feel such lightness in my heart,
that if speech didn't stammer I'd impart
new love to those who are not lovers yet.
(trans. Andrew Frisardi)

In *Vita Nuova*, Dante traces his growing maturity as a poet of love. The book collects his best work from the age of eighteen until his mid-twenties. In its final chapter, Dante discloses his new recognition that experiencing earthly love for a woman—in his case, Beatrice—is a preparation for eternal life, for union with God. The poet concludes by saying that after finishing the book's final sonnet, he had "a marvelous vision" in which he saw "things that made me decide not to say anything more about this blessed lady until I was capable of writing about her more worthily."

He said nothing else of Beatrice for at least a decade. The next thing he wrote about her was the *Commedia*, the greatest love poem ever composed.

Mastering sexual desire was a problem for me in my youth, for a reason not foreign to Dante in the same period of his life: I could not resolve the tension between the clean ideals I had of love with the messiness of real life. I was no kind of lothario. Far from it: I was far too knotted up by my own insecurities and intellectualism to be the roué of my dreams. Yes, I had my share of hookups, but they never produced anything more than hangovers and guilt, mostly for the lies I told to avoid subsequent emotional entanglements with these women. "It's not you, it's me," I would say, which was true, but not in the self-serving way I meant it.

The women I wanted most were those I couldn't have, because they allowed me to spiritualize my desire without having to test it. When I finally was rid of my two-year unrequited infatuation with one of these goddesses, I shamefacedly wrote and asked her (her name, if you can believe it, was actually Beatrice) to please return my love letters. She did, graciously, though under protest, and I destroyed them all. You probably could have spotted that bonfire from space.

In Love with Love

I joke about the bonfire, but the fact is, in my late teens and twenties, I poured an enormous amount of creative passion into the pursuit of women, especially through writing. So did Dante Alighieri; in fact, devotion to the cult of romantic love defined his early poetry. The courtly love tradition in European poetry began two generations before Dante's birth, when Provençal troubadours began to exalt romantic love in their songs. By Dante's day, the imagination of poets encompassed the nature of a man's love for a woman like planets wheeling around a blazing sun. They worshiped the ideal personalized as "Lord Love" in their poetry. Young Dante, possessed by the spirit of love when he first saw Beatrice, devoted his art to its praise and glory, and his passion to its pursuit.

That was me, back in the day: in love with love, and consumed by a desire to find the one who would complete me by absorbing me fully within herself. I approached women like a reckless child hunting for Easter eggs, taking no notice of whom or what I trampled to find what I wanted. And because I did not want sex, primarily, but the holy grail of love, I told myself that my quest was noble. It was the icon of my personal religion.

It sounds strange to put it that way, but for me, sex was only the outward manifestation of the inward state for which I longed intensely. Sex was always disappointing to me, because no matter how intense the physical pleasure, the absence of spiritual communion left me with a sense of melancholy and alienation.

I tried to make myself believe that the cause was my inability to shake off Christian guilt from my childhood, but deep down I knew there was something else going on.

Now it is clear to me that I was desperate for a God I would not have. Instead, I wanted not simply to be in love but to be utterly consumed by it. In the music, films, and books closest to my heart, becoming a slave to Lord Love, was the summit of all human experience.

One of my favorite movies back then was a 1986 French romance, *Betty Blue*, about the combustible relationship between an extravagantly sexy but unstable woman and the writer who was obsessed by her. I loved the movie so much I bought a giant poster of the film and tacked it above my bed in my dorm room and in every bedroom I slept in for years afterward.

The Cad Crashes

When I was twenty-five, I crashed into the consequences of my folly. I became involved with a beautiful and intelligent woman, a sunny blonde with an irresistible smile and wide, trusting blue eyes. She fell hard for me, and though I liked being with her, I didn't have the patience for anything short of instant, head-over-heels rhapsody. I broke it off long after I should have, hurting her badly with my dallying. She had told a mutual friend that she thought I might be the one she would marry. The guilt I had over the way I treated her was intense, and I carried that weight with me for a decade, until I found her online and asked her forgiveness (she kindly gave it).

You could say it was just an ordinary breakup, and you would probably be right. But I knew the sweetness of my girlfriend's heart, and I knew I had treated her shabbily. When my self-tortured utopian romanticism hurt me, that was one thing, but when it hurt others, especially one as gentle and as kind as my then-girlfriend, that was something else. Was that the kind of man I wanted to be?

And then there was the drunken hookup at a party with a woman I barely knew that resulted in a pregnancy scare.

"Don't worry," she said. "I'll have an abortion if it comes to that."

"You can't!" I said, stunned. "It would be . . . it would be our baby."

"It's my body, I'll do what I want," she fired back. And I knew that as a matter of law, at least, she was right. But if she went through with it over my objection, that would not release me from moral responsibility for the death of what I believed would be my own son or daughter—a child who would not have come into the world had I not been so careless.

There was no pregnancy, but waiting for the news was the longest two weeks of my life. I knew that I could not carry on like this.

I had been praying for a sign that God was there and, if he was, that he would throw me a lifeline. By then I was sick of myself and eager to change my life.

The Interview

One day, someone tipped my editor off that a local priest in his nineties had an interesting story to tell, and my boss dispatched me to see if it was true. I went to interview Monsignor Carlos Sanchez, who lived in a retirement facility in Baton Rouge.

Monsignor Sanchez was a frail, tiny man with delicate skin the color of milky coffee and a reedy voice abraded by old age. Over tea, he told me his story. He had been born in Guatemala in 1898, to a wealthy coffee planter and his English wife. They sent him to Dartmouth to study engineering.

"Those brilliant minds made a lot of boys lose their faith," he told me. "They made me lose mine. Everything became so uncertain."

Sanchez, who had a master's degree in architecture, joined the team designing the Empire State Building. Then, following his passion for painting, he worked closely with the Mexican muralists Diego Rivera and José Orozco.

Once, on a visit to Guatemala, he accompanied family members to mass, hiding his atheism from them out of courtesy. As Sanchez kneeled to receive communion, a life-size image of the crucified Christ appeared at his side. The old man recalled, "He said, 'I have always loved you.' Simple as that. No reproach, no nothing." In an instant, twenty years of unbelief evaporated.

Years later, a second mystical experience at the same communion rail spurred Sanchez to seek ordination to the priesthood. "When the priest came to give me communion, his arm, his alb became dazzling white," the monsignor told me. "Then Our Lord said to me, 'Why don't you do what I tell you?' As distinctly as I hear you. He wasn't threatening me, you understand. But that really was terrifying. I knew I had to do something right away."

It took years to convince the Church to receive a man of his age into the seminary. But, eventually Archbishop Joseph Rummel of New Orleans ordained him at the age of fifty-one. After decades of priestly service, Sanchez retired to the little apartment where we were drinking tea.

When he finished his story, the old monsignor's face glowed and his cheeks were wet with tears. It was as if all those things had happened to him only the day before. By the light in Monsignor Sanchez's eyes, I could see that all my intellectual doubts about Christianity amounted to nothing more than a problem of the will: I didn't want to believe, because then I would have to change my life.

But I wanted the peace that old man had more than I wanted to pursue my own desires. I wanted light. I wanted clarity. I resolved to become a Catholic.

For me, Catholicism offered beauty and mysticism upon a doctrinal foundation—a testimony of truth—that seemed as solid as rock. Despite his intense disgust with corruption in the papacy and the institutional church, and contrary to the practical atheism of some of his literary and social circle, Dante remained a stalwart Roman Catholic. He accepted the ancient and unbroken Scriptural teaching that the church is the mystical Body of Christ, the embodiment of a covenant God made with humanity that cannot be nullified no matter how wicked the church's leaders may be.

In fact, Dante held firm to the orthodox Catholic teaching that following the Roman church and its Supreme Pastor, the pope, are as important to eternal life as the Bible. The poet has Beatrice advise Christians to shun innovations:

> *"You have the Testaments, both New and Old,*
> *and the Shepherd of the Church to guide you.*
> *Let these suffice for your salvation."*

> [*Paradiso* V:76–78]

In 1921, Pope Benedict XV issued an encyclical—the highest form of papal teaching—in praise of Dante, calling him the greatest Catholic artist of all time. "The divine poet throughout his whole life professed in exemplary manner the Catholic religion," the pope wrote, noting in jittery passing that Dante had severe words for some of Benedict's predecessors on the Petrine throne.

It is impossible to pin an artist and religious reformer as subversive as Dante Alighieri down as a simple son of the church. Nevertheless, the Holy Father's glorification of the troublesome Tuscan whose poem put some popes in hell is sublime vindication for Dante, who suffered a kind of bloodless martyrdom for his Catholic faith. Six hundred years after his passing, the precious stone rejected by the church's fourteenth-century builders became by papal recognition a cornerstone of Catholic art.

It was the testimony of Catholic art—that is, the French Gothic cathedral—and a priest-artist named Carlos Sanchez, that lit the spark of conversion within me, and made me, at last, want the Catholic faith more than anything else.

The Inconvenient Truth About Sex

By the time I was received into the Catholic Church in 1993, I had committed to live chastely until marriage. I was twenty-six years old. It was one of the hardest things I've ever done—and one of the best.

Many Catholics think the Church makes too big a deal about sex; some think the Church should say nothing about sex at all. But practicing chastity after my experience with sex, I understood the wisdom of the Church's teaching. All the lies I had told myself, and that our culture tells us, about what sex is for left me feeling hollow and unsatisfied.

I didn't want sex; I wanted love. I mean, yes, I wanted sex, but when it was decoupled from love, that desire was a counterfeit, a false idol. It was destructive to me and to the women I had been with. I realized around this time that by trying to banish that guilty feeling so I could be as free as I wanted to be and thought I had a right to be, I was killing off the most humane part of myself.

When I embraced chastity, I had no idea if I would ever get married. The thought that this might be a lifetime thing filled me with dread. But the prospect of going back to the Egypt from which I'd just been delivered was worse. So on I went, trusting that God knew what was best for me, and knowing that I would rather die to my body with him than live in my body without him.

I was not entirely successful in those first years, but I was a lot better than I had been. Prayer and the confessional helped me with my repentance. Learning to tell myself no was a new thing, and an important one. I learned to steer myself away from getting involved with women who didn't share my faith and my commitment to chastity before marriage.

My secular friends thought I was a very odd duck because of this. But I didn't care. I knew what I was being saved from. I knew the kind of man I was and the kind of man I wanted to be. By practicing chastity, I began to understand better the workings of my own heart, and how I had fallen into self-deception (and deceived others) in past relationships.

But here's the thing: I was still blinded by my habit of exalting romantic love. For my twenty-eighth birthday, my friend Tom Sullivan gave me a copy of *The Letters of J. R. R. Tolkien*. On a cold February morning, I sat in the living room of my Capitol Hill apartment and cracked open the book. A 1941 letter Tolkien wrote to his son Michael caught my attention. The older Tolkien warned his son to be wary of courtly love, which exalts "imaginary Deities, Love and the Lady."

"The woman is another fallen human being with a soul in peril," Tolkien wrote, adding that the courtly ideal "inculcates exaggerated notions of 'true love,' as a fire from without, a permanent exaltation, unrelated to age, childbearing, and plain life, and unrelated to will and purpose."

That was an epiphany. I had thought my high view of women and love was something wholly noble, especially when joined to Christian conviction. Tolkien showed me that I was actually engaged in idol worship of "Love and the Lady," obscuring the truth and making it harder for me to find what I deeply desired: true love and companionship with a woman.

That morning, I took the *Betty Blue* poster down. I was turning away from the vision of romantic love that books and movies told me was true, because now I knew better.

Later that year, I took a journalism job in Florida, where I made great friends, but none who shared my faith. I had no religious community. From a spiritual point of view, this was the desert. I was all alone, and agonizingly lonely. This was when the purifying flame burned the hottest. All I could do was pray, hope, and keep struggling.

A Lone-Star Beatrice

And then I flew to Austin, Texas, one weekend to meet Frederica Mathewes-Green, a friend who was giving a speech. The Texas capital is one of my favorite towns, and I wanted to show her around. On a Friday night, Frederica, a writer, gave a reading at a bookstore. There I met a University of Texas journalism undergraduate named Julie Harris. The moment I took her hand, I knew that something unusual had just happened.

"Here is a god stronger than I who is coming to rule over me," said

Dante to himself when he first saw Beatrice. That's how it was with me when I laid eyes on Julie. Nothing like that had ever happened to me—or, as it turned out, to her.

We went to dinner that night, and out for a late coffee on Saturday. We spent Sunday together, and had our first kiss in the parking lot of Waterloo Records. Three days later, me back at my job in Florida and her in Austin, we were emailing, talking about marriage.

It was crazy. But we both knew. Four months later, after only a few weekends spent together but many, many emails and phone calls, I flew to Austin and, kneeling in a chapel in front of an icon, proposed marriage. She accepted. We drank Veuve Clicquot and ate chips and salsa. Later that same year, 1997, we married, and began our life together.

How in the world had that happened, and happened so quickly? Sure, I'm a hopeless romantic, but I am convinced that if my own heart had not been purified by those three years I spent walking through the fire, I would not have recognized the smile of the beautiful, pure-hearted woman who was my own Beatrice, for whom I had been praying and longing for many years.

So when the pilgrim Dante meets two condemned lovers in the Circle of Lust, they were not strangers to me. I could easily have been one of them. Standing on the edge of the tempest, watching the souls of the lustful whirl by, Dante calls out to a pair physically bound together for eternity to descend and speak to him.

The Real-Life Lovers of "The Kiss"

They are Francesca da Rimini and Paolo Malatesta, who were a real-life scandalous couple in Dante's day. Francesca's husband, Giovanni, caught her in an adulterous clutch with Paolo, his brother, and murdered them both. They lived for lust, and now they live chained together in eternal death.

Everybody knows Rodin's famous sculpture *The Kiss*, but few realize that it depicts Francesca and Paolo. I first saw *The Kiss* as a teenager, in a

Paris museum, and thought it was a romantic image, a positive one, a symbol of the kind of love I longed to have carry me away one day.

In reading the *Inferno* nearly thirty years after that Parisian encounter with *The Kiss*, I learned that Rodin's masterpiece actually depicted these two damned lovers. The original title of the piece was *Francesca da Rimini* (by the way, Rodin's *The Thinker* is modeled after Dante himself). Now where I once saw ideal romantic love, I see a consuming passion, an adulterous distortion of true love. In our time, we can't help regarding these lovers as anything other than objects of ravishing beauty. That is how Francesca and Paolo saw themselves. They were so focused on each other, and on satisfying their desire for each other, that they saw nothing else.

In the poem, when the pilgrim Dante begins to question Francesca about how she and her silent lover ended up in hell, she answers with baroque flattery, praising Dante for being more compassionate than God. She goes on:

> "*Love, quick to kindle in the gentle heart,*
> seized this man with the fair form taken from me.
> The way of it afflicts me still.

> "*Love, which absolves no one beloved from loving,*
> seized me so strongly with his charm that,
> as you see, it has not left me yet.

> "*Love brought us to one death.*"

> [*Inferno* V:100–106]

Francesca states the courtly view of love that was all the rage in Italy of the High Middle Ages. Lord Love seized the two innocents and carried them off in bondage. *How can you blame us?* Francesca says. *We couldn't resist.*

And then she tells Dante about the deed that led to their affair. They were reading together about Lancelot's adulterous affair with Queen Guinevere, and in turn became enflamed by mutual desire. They kissed, and were carried off by their passion to what would be their deathbed.

When Dante hears all this, he faints. Is it out of pity? Probably. But there may be something more complicated in his reaction? After all, Dante had been a bright light of the courtly love movement and could have written some of the poetry that misled her to damnation.

The *Commedia* is a poem about connections. However self-serving it is for Francesca to blame the books for her fate, art really does instruct us in how to think, feel, and behave. To be an artist is to have great power, to be the creator of others' dreams; it is a responsibility that must not be taken lightly.

What's more, Dante had made a god out of love, just as Francesca had. In her fate he could see a preview of his own if he did not turn back.

The famed Francesca episode is a good introduction to Dante's way of thinking. The pilgrim enters into Francesca's story and is overcome, just as Francesca was in reading the story of Lancelot and Guinevere. *That could have been me,* I thought, *half a lifetime ago.* In those callow days, I comprehended neither the nature of love nor the difference between it and lust. I gave myself over to popular books, music, and movies that catechized me in that confusion. Like Francesca, I cloaked my baseness in poetry and philosophy. I was adrift in a turbulent sea of selfishness, sentimentality, and desire and had no idea how lost I was, until my recklessness beached me.

Unlike Francesca and Paolo, I knew the truth: that my troubles were avoidable and were nobody's fault but my own. That self-knowledge was the line that God used to tow me back to solid ground. Reading the "Lust" canto in *Inferno* showed me the man I had once been, and it taught me to trust Dante. My new guide may have lived in a distant time and a foreign land, but to my great surprise and pleasure, I was no stranger to him.

HOW TO TELL THE DIFFERENCE
BETWEEN LUST AND LOVE

Problems of intellectual belief are sometimes really problems of the will. We tell ourselves that we cannot believe something when the truth is that we *will* not believe it, because believing it would require us to change our lives in ways we would rather not.

Perhaps no sin confuses us this way more than lust. Lust makes you stupid. Sexual desire is not the same thing as love, but it's easy to think so. If you lust after someone, you want the pleasure of erotic coupling without the responsibilities of love. Love binds; lust separates, and worse, separates under the illusion of unifying. If you want to find true love, stop indulging your lust.

Don't think that romantic love can save you, though. Your partner is not a god or a goddess, but rather, as Tolkien says, a companion in shipwreck. If you think that falling in love will bring you ultimate fulfillment, you will be disappointed, and end up hurting more than just yourself. And the fault for that will be your own.

8

UNCLE JIMMY VERSUS
THE GOLDEN CALF

———

As avarice quenched our love of worthy things,
wasting our chance to do good works,
so justice here has bound us fast.

[*Purgatorio* XIX:121–123]

Why Wealth Has Nothing to Do With Money

My chronic fight with the Epstein-Barr virus kept me house-
bound for much of the twenty-two months I grappled with it.
Spells of fatigue would announce themselves with dark
patches appearing under my eyes, like the black greasepaint football
players smear on their faces. Minutes later, I would feel the tissues in my
nasal passages swelling, then a headache would gather in the center of my
forehead. And then my muscles would turn to dishrags, my bones to
rubber stalks. The only thing that brought relief was sleeping, often for
hours at a time.

The episodes were unpredictable. Many times we would have a family outing planned, but I would have to tell Julie at the last minute that I
needed to stay home. She never complained, but I could see the strain it
was placing on her.

I was too sick to do physical labor, especially in the Louisiana heat,
but driving was usually no big thing, so I jumped at every chance to help

out in that way. In the spring of 2013, my mother phoned to say that Uncle Jimmy had died. Did I feel well enough to drive her tomorrow to West Monroe for the funeral? "Yes," I told her, "let's go. If I get sick on the road, we'll just deal with it."

The Little Way of James Fletcher

James Fletcher, who was ninety-two when he died, was Mama's uncle on her mother's side. I had met him only once or twice as a small boy. About all I knew was that he and his wife, Aunt Ethel, had meant the world to Mama as a girl. On the long drive through the Mississippi River delta, including the bean fields and beat-up towns of northeast Louisiana, Mama talked about him—talked about *them*, because it was hard to speak of one without speaking of the other.

My mother's childhood was bleak. She grew up in rural poverty, in a household lorded over by a truck-driving father who had a rough tongue and a hot temper and was quick to use his belt on his children. To Mama, Uncle Jimmy and Aunt Ethel represented everything she lacked in her meager life: light, and kindness, and tenderness. They were working people too—Uncle Jimmy put in long shifts at the paper mill on the banks of the Ouachita River—and Southern Baptists who took their faith seriously.

"They were so *good*," Mama reminisced. "I just loved being around them. You have to imagine what that was like for me," she continued. "I was so afraid all the time. When we would go visit Uncle Jimmy and Aunt Ethel on the weekends, there was love in that house. Nobody yelled and nobody cussed. I knew he and Aunt Ethel cared about me. As long as they were in the world, I knew there was hope."

Just before two that afternoon, we pulled into the parking lot of the Trinity Baptist Church, a redbrick temple in a working-class West Monroe neighborhood that had seen better days. A weary-looking church sign, its white plastic faded to a brownish yellow from decades in the hot summer sun, stood tall out front, pleading, GOD HELP AMERICA IN JESUS HOLY NAME. This was Uncle Jimmy and Aunt Ethel's church, and had been for many, many years.

Mama and I walked in about ten minutes before the service began. As we made our way to the front to pay our respects to Uncle Jimmy and to greet Aunt Ethel, someone introduced me to Mildred Chapman, an elderly woman as thin and dry as kindling. She was Jimmy and Ethel's neighbor.

Mildred said that her late husband, Peewee, had led his fellow mill worker Jimmy to the Lord when they were young men. Peewee had walked across the street and asked Jimmy if he knew Jesus, just like that. Soon after, Jimmy and Ethel were baptized in the Trinity church and became faithful members.

A Man in Full

During the funeral service, a number of people stood to testify what Uncle Jimmy had meant to them. One older woman said she had grown up in the church and that the thing she remembered most was that Brother and Sister Fletcher had always been there. Always. Over and over, the same theme from the congregation: the steadfast presence of James and Ethel Fletcher, married seventy-one years, in the life of this congregation.

Uncle Jimmy had been a presence in the community too. He lived on Nat Street, a short walk from the mill. He was a genius with car engines. On the weekends, cars would line up on Nat Street for Uncle Jimmy to give them a tune-up, which he did for free, because this was something he could do for people.

And then frail Mildred Chapman stood up behind me to tell her story. Holding on to the back of our pew to steady herself, Mildred said Peewee had died in an automobile crash when she was pregnant with their twin boys. Jimmy became a father figure to her sons, she said. Once he rebuilt an old bicycle for the kids so beautifully that it looked brand-new. Those fatherless boys living on Nat Street in the 1940s wouldn't have had anything if not for Uncle Jimmy.

That did it. I began to cry over the life of the great-uncle I'd barely known. The stories kept coming. Mourners spoke of his abiding sweetness. His daughter Linda recalled how much love her parents had for each

other, and showed to their children. How the only disa
had amounted to each raising his or her voice once, anc
How Uncle Jimmy had been able to build anything, how h
had loved making quilts together, and how the children's
dren's closets were full of their homemade quilts. How tl
their children to pray, and how their children had seen
praying all the time.

Now, Linda told the congregation, all the children and gr
and even the great-grandchildren were faithful to the Lord—
their mother and father were not only steady in their prayer.
also made their piety real by their love for each other, and for

Toward the end of the service, their son Ken, a musician, sa   ng
to his mother, there to bury the love of her life, thanking her and his
father for all their love and sacrifice. In the song he named the things
Uncle Jimmy and Aunt Ethel had done for him and his siblings. It was a
moment of almost unbearable tenderness.

Uncle Jimmy's grandson Richard told the congregation that over the
years, when Richard and his family would drive down from Arkansas to
visit, Uncle Jimmy would always tell them goodbye by saying, "Y'all have
a safe trip home. I'll be praying for you. Please call when you get there."
Every time.

A week earlier, with Uncle Jimmy near death, Richard and his family
had made the pilgrimage to West Monroe for what turned out to be the
last time. As they stood at Uncle Jimmy's bedside to bid him farewell, the
old man had said to them, "Y'all have a safe trip home. I'll be praying for
you. Please call when you get there."

Choking back sobs, Richard said, "In those words is that man's legacy."

One of Uncle Jimmy's former pastors rose to praise him as a model
of what it means to be a good man. We look to the athletic field, the stage,
or the screen for role models, the preacher said, but nobody much looks
at a mill worker from Nat Street. Yet anyone who knew James Fletcher
had seen what it meant to be a good man and a faithful Christian.

"As Christians, we should look first to our Lord Jesus Christ for what we should be like," he said. "But after that, look to our brother James. You can't find a better role model than him."

The thing is, those words carried weight. They weren't just something nice a clergyman said at a man's funeral. This service lasted nearly two hours, with people standing up talking about Uncle Jimmy's deeds, the purity of his heart, and the constancy of his love for Aunt Ethel, his family, his church, and everyone he knew. I kept thinking about my late sister, Ruthie, and what she and Uncle Jimmy had had in common: how they both embodied the principle that there are no sermons more powerful than the loving deeds of a righteous soul.

In a back hall of the church, I saw a Charles Wesley quote pasted to the wall: "Catch on fire with enthusiasm and people will come for miles to watch you burn." I don't know that Uncle Jimmy burned with enthusiasm, but it was plain to me that the man's heart was an extraordinary source of light and warmth to all who knew him.

I wished I had known him. I sat in my pew wiping away tears and thinking how the story of Uncle Jimmy made me want to be a better man. Uncle Jimmy hadn't had much of anything in the way of education, wealth, standing, or influence in the world. But through the steady practice of faith, hope, and love—active love, in service to his family and his community—he had become holy.

Ken Fletcher closed the service by telling the mourners that there was nothing anyone can take out of this life except what they pour into the people they know, and the ones they leave behind. I did not know Uncle Jimmy, but on the evidence of the love he left behind, and to which so many testified today, he walked the little way to heaven right down Nat Street, and went into glory laden with treasure.

When the congregation sang "Amazing Grace," Mildred Chapman's withered voice rose softly, barely more than a sigh. It was one of the most beautiful sounds I have ever heard. And then they closed the casket and carried James Fletcher out of his church for the last time. *Surely*, I thought, *these must be the richest people in the world.*

On the drive home, I thought about how Uncle Jimmy had followed a "little way," just like Ruthie. Nobody looks for saints in out-of-the-way places like Nat Street or Starhill, and nobody expects spiritual grandeur in the lives of mill workers and math teachers. But it's there. I had seen it that afternoon in West Monroe, just as I had seen it in West Feliciana, and I had moved my family there to become part of the story Ruthie left behind.

Hoarding Love, Squandering Opportunities

Mama and I stopped in Natchez on the drive home to eat a burger. Back on the road, we turned south onto Highway 61 and fell into conversation about the stalemate in our family.

"I hate this," she said. "I just hate this."

"I'm not having fun either, believe me," I said.

"I just don't understand why it has to be like this," she said.

"If you don't understand why, then it's because you don't want to understand why," I said sharply. "I have told you over and over, and you don't want to accept it."

"Don't fuss at me," she said. "I feel like I'm trapped in the middle here. I love all of y'all, and want to see my family together."

"Mama, don't you think I do too?" I said. "We moved here to be together. But there is not a damn thing more we can do to make that happen."

She fell silent. I felt guilty for speaking so harshly to her. But in the next moment I was angry at myself for the guilt. It was an endless spiral. These conversations never went anywhere. She was hurting, Daddy was hurting, and I was hurting, all over the same thing—but our conversations about it did nothing except weary us and depress us all.

My parents seemed determined to sidestep the heart of the problem and pass the blame on to Julie and me. They wanted to have the image of a harmonious, happy family, and faulted us for not giving it to them. I would point out that Ruthie's children were behaving toward us exactly as she had raised them to. They refused to accept this and could not believe that Ruthie, her family, or they themselves had done anything wrong.

The problem, they felt, was my selfish obstinacy. If I loved rightly, I would see this. From my point of view, they preferred the misery they knew to the possibility that they might have been mistaken about us. Always sinned against, but never sinning: that was my family's way. We were at loggerheads.

One late summer day, I sat on a rocking chair on my front porch reading *Inferno* and following Dante and Virgil into the next circle of hell. There the hoarders and the squanderers rage, shoving heavy weights forward with their chests, but in opposite directions, endlessly crashing into each other and cursing. Says Virgil:

> *"Now you see, my son, what brief mockery*
> *Fortune makes of goods we trust her with,*
> *For which the race of men embroil themselves.*
>
> *"All the gold that lies beneath the moon,*
> *or ever did, could never give a moment's rest*
> *to any of these wearied souls."*

> [*Inferno* VII:61–66]

These are sinners whose damnable fault had to do with worshiping money and possessions. Either they were greedy (the hoarders) or they were spendthrift (the squanderers). Virgil tells Dante that in life, fortune waxes and wanes, and people have no business blaming bad luck for their situations. Everything that rises must converge. Things happen. The world passes away. We lose ourselves by caring too much for the transient things and ignoring the permanent things, the things of heaven. This is how the hoarders and the squanderers have come to eternal grief. Dante scholar Anthony Esolen reads this as saying that what to unbelievers is blind luck, people of faith regard as the outworking of divine providence. That is to say, all things, even terrible misfortune (such as Dante experienced in his exile), can work to the good if we accept it in the right frame of mind.

I set the book down and stared at the neighbor's house in the distance. On this same front porch, with me sitting in this same rocking chair, my sister's physician and I had talked about Ruthie's legacy. I had asked Dr. Tim Lindsey, an evangelical Christian and a young doctor beloved by our town for his generosity, what he thought the most important lesson of Ruthie's life and death was.

He had rocked in his chair for a few seconds. "That the American dream is a lie," he said at last. "The pursuit of happiness doesn't create happiness. You can't work hard enough to defeat cancer. You can't make enough money to save your own life. When you understand that life is really about understanding what our true condition is—how much we need other people, and need a Savior—then you'll be wise."

Tim was right about Ruthie. Whatever her faults, she was not one to tie her happiness to money or its lack. She taught in a public school, and her husband, Mike, was a firefighter. They were neither rich nor poor, but they were extravagantly wealthy in terms of friendship. The friendships that sustained Ruthie and her family through her long march to death, and their cultivating of the roots that made those friendships possible, were some of the reasons I had moved back here.

Yes, I had been poleaxed by Ruthie's hidden resentment toward me, but I could not let that overshadow the great good in my sister's character. *The Little Way of Ruthie Leming* was a true story; I could not deny that. The woman I wrote about in its pages had really lived and been every bit as loving and as loved as I had written.

She was famously thrifty about her own purchases, but she freely spent on her students, quietly making sure the poorest children in her classroom never missed a field trip for lack of money. Her humble, country life devoted to family, friends, and her students—especially the poor ones—was a resounding rebuke to greed. Cancer stole her health and eventually her life, but when we would lament this curse that had fallen on her, Ruthie would shake her head and say, "But look at all I have"—and then talk about all the love her friends, family, and community had showered upon her as her body withered.

I could not let myself forget this truth. The pain and anxiety were real, and they blew like a bellows on the anger in my heart. But the good that Ruthie did, the good that she lived, was more real.

This tercet made me think of my parents and me, and our pointless talks about the family mess:

Thus they proceeded in their dismal round
on both sides toward the opposite point,
taunting each other with the same refrain.

[*Inferno* VII:31–33]

In my family, who were the hoarders? And who were the squanderers?

When Money Is Not Currency

We were not particularly tied to money or possessions, but love and loyalty were the currency within my family system—and there Dante's insights hit home. None of us knew how to manage our love for one another. I thought they were hoarders, who would only share love if they could have their own way, and squanderers of the opportunity Ruthie's tragic death gave us for reconciliation. In my view, they were willing to let the treasury of love drain away out of pride.

They must have thought me a hoarder for leaving Louisiana in the first place, keeping myself from them all those years to pursue what they saw as the false values of worldly success. And they must have seen me as a squanderer for coming home and wasting these days in worry and bitterness.

It occurred to me that the idea of all of us living in harmony in one place was our family's golden calf—the idol around which we all had danced for as long as any of us could remember.

Later that evening, making supper with Julie in the kitchen, I told her about my Dante reading, and how the poem was forcing me to think about the intractable situation with my family in new and unsettling ways.

"It would be so much easier if they were all just bad," I said. "But it's not true." The canto about greed had made me think about how generous Ruthie was, I told her.

"You can't lose sight of that," Julie replied.

"Yeah, but the double vision is so hard for me to pull off," I said. "I feel like if I only focus on the good, I'm whitewashing the bad."

As I would discover the further I went into the *Commedia*, Dante's gift for showing how the virtues of some of his poem's greatest sinners are inseparable from their vices helped me to make sense of the nuances in my own situation—and in my own divided heart.

"Can I say something good here?" Julie said that night. "It makes me happy to see you get so excited about fiction, for a change."

"It's weird, isn't it?" I told her. "I could be reading all of this in a book of philosophy, but it wouldn't have the same effect. Dante is getting inside me and messing with my head."

"That's not a bad thing, is it?" my wife said.

"No, not at all," I said. "It's just that it kind of feels like this book is taking over."

HOW TO DIE RICH

What are they going to say about you at your funeral? Nobody is going to praise you for the size of your house, the money in your bank accounts, the cool places you vacationed, or your exemplary collection of cars, guns, wines, or clothing. Nor will they rise in tribute to the numerous or fancy gifts you gave on birthdays and at Christmas.

Nobody will care. What they will care about is how well you loved—and love is not measured by how much money you made or gave away. "Getting and spending, we lay waste our powers," said the poet Wordsworth. Quit trying to control material things and manipulate material conditions, and you will be happier. Naked, poor, and powerless you came into this world, and naked, poor, and powerless you will leave it. To be poor in spirit—that is, to be detached from material wealth—is to possess all that matters.

9

THE LIFE OF BOOKS,
THE BOOKS OF LIFE

In its depth I saw contained,
by love into a single volume bound,
the pages scattered through the universe . . .

[*Paradiso* XXXIII:85–87]

The Promise and Peril of Bibliotherapy

The deeper I descended into the *Commedia*, the more I wanted to know about Dante and the book. His language is straightforward, but it is hard to grasp the fullness of his meaning and message without help. I began ordering different translations of the *Commedia*—the Esolen, the Ciardi, the Musa—to go with my Hollander, and delighted in seeing how each version differed from the others. Every time Julie would bring in the mail and drop the Amazon box in my lap, it felt like my birthday.

The commentaries on the *Commedia* also began stacking up at my bedside and on the bookshelf next to my chair in the den. There was Charles Williams's *The Face of Beatrice*, Harriet Rubin's *Dante in Love*, Yale scholar Giuseppe Mazzotta's *Reading Dante*, and later the galleys for English Dantist Prue Shaw's *Reading Dante: From Here to Eternity*. Most important of all, I began listening to the Great Courses audio lectures by Bill Cook and Ron Herzman, which made the poem come alive like nothing else.

At first Julie was amused by my Dante fascination, then delighted that I was discovering the joy of fiction, but when it was clear that obsession had taken hold, she asked me what it was about Dante that drove me so hard.

"I feel like I'm reading to save my life," I told her. "I mean, I'm not going to die if I don't read Dante, but I have this feeling that there's something in this book that is going to make things different."

"Careful with that," she warned. "You know how you are."

She didn't have to explain what she meant. Julie and I had long laughed at our shared faith in books to explain the world to us and solve our problems. For bibliophiles like us, books were a source not only of pleasure but also of wisdom about life and how to live it. "Bibliotherapy"—using books to treat psychological disorders—may be a new trend, but for me, it came naturally.

To Read Is Not Necessarily to Live

Yet we had both come to understand the limits of that approach. When we became Orthodox Christians in 2006, one of the first things we learned was the distinction between knowing God and knowing *about* God. Orthodoxy does not demean intellectual knowledge, but it insists that knowledge of God with the heart takes priority. Conversion is not so much a matter of believing the correct doctrines (though that is important) as it is of surrendering one's will to God. That is something that only happens through purification of the heart, prayer, fasting, receiving the sacraments, repentance, and loving others actively. You can't read that in a book; you have to do it. The spiritual life in the pages of the book is just writing; it's not the spiritual life.

I saw this clearly when Ruthie received her cancer diagnosis. From the beginning, she maintained that she didn't know why God allowed this to happen to her, but she knew that he loved her and would not abandon her. And that was that.

Me, had I been told I had stage IV lung cancer, I would have scoured every book looking for meaning, for clarity, for perspective, for deliverance. And if I was lucky, at the end of all my searching I would have arrived at the place where my sister started: accepting fate's verdict with as much serenity as I could muster, and trusting God to bring good out of it.

In *Little Way*, I made fun of my bookishness, comparing my intellectual busyness unfavorably to Ruthie's simple faith. But now I was starting to reconsider. When I was a child, Daddy prodded me often to get my head out of books and participate in "real life." But for me, books *are* real life. For a professional writer who dwells so fully in his mind, in the realm of ideas, the written word is how I connect to the world around me.

This bookishness has not always served me well. Back in Baton Rouge, when I felt the first stirrings of a call to Catholicism, I immersed myself in books about the faith. A colleague at the newspaper invited me to join her one Saturday afternoon at the downtown soup kitchen run by the Missionaries of Charity (Mother Teresa's religious order), to help out with chores. I spent hours there peeling potatoes and washing dishes. *That was fine*, I thought then, *but my time would be better spent reading theology and apologetics.*

Years later, after the sex abuse scandal had destroyed my faith in the Catholic Church and made it impossible for me to remain a Roman Catholic, I reflected on how all that intellection had not saved me. I had always believed that as long as I had the syllogisms straight in my mind, my faith could withstand any challenge. But all that time I devoted to talking and reading about Catholicism, especially the theological politics within the Church, was not the same as living out Catholicism. I should have prayed more. I should have peeled more potatoes.

It was a mistake I was determined to avoid as an Orthodox Christian, but doing so would mean going against my natural inclinations. And it would take a spiritual guide who would not let me fall back on my bad habits. That guide was Father Matthew Harrington, the pastor of our mission parish.

A Priest With Backbone

In Orthodox Christianity, your priest, or perhaps a monk with whom you have a special relationship, may be called your "spiritual father." It was hard to think of a bearded and ponytailed man about a decade younger than I as my spiritual father, but this priest had authority, and not just the kind you get from ordination.

Father Matthew had a blue-collar upbringing and had been a cop for years before all the violence and human brokenness he dealt with burned him out. He put down his gun and his badge and chose to fight evil with spiritual firepower, as a priest.

Father Matthew was friendly, but he made it clear to our congregation from the beginning that he wasn't here to be our friend; he was here to help save our souls.

"The Church is the hospital," he told us. "You come here to get well. Sometimes it takes a little pain to get the healing started. There are going to be times when you don't like what I have to say, and that's fine; we can work through that. But I will always tell you the truth as I see it. My responsibility is the care of your soul."

That made a powerful impression on me. We were not going to have any Jesus-is-my-brunch-buddy silliness in this parish. This guy had a backbone; he was for real. As our little flock soon learned, Father Matthew was a powerful preacher and an unusually good confessor. In the confessional, his insight was often piercing. Through patient questioning, he took as much time as both you and he needed to get to the bottom of the sins that troubled you. The congregation agreed that our priest seemed to know exactly when to show mercy and when to be tough.

It was hard to believe that Father Matthew had not been a priest for long, but when he told us stories about situations he had dealt with as a police officer, I understood why he practiced tough love on us. Here was a man with a big heart for others, especially the poor, but who also had seen firsthand how sin destroys lives, families, and communities. When this priest talked about hell, you had the impression that he had been to its outer precincts many times.

After the Sunday morning liturgy, most of the congregation—usually between ten and fifteen people in our mission parish—sticks around for coffee hour. It gets cozy in the fellowship hall, which is actually a small room linking the church and the rectory. Many decades ago, my father's uncle Euwin Poche, who was a talented woodworker, had constructed the building himself out of cypress lumber as a home for him and his wife, Rita. Euwin and Rita moved away and sold the property to a Starhill neighbor, who rented it out.

When we founded St. John the Theologian parish, Uncle Euwin's place seemed like a good home for us. The building, which sits in an oak grove facing Highway 61, had been empty for some time and needed fixing up. Father Matthew, his wife, and their children lived in one end of the building, Uncle Euwin's old woodworking shop at the other end became our worship space, and the room connecting the two served as the fellowship hall. It was an exceedingly modest place, but it had a special beauty for us, because we had made it with our own love and labor.

Police detective Shannon Tilley, sheriff's deputy Jack Cutrer, and firefighter Casey Cleveland, all of whom had read their way into Orthodoxy, did the cleaning, painting, repairing, and other hard physical labor to make the house and church ready. Chris and Christi Dantin, an evangelical couple converting to Orthodoxy, and my wife, Julie, rounded out the work crew. I was too physically ill to help, and felt ashamed because of it. But I did write checks, which were also needed.

One Sunday morning, we Drehers were the last parishioners left at coffee hour. Julie and Anna were in the kitchen cleaning up, and the kids were running around outside under the oaks. Father Matthew and I stood in the fellowship hall near the coffee urn.

The Discipline Of Prayer

"Benedict, you asked me once for a prayer rule," he said, using my patron saint's name, as is the Orthodox tradition. "I have one for you."

"Great!" I said. "What is it?"

A prayer rule is nothing more than a daily prayer discipline. It can be short or long, depending on the spiritual need and capabilities of the individual. I did not know what to expect from Father Matthew, but I certainly did not expect what he handed me.

This rule required me to pray five hundred Jesus Prayers a day, a demanding discipline. If done with the proper attentiveness, this takes about an hour. To pray in the right way, you have to clear your mind of all thoughts and images and let nothing but the words "Lord Jesus Christ, have mercy on me" (the shortened version of the prayer that I used) pass through your mind like the coming and going of the tide. Most people use a prayer rope, a kind of Orthodox rosary, to help them keep track of their prayers.

"Five hundred Jesus Prayers?" I said, nonplussed. "How long do you want me to follow this rule?"

"Every day for the rest of your life."

This seemed ridiculous, but I didn't show how I felt. I resolved to obey. It wasn't like I could do much more than sit around the house anyway.

How hard can it be to sit still and pray in a focused way for an hour? Try it. Your thoughts will swarm around your head like a cloud of stinging wasps, distracting you every two seconds. Still, you press on. The goal is to achieve inner stillness and connection with God. On most days, I would lie in one of the alcove beds in the darkened bedroom, with the light out and the curtain pulled, and silently pray on my prayer rope. As each tiny knot of the black woolen rope passed between my thumb and forefinger, I would breathe in on "Lord Jesus Christ, Son of God" and exhale on "have mercy on me, a sinner."

I felt stupid. I could not settle my mind. It seemed at first that I would have to stop after every five or six prayers to refocus. This was work! But after a couple of weeks, I noticed that I felt slightly less tense. The prayer worked like a hatchet, chipping away at the ice encasing my heart.

Until I began to pray the Jesus Prayer diligently, I had not realized how captive I had been to unwanted thoughts. In time, the prayer discipline trains your mind to deflect these thoughts to protect your inner stillness. One benefit of this technique is acquiring the skill to maintain inner stillness no matter how distracting or upsetting the world can be.

"Following a prayer rule helps us see the movements of our heart, movements of our soul," Father Matthew explained to me. "It makes us quiet. We ask ourselves, 'Why does my heart keep going back to that one thought?' It allows us to see what we're fighting. And then there's the asceticism of it: 'I'm going to make myself do my prayer rule.' You have to fight through it sometimes, and it's that asceticism that causes us to appreciate and deepen our life in the Church.

"This is a struggle of the heart, Benedict, not the intellect," he said, as if he could read my mind.

Since Father Matthew arrived in Starhill, shortly before Christmas in 2012, he had been dealing with my sickness and depression, mostly in the rite of confession. In the Orthodox tradition, the faithful regularly meet with their priest to tell him their sins. It is an essential part of Orthodox spiritual life, and most priests will not permit you to take communion if you have not recently been to confession.

In confession, the penitent stands next to the priest at the front of the church, before the altar, near a stand atop which sits a Gospel book and a metal cross. Speaking quietly, the penitent tells the priest the sins he has committed since his last confession. Sometimes the priest asks questions, and he usually offers counsel for how to struggle against sins more effectively. Then, in the name of Jesus Christ, the priest pronounces God's forgiveness.

From Cop to Priest

St. John the Theologian is Father Matthew's first parish. When Father Seraphim Bell, a Walla Walla, Washington, priest who is Father Matthew's own spiritual father, dispatched the newly ordained Matthew to us, he told me that the former police officer was a naturally gifted pastor "because he has suffered."

After we had known each other a while, I asked Father Matthew what

Father Seraphim had meant by that. I knew that Father Matthew had been raised by his grandparents and had never known his father. And I knew that he had been a police officer. One afternoon, sitting alone with him in the fellowship hall, I asked him to tell me his story.

"I was a very capable police officer, but I always felt like I was being punished for doing my job," he said, squaring his shoulders under his black cassock. "I would arrest some city bigwig for drunk driving, and my boss would fuss at me. Why? It really aggravated a sense in me of deep mistrust of authority.

"And there were other things that are normal in police work but that started to get to me. I would think, 'Why did that guy try to kill me? Why couldn't I have saved that person?' As I progressed in police work, I felt more and more of a sense of being orphaned. It all came out of self-pity, but those are real, hard emotions that being a cop coughed up."

"Tell me about the breaking point," I said.

"It was the second-to-last call I ever took," he told me. "It was a little girl. She lived right by a big aqueduct, and fell in and drowned. I never saw her body, but by then I was so emotionally fragile that the pictures by themselves shook up me up pretty bad. She had on these pink sandals with flowers on them.

"That was a Saturday. The next morning, I went to liturgy, and in front of me was a little girl wearing the exact same shoes," he continued. "I came undone. That was the end of my career. It really was. My wife knew. I knew. It was just how I navigated the exit."

Father Matthew's last deed as an active police officer was to chase two suspected thieves who were escaping on bicycles. They dropped their bikes and slipped away. Enraged by this, he took out his knife and cut their tires.

"Just like that," Father Matthew said, shaking his head. "Then I realized that I had become what I was fighting. I couldn't be a cop anymore. I talked to my chief and told him I couldn't go on. I wasn't a bad cop, and I wasn't a malicious cop, but I was a suffering cop, and I needed out."

Father Matthew and his wife, Anna, had discovered the Orthodox Church through the parish pastored by Father Seraphim. As the young police officer's emotional life disintegrated under job pressure, the con-gregation held him up.

"What I thought was a strong wall cracked, and I fell apart," the priest told me. "They didn't judge me when they saw me bawling through vespers and liturgy, just bawling."

"Wait," I said. "*You*? You cried in front of all those people?"

Tall and stern, with a piercing gaze, Father Matthew is not the kind of man you imagine crying in public, if at all. Though he wears a cassock now ("my dress," he snarks), this priest does not look like the sort of cleric fat-mouthing heretics would want to mess with.

"Yeah, I cried," he said. "I was broken. I still am broken. I can't watch war movies or anything like that. It's a humbling experience to know that you're in the prime of your life and you're broken."

Meeting Father Seraphim had made all the difference in his life. "He tells it like it is," said Father Matthew. "He made me face myself, and all my pride and anger. Man, was I ever angry. Orthodoxy allowed me to come out of that."

"Dante would call it a dark wood," I said. "So is that why you became a priest?"

"I haven't thought about it," he said. "It was a response to the love I received from Christ through the Church. If anything, my time in the civil service showed me that the only way I could help people was to heal my own heart. I had to seek the fullness of life in Christ, to be able to see the divine light in anyone. Otherwise, all they're getting is the blind lead-ing the blind."

God Can Work With Mysterious Tools

I craved Father Matthew's brand of spiritual leadership. He reminded me of what was best about my father: his gentle but firm masculine confi-dence, and a sense that his authority was trustworthy. But he had some-thing my iron-willed father did not. Suffering had broken Matthew Harrington and driven him to his knees. The humility that came from that weakness made him strong.

He was particularly qualified to be one of my three Virgils—the poet Dante Alighieri and the therapist Mike Holmes were the others—who led me out of the dark wood. Though the *Commedia* is perhaps the most philosophically and theologically informed poem that has ever been written, Dante makes his fictional version's guide neither a priest nor a philosopher but a poet. This was Dante's way of asserting that poetry can be a superior way to approach and meet an individual's challenges.

My priest, obviously, was far closer to a theologian than to a poet, but he was in tune with Dante in one important way: he pressed me to turn away from abstract intellection as the way to resolve my inner crisis. This is one reason he gave me such a strict prayer rule: to compel me for at least one hour each day to turn off my mind, to abandon the compulsion to analyze, and instead simply to practice the presence of God.

He was never enthusiastic about my reading Dante, though he never discouraged me from doing it. I once asked him why he seemed so reticent to embrace the poet. For one thing, he said, he found reading fiction as difficult as I did. More important, he said, it was hard for him as an Orthodox Christian to see the appeal of a poet whose work is so suffused with Roman Catholic theology, which is alien to him.

"But it doesn't really bother me that you're so into Dante, because it seems like you're making spiritual progress," he said. "Who am I to say what God is and is not doing? If God can work through a slashed tire, he can work through a book of poetry."

HOW TO STOP THINKING
AND START DOING

Books—even works of fiction—can be do-it-yourself manuals for people searching for the wisdom to fix their lives. Some of the best self-help books are not shelved in the self-help section. But don't think that reading is the same thing as doing. When thinking about taking action is a substitute for taking action, reading is an obstacle to getting better. Reading a recipe and learning it back to front is not the same thing as baking a cake.

Read, certainly, but make sure you take time to contemplate in stillness and prayer (if you pray) what you have read, and how to implement it in your life. The best books offer a window into life and truth, but their lessons only become alive and true for us if we take them into our hearts and, by force of will, turn them into action. The key is to know when to turn off the analytical mind and when to engage the will. The Jesus Prayer is an ancient Christian contemplative practice that opens blocked pathways between the mind, the heart, and God.

10

THE POWER OF THE IMAGE

Turn your back, and keep your eyes shut,
for if the Gorgon head appears and should you see it,
all chance for your return above is lost.

[*Inferno* IX:55–57]

Meddling With Medusa Is Risky Business

In 2006, when Callen Taylor taught social studies at a San Francisco high school, she started a Saturday morning Dante Club for students. The club members were high school seniors, mostly immigrant kids from poor or working-class families. They found in Dante a way to connect with Western culture. They also found reading *Inferno*, with its baroque descriptions of tortures suffered by the damned, to be great fun.

The Dante Club was a big hit. When the *San Francisco Chronicle* wrote about it, readers raised enough money to send the students, most of whom had never left San Francisco, to walk the Dante trail in Italy. Eight years later, the newspaper did a where-are-they-now piece on the students, all of whom had defied the odds and gone to college.

"This club provided me a different perspective and outlook on life," said Chelly Lim, a member of the club. "Who would have thought that a few inner city students would learn so much from the work of Dante Alighieri?"

I knew just what she meant. Curious to learn more, I found Taylor, the teacher, and wrote to ask her what her students responded to most in Dante.

"They love the *Inferno* because it is so graphic," she responded. "And young adults are all about justice. If one student gets in trouble for talking back, that same student will watch so intently the next time a student talks back to see if that student gets punished too. The idea of crime and punishment is a real draw to students, and how *contrapasso* works fascinates the kids."

Those kids understood what Dante is up to with his storytelling technique, which is called *contrapasso*, meaning "to suffer the opposite." The poet doesn't present us with gruesome images for the sadistic fun of it. The images and the punishments convey meaning about the character of the sin for which the damned suffer. The punishment, in other words, fits the crime.

For example, when Dante and Virgil come upon the flatterers, they see these wretches facedown "in a ditch below . . . plunged in excrement that could have come from human privies." They live eternally with their mouths full of feces—this for spending their lives telling lies to curry favor with the powerful. The traitors live frozen in a lake of ice at the bottom of the infernal pit, just punishment for the coldness of their hearts. In purgatory, where the punishments are only temporary, the envious, who in life sowed division by looking upon others spitefully and begrudging them their good fortune, dwell huddled together on the edge of the mountain, their eyes sewn shut with wire. Because of their blindness, they must cling fast to each other to keep from falling off the precipice.

Dante's purpose is to demonstrate to the reader the disfiguring nature of sin. What they chose to be in life, they became in the afterlife. When Dante shows his readers the terrifying punishments of the damned in hell and the penitents in purgatory, he is trying to shock us into recognizing that this is what our souls look like when we sin.

For Dante, the power of images is supremely important. Dante shows us like nobody else that good and evil are not abstractions but that they take particular forms. An image is never just an image; it always points to something else.

In the realm of Dante's afterlife, images are reality. The pilgrim's movement toward unity with God is measured by his increasing ability to see things as they really are. Believing is seeing. Not so in the mortal life, when images can serve as a veil hiding the true nature of the evil men do.

The French have a saying: "To understand all is to forgive all." In one sense it's an exhortation to empathy: if we truly put ourselves in the shoes of a wrongdoer, we may find it easy to forgive. In another sense it is a warning against too much empathy: our identification with a wrongdoer may blind us to the seriousness of that person's sin.

Consider one notorious example: In 1996, Boston's Cardinal Bernard Law penned a letter to Father John Geoghan, granting him early retirement. "Yours has been an effective life of ministry, sadly impaired by illness," the cardinal wrote. You would never know from the gentle, fatherly tone of the letter that Father Geoghan had spent his priestly career raping and sodomizing children in multiple parishes in the archdiocese, and that Cardinal Law and his predecessors had full knowledge of his actions. They had simply moved the pedophile from parish to parish. This kind of thing happened over and over: bishops seeing sexually abusive priests with sympathy, and regarding victims and their families as abstractions at best and at worst as enemies of the Church.

Do I believe that these bishops wanted to see children abused? No. I think they were so corrupted by the image of the priesthood and the Church as something wholly noble, pure, and good that their will to act was paralyzed in the face of information that challenged the truth of that image.

The Medusa Effect

The malign power of the image is the next challenge Dante and Virgil face in *Inferno*. They approach the city of Dis, a citadel protected by walls of iron glowing red from the heat of the inferno. Till now, the sins Dante and Virgil have faced are connected with the appetite. The iron walls of Dis symbolize that beyond this point, the sins punished are those having to do with a hardened will.

The demons guarding Dis will not grant them entrance. Virgil's powers fail him for the first time on the journey. The pilgrim turns white with fear, but anxious Virgil bucks him up by telling him God has promised to send help.

Suddenly "three hideous women" appear, warning the two travelers to leave, or else they will summon Medusa, the monster from Greek mythology, whose gaze turns all those who meet it to stone.

"Turn your back and keep your eyes shut," Virgil orders. He is so afraid for Dante that he puts his own hands over the pilgrim's eyes to protect him.

The meaning of this dramatic moment has to do with the limitations of both intellect and the power of reason. Here at the gates of Dis, Virgil, sometimes considered the embodiment of reason, is up against a force too great for his considerable powers. Only divine assistance can save them now.

This Medusa moment has roots in Dante's youth. Earlier in his life, the poet wrote a series of dazzling poems about the *donna pietra*, or stone lady. She was a heartless woman who would not return his obsessive love, thereby leaving his will powerless before her image. Here in *Inferno*, the pilgrim Dante faces a legendary woman with the power to freeze him in place with a single stare. And reason cannot help him conquer her.

We often underestimate our own weakness in the face of compelling images. In his *Confessions*, the fifth-century saint Augustine of Hippo wrote about his young friend Alypius, a Roman law student of strong moral convictions. His friends invited him to go to the gladiatorial games at the Colosseum, and after first refusing, Alypius agreed, saying that he would keep his eyes closed during the gory parts.

At the games, a roar from the crowd was too much to resist. Certain that he could handle what he saw without losing control over his will Alypius uncovered his eyes. It was a terrible mistake. Augustine writes:

> He fell more dreadfully than the other man whose fall had evoked the shouting; for by entering his ears and persuading his eyes to open the noise effected a breach through which his mind—a

mind rash rather than strong, all the weaker for presuming to trust in itself rather than in [God], as it should have done—was struck and brought down. As he saw the blood he gulped the brutality along with it; he did not turn away but fixed his gaze there and drank in the frenzy, not aware of what he was doing.

[St. Augustine, *Confessions*, trans. Maria Boulding]

Custody of the Eyes

There's an old-fashioned Catholic phrase, "custody of the eyes," that refers to one's obligation to be careful what one allows oneself to see. It's a quaint-sounding concept today, but a surprisingly useful one.

One of the best things my wife ever did for me was to challenge me early in our marriage about my habit of watching *Jerry Springer* and other trash-TV shows. I got a big kick out of laughing at the dolts and mouth breathers confessing their sleazy sins on TV and getting into fistfights. I was watching it ironically, or at least that's what I told myself.

Julie wasn't having it. "You don't want to be that guy," she said. "You don't want to be the guy who takes pleasure in watching people degrade themselves and behave like animals." Actually I didn't mind being that guy at all. It was fun. But my wife showed me that I was training my conscience to find amusement in things that ought to horrify me, or at least move me to pity and compassion for people who degrade themselves publicly.

My sister, Ruthie, was no stick-in-the-mud, but she hated those who laughed at the expense of others, especially those who ridiculed poor people. So did my father. I found it far too easy to treat those I didn't know as abstractions.

One night the summer after I graduated from college, I was in St. Francisville with my father and some Baton Rouge friends drinking at a saloon. My pals and I had had far too much to drink, and one of our group, the cleverest, was leading a tipsy old farmer to make a fool of himself in conversation. My buddies and I thought it was hilarious. Daddy took me aside for a word.

"You boys leave that man alone," Daddy said. "Y'all are being cruel."

"Oh, come on, Daddy, he's just an old drunk."

"He's got dignity, son," my father said. "If he wants to get drunk, that's on him. Y'all got no business helping him act like an idiot. Now stop it."

I eased back to the bar and quietly called my friends off. We all went back to Mama and Daddy's place that night and crashed. The next morning at breakfast, I remembered what my father had said to me, and was ashamed. I had reduced a human being to an image for my own amusement.

In a much more serious vein than slumming with *Jerry Springer,* I fell victim to my own hubris in reporting on the Catholic sex abuse scandals. In 2001, when I first began to write about the scandal as a *New York Post* columnist, I interviewed Father Tom Doyle, a courageous Catholic priest who destroyed his own clerical career to take a stand for abuse victims. When I told Father Doyle that I was a Catholic who was serious about my faith, he warned me to be very careful going forward.

"If you go down this path," he said, "you will go to places darker than you can imagine."

He knew; he had been there. I took the priest's warning with care, but felt that it would be cowardice to turn back. These were terrible crimes committed by priests of my own Church against innocent children—and the bishops were accomplices. I had the courage of Alypius, confident that I could see anything and not have my moral resolve shaken.

I was wrong. The evil I examined as a journalist—in reading court testimony, accounts of abuse survivors, and once-secret church documents detailing sexual attacks on children, and in personal interviews with the families of victims—destroyed my ability to believe in the Roman Catholic faith, and almost did the same to my capacity to believe in Christianity at all. I did not seek out the scandal details for the sake of curiosity. I sought them out to do good, to help the helpless. My motivations didn't matter. What I saw turned my faith to stone—and there was nothing my reason could do about it.

If I had taken Father Doyle's advice, I would have spent far more time strengthening myself in prayer as I carried out my investigations. This, I think, is what Dante would have advised. Some threats are so potent that only the grace of God can deliver us from them—and that's what happens to Dante and Virgil.

Memories Are Not Your Master

The sudden appearance of an angel saves Virgil and Dante from the Furies and opens the gates of Dis for them. There are times when only an infusion of divine grace can give us the strength to overcome what we cannot conquer through our own power.

The showdown at the gates of Dis revealed to me my own personal Medusas: memories that rendered me helpless to act to free myself. Why was it that so many of my sessions with Mike returned to the same family stories—the hunting trip, the bouillabaisse insult—and the same arguments, jibes, and rude gestures? And why did so many of my confessions with Father Matthew double back to those same stories?

My sins always emerged from anger at the unjust way I had been treated and impotent rage at my inability to change my family's minds or to overcome their power of these memories over my emotions. "The bouillabaisse story is the template for my relationship with my family"—if I told Mike and Father Matthew that once, I told them a hundred times. And it was true! But it had turned from an icon disclosing the emotional and psychological dynamics within the family system into a monster whose gaze I could not turn away from, and who turned my legs to stone.

"You think you can't move," Mike told me, "but those memories only have the power over you that you allow."

"Do you think I want to hang on to them?" I said. "They're making me sick as a dog, and miserable. If I knew how to let them go, I would. It's not so much that those memories stick around, but that they explain so perfectly everything that has happened since I came back. One way or another, the bouillabaisse story happens every few days."

"I get that," Mike said. "I'm not denying that what you're going through is real. What I'm saying is that you need to decide what you believe about memories. They aren't who you are. They aren't who you have to be. Even if things like this keep happening, and they likely will, you have to decide how much you will internalize them."

I could see his reasoning, but I still did not know how to break the spell. I wanted a quick fix, a eureka moment that sorted everything out and set me aright. This was unrealistic.

Reason Aided by Grace

Week after week, I would drop my son Matt off at his Thursday morning tutorial, then drive down to Mike's office. I would tell Mike what had vexed me in the past week, and we would rationally analyze those events and anxieties in light of what we had established in our early meetings was true about myself.

The method worked something like this.

Me: My mother and father accused me of X this week.

Mike: Is it true?

Me: No, but they refused to listen to my explanation.

Mike: Okay, let's break this down.

Then we would talk about the situation from several angles, including the possibility that the fault in the argument was my own. It frustrated me at first, because Mike wasn't telling me what to do (nor, interestingly, does Dante; like an experienced therapist, he lets us arrive at these conclusions under our own power). We more or less talked about the same things week in and week out, without a firm resolution. It seemed so simplistic. If I was going to submit to this therapy thing, then I wanted to be bum-rushed with applied psychoanalytic theory of the sort wielded by Viennese eggheads in hipster glasses, an intellectual adventure worthy of a novel and my grandiose sense of self. Instead, I was stuck there on that flowery sofa, washing dishes and peeling potatoes.

After a while, though, I began to see what the therapist was up to. He *was* applying psychoanalytic theory, but flying below my radar. The real work of therapy was taking place not in Mike's office but in the hour after our meeting ended, when I would drive to a Starbucks and think about all that had been said. That's when the firm resolutions began to emerge. That's when I would decide in advance how I was going to act the next time one of these depressingly familiar clashes arose.

Eventually it became clear that Mike was showing me how to use reason to help me distance myself from the things that caused me such overwhelming stress. The rheumatologist had advised putting geographical distance between the stressors and myself. Mike was teaching me how to use reason and the growing power of my will, my free choice, to face down my own Medusas.

"You need to let your beliefs lead your emotions," Mike said. "Once you see that you are free to choose your response to your environment, you won't act so impulsively in regard to it."

That made sense to me. I prayed constantly for God's help, for the same divine assistance that rescued Dante and Virgil at the gates of Dis. In my exasperation, I was still hoping for a miracle. Only gradually did I see that healing grace emerging through the patient work my therapist and I did together.

Time Defaces a Beautiful Image

That healing grace also emerged through study. As I read through the small library of books about Dante I had assembled, I discovered that in a version of the Greek myth told by the Roman poet Ovid—who influenced Dante greatly—Medusa was a once-beautiful woman who had been raped by Poseidon in the Temple of Athena, and as revenge made hideous by the furious goddess. Could it be that in the *Commedia*, the face of Medusa stands for something that was once a thing of beauty but had been disfigured, and thus held a terrible power of fascination?

If so, then Medusa symbolizes the passions of Dante's past and his inability to get free of them. Dante's journey is a psychological one; the

Medusa is the defaced image of a past obsession, one whose dark power threatens to end the entire pilgrimage.

Suddenly it hit me: my Medusa had begun as the beautiful dream of returning home to my family, a fantasy that had captivated and motivated me for years. When it finally came true in the wake of Ruthie's death, I thought the realization of my dream was at hand. When it all turned sour and ugly, I was still captivated by the image of a loving, united family, but in a disfigured way that imposed a curse I was powerless to defeat.

The Hidden Source of My Medusa's Power

The Dantist John Freccero says that Dante's Medusa symbolizes hardness of heart as an obstacle to conversion. In my confessions and our conversations in those days, Father Matthew acknowledged my hurt, but he also insisted that as a Christian, I could not be satisfied to rest in a place of resentment.

"You have to love them, no matter what," my priest said. "Just as God loves you."

"I know," I told him. "I do love them. But it's so hard to figure out how to love when it hurts so much and I'm so mad about everything."

"It is," he affirmed. "It will take time. Don't stop fighting, though. Keep praying. Keep coming to confession. As long as you confess your sins sincerely, you're in the arena fighting. It's when you stop believing you have any sins to confess that the enemy has won."

"But I haven't done anything to them," I said. "I came home for them. I wanted to be part of their lives. They didn't want me."

"Are you angry at them?"

"Yes."

"Are you so angry at them that it interferes with your ability to show love to them?"

"Yes."

"Then you are in sin, my friend."

I thought about this for a moment. "I see your point," I said. "In

Dante, sin is a distortion of love. You're saying that if my love for my family is distorted by my anger, then I am guilty."

"You got it."

This was a bitter truth that I struggled to choke down. I would confess my anger, but I could not yet master it, and did not understand why. But I sensed that deliverance from my personal Medusa would somehow come when I penetrated the mystery of why the dream of home had always been so potent in my mind. And I was certain that if I had any hope of breaching the iron walls that had broken my will on every prior assault, it was through prayer. So I prayed, and read, and waited, and followed Dante deeper into the pit.

HOW TO STARE DOWN MEDUSA—AND WIN

"When you gaze long into an abyss," Nietzsche said, "the abyss also gazes into you." The philosopher's line is a warning to keep our eyes away from dark things that fascinate. Stare at something long enough and you will become its prisoner.

Sometimes even good memories and worthy ideals hold our minds captive, and prevent us from moving forward with our lives. How do we defeat their hold on us? Use your free will to separate yourself from that image, and subject it to the scrutiny of reason. Is the image, belief, or memory true or false? The power is within you to decide. Ask for God's help in activating it. After all, in the Greek myth, a gift from the goddess Athena gave Perseus the ability to look upon Medusa's face and slay the monster.

11

FALSE GODS AND HERETICS

The ancient blood and gallant deeds
done by my forebears raised such arrogance in me . . .
And for this pride, here must I bear this burden—
here among the dead, since I did not
among the living—until God is satisfied.

[*Purgatorio* XI:61–62, 70–72]

The Damnable Worship of Family and Place

In making your way through the *Commedia*, you will inevitably confront a sin that has deep personal relevance to your own struggle. You stumble into it and think, *Ah, yes; this must be the place.* For me, it was the sixth circle, the abode of the heretics, people damned for believing things opposed to religious truth.

Dante here only deals with one sort of heretic: the Epicureans, who denied the immortality of the soul, teaching instead that all that is for us exists in this world and should be enjoyed. "Eat, drink, and be merry, for tomorrow we die"—that's the classic Epicurean sentiment. In this exquisite canto, Dante doesn't render the two Epicureans he meets as mere hedonists. Rather, they are a pair of refined *grandi*—great men of Florence. Had they simply been hedonists, Dante might have placed them in the circles where sins of the flesh are punished. Theirs is an intellectual sin, which puts the confrontation in a different light. It is fitting, then, that they dwell eternally in a grave, as that is what they expected out of the afterlife.

Because they wrongly and adamantly professed that the grave was the end of human existence, the Epicurean heretics are condemned to spend eternity amid flames in an open tomb. As Dante and Virgil make their way through tombs burning like braziers, a nobleman rises out of his grave and addresses Dante in a pompous tone, greeting him as a fellow Tuscan (he can tell by Dante's accent).

This is Farinata degli Uberti, the patrician who led the Ghibelline faction in Florence for much of the thirteenth century. He had betrayed Guelph-led Florence to its Ghibelline enemies in Siena, but when the victorious Sienese wanted to destroy Florence, Farinata successfully prevented it. They compromised by leveling all the homes of the leading Guelph families. Later, when the Guelphs came back into power, they repaid Uberti by demolishing his family mansion.

Here is how Dante describes Farinata's appearance in hell:

Already I had fixed my eyes on his.
And he was rising, lifting chest and brow
As though he held all Hell in utter scorn.

[Inferno X:34–36]

Surging as if he held all hell in scorn: Farinata is an aristocrat of sublime haughtiness. The portrait Dante paints of him in just a few lines is indelible.

When I stood at the foot of his tomb
he looked at me a moment. Then he asked,
almost in disdain: "Who were your ancestors?"

[Inferno X:40–42]

Think of it! Farinata is living for all eternity in hell, and the first thing he wants to know is whether or not this extraordinary visitor from the mortal life is sufficiently highborn to engage in conversation. Farinata is keeping up appearances; he still believes that distinctions he held on earth matter here in hell. And why not, given his belief that the earthly life was the only one that mattered?

Farinata shares his tomb with Cavalcante de' Cavalcanti, a fellow Epicurean but, as a leading Guelph, one of Farinata's bitterest enemies in the factional politics tearing Florence apart. They could not bear each other's company in life; now they share a fiery sepulcher—and refuse to acknowledge each other's presence.

Theirs is much worse than a political rivalry. Cavalcante married his son Guido off to Beatrice degli Uberti, Farinata's daughter, to resolve a dispute between the two families. Not only did the men share a family bond, but they were also neighbors in Florence. To this day, you can see what is left of the Cavalcanti family palazzo in the Via del Calzaiuoli. The Uberti palazzo was a short walk away, in what is now part of the Piazza della Signoria. After the Guelphs returned to power, they leveled the Uberti family compound and passed a law forbidding anyone from ever building on that unholy ground again. And no one ever did.

In the duo's conversation with Dante, we see that all Farinata cares about is his family, his political party, and his personal status in Tuscany. All Cavalcante cares about is his son's status as a poetic genius. They cannot care about anything else, because they believed that the mortal life was all that existed, and that the point of that life was to enjoy the things that gave them pleasure. Dante the poet points out that their heretical belief that life on earth is all that exists led them to embrace with passion the things of this world—and that, in turn, led to their blind and destructive egotism. This had dramatic consequences for their families, their city, their region, and their Church. The pilgrim Dante is moving toward a vision of cosmic harmony, but first he has to see the consequences of division, of people being so passionate about the things they loved in the world that they made life for everyone a living hell.

One way to think of the sin of heresy is mistaking one part of the truth for the whole truth. In this sense, the heresy of Farinata and Cavalcante includes believing that truth consisted in their all-consuming love for family, party, social status, and so forth. The thing is, there is nothing wrong with loving your family, your party, your city, and your creed. In fact, there is nobility in Farinata's character: his love of Florence once saved it from total destruction, and he is honored today by a statue next to the Uffizi Gallery there. The error comes in believing that these are *ultimate* ends. To let this disorder reign in one's heart inevitably results in disorder in the family, in the community, in the city, in the country, everywhere—because everything is connected.

Though the pilgrim Dante can see where Farinata's obstinate devotion to the things of the world has landed the Florentine noble, he can't help engaging in some Guelph-Ghibelline trash talk himself. At this early stage of his journey, the pilgrim too is bound tightly to his status as a Florentine player. This is the poet Dante's commentary on his younger self and the attitudes that led to his near-ruin.

This Dantean insight proved incredibly helpful for me in trying to untie the knot that bound me after my return to my hometown. The divisions between my Louisiana family and me that had been there for most of my life proved impossible to bridge. I couldn't figure this out. I had no doubt that my sister loved me, though she didn't much like me, nor did I doubt that my dad loved me, though he had always disapproved of me. And I loved them too, though I found their judgmentalism hard to take. Still, with all that love, why did we struggle so intensely?

It was, I think, because our loves were disordered in the same way Farinata's were. We loved good things—family and place—too much.

In the house of my father, family and place were at the center of our life together. It is traditional for southerners to hold a high view of family, but Daddy was even more idealistic than most. He worked hard in his job and on his land to provide for us kids and to help other members of the Starhill clan. Daddy told Ruthie and me stories about growing up in the country during the Depression, and how everyone in the family had had to pull together for survival. To him, sundering the family bond was an unforgivable sin. The world was the family and Starhill, and as long as we kept that straight, he taught, all would be well.

I believed that as a child, but when I became a teenager, I drifted. There was no room in Daddy's mind for dissent or doubt on this subject, however. He had the answers, and my refusal to agree with him marked me out as a heretic. Back and forth we battled, with him asserting that my unwillingness to agree with him on all things was a failure of love on my part. I thought his unwillingness to see me as a distinct person—a young man of worth, even though I was not the same as he—was a failure of love on his part. The clash was irresolvable.

Ruthie was unswervingly aligned with our father on this. She held his strong views about family and place. She possessed his scorn for and skepticism of anything and everything that challenged our family's way of life. And she was supremely untroubled by self-doubt. They led with their hearts.

Daddy and Ruthie were bayou Confucians: they believed that there was a natural order to the universe, and that the purpose of life is to conform dutifully to its prescriptions. I too believe there is a natural order to the universe, and that the purpose of life is to live in harmony with it. The difference was where we located the source of that order and where we drew its boundaries.

For them, the family and its traditions were at the center of all that is good and right, and the boundaries were those of West Feliciana Parish. I did not have the settled confidence that they did. I was a seeker; they were abiders. Now I understood what a threat the choices I made had been to them.

After all, by the time of Ruthie's diagnosis, I was living in my sixth city in twenty years; they had stayed in Starhill. I was on my third different form of Christianity; they were still Methodists. They achieved this stability, this deep rootedness, in part by remaining steadfastly incurious about the world—at least outside of science and mathematics, which are fixed and knowable—and never questioned the verities by which they understood the meaning of life.

"Y'all made us so nervous when you would come visit us from Dallas," Hannah once told me. "It sounds horrible, but we were always relieved to see you go."

"Why?" I asked.

"You were so different from us," she replied. She could not explain further, because there was nothing more to explain. It wasn't the way in which we were different; it was difference itself. My mother did not share this view, as far as I could tell, but Daddy and Ruthie, with their strong personalities and unbending convictions, set the tone. In my family's eyes, if I had loved as I ought to have loved, I would have wanted what they wanted and lived the way they lived.

Standing at Dante's side as he bantered with Farinata, I found things beginning to come into focus for me. I too had internalized Daddy's values. Though I had rebelled, deep down I had accepted the critique my father and my sister had of me and the way I saw the world. They believed strongly in order and justice; if you did the right thing, as they saw it, you would prosper. If not, you wouldn't. But Ruthie had lived by the code, and she died young, in agony. I had not lived by the code, but I prospered. Both my niece Hannah and my parents told me that Ruthie resented me in part because everything seemed to come easily for me, though of course that wasn't true.

What I hadn't counted on was this state of things existing even after Ruthie's death. Her death changed me, and I assumed it would bridge the chasm between me and my Starhill family.

While she was sick, Ruthie told everyone that God had a plan here and that good could come out of it, even if she didn't survive. I believed that, and I think she did too. However, it emerged after her sudden passing from an embolism that despite having lived for nineteen months with Stage IV cancer she had made no provisions, financial or otherwise, for what would happen in the event of her death. In her heart, she still believed that a miracle was going to happen and that death would pass her by.

Her death was a shattering event on all fronts. For me, the grace with which she died, and the generosity that her friends and neighbors showed her and her family during her cancer fight, broke through my own settled certainties about the meaning of life. When Julie and I came down from Philly for the week of her burial, Starhill was glowing with love. I mean that: the place and the people were ablaze with a brilliance that almost hurt to look at. I didn't care about past hurts and failures; I wanted to be a part of this. I wanted to be with my family. I wanted to walk the little way of Ruthie Leming. And so did Julie.

I was not driven home by duty but lured there by love. It transformed everything—or so I thought. But after I returned home and reached the end of writing my book about Ruthie and the life-changing power of her love, I learned that my Louisiana family dealt with the world-collapsing fact of her death by doubling down on the code of order by which they made sense of the world.

Two and a half years after Ruthie's death, I sat at my mother and father's table after Sunday dinner—we had a standing invitation but rarely went because we felt out of place—talking to my niece Claire. The meal was over, and everyone had scattered. She was fourteen now, a sweet kid, but a stranger to me. I hated that. I hoped that I might be able to break through to her.

After a few lame attempts to start a conversation, I finally said what was on my mind.

"You know, the main reason Aunt Julie and I moved down here was to be a part of you girls' lives, and to help out," I said gently. "We never see you. I hate that. We want to be a part of y'all's lives, but I don't get the feeling that you want us to be."

Claire sat still, her big brown eyes staring at me with a look of innocence and openness. She had nothing to hide, but nothing to say either.

"Hannah told me you and Rebekah would stay away from us because your mother raised you all to think that we were bad. Is that true?"

She shrugged. "Yeah, it is."

"And she also told me that y'all were staying away from us because you want to honor your mother's judgment. Is that true, babe?"

"Yeah, I guess it is." There was no malice in her tone.

I did not know what else to say, and an uncomfortable silence hung in the air between us.

That was that. My Starhill family fiercely loved the world they had created for themselves, and they held on to it with unyielding defiance. And rather than providing an opening, Ruthie's death seemed to have entrenched their belief in the code of loyalty even deeper.

It had not occurred to me that disordered love could be so destructive. In this rootless era, how could you love the idea of family too much? Or the idea of place? I was confused. I knew my Starhill family were good people, and I knew that they loved me. But what kind of love was it that would treat others like this?

I used to find admirable the kind of tenacious conservatism that held on to ideals of family and place in a culture that made both increasingly irrelevant. Since 2002, my journalism career has been in part devoted to promoting a return-to-roots traditionalism that puts family and place first. But when I chose to live up to my own ideals, I had wandered triumphantly into disaster.

Now, through the negative examples of two Florentine lords who epitomized devotion to family and place, Dante was showing me why. When family and place and a way of life centered around them become ends in themselves rather than the means to the good, they turn into idols. Meeting Farinata and Cavalcante in hell, and thinking about my own condition, I began to appreciate the meaning of historian Jaroslav Pelikan's line: "Tradition is the living faith of the dead; traditionalism is the dead faith of the living."

My sister's life and death converted my heart, allowing me to embrace the tradition that had been reserved for me, and to make it my own. What I found when I came home, though, was not tradition but traditionalism. To change their minds about me, I now saw, would have been to violate their loyalty to Ruthie's memory and deny everything that gave shape and weight to their worldview.

I had done all I could to bridge the chasm, and it still had not been enough. It was time to move on in my heart, for my own good and the good of Julie and the kids.

And yet there I was, behaving like Dante, standing at Farinata's tomb arguing over things that once were but were no more. I too was caught up in the world that used to be: a world in which I tried to appease the household gods of family and place, thinking that if only I worked at it a little harder, they would accept me. Farinata could not move; Dante still had the freedom to walk on. I needed to get on down the road, so to speak.

What I could do, and what I did, was to recognize the extent to which in my heart of hearts I had always accepted this judgment and oriented my own interior life around it. The division existed tangibly in the world, and because of that, it existed in my soul as well. It came between God and me. I had always believed that God loved me but that he couldn't possibly approve of me, no matter what I did. My spiritual life, I came to see, had been for many years oriented around appeasing a father God who was unappeasable. It had been built around the idea that if only I did the right thing to prove my love and loyalty, he would find me worthy of his love.

Once Dante unmasked this within me, I saw that I too had made false idols of family and place. It's not that loving family and loving place are bad, but that they are only good relative to the *ultimate* good, which is unity with God. We were all professed Christians, but it sometimes seemed that the family's real religion was ancestor worship.

In his beautiful little book *The Return of the Prodigal Son*, the Catholic priest Henri Nouwen writes of the exiled wastrel in the Gospel parable:

When the younger son was no longer considered a human being by the people around him, he felt the profundity of his isolation, the deepest loneliness one can experience. He was truly lost, and it was this complete lostness that brought him to his senses. He was shocked into the awareness of his utter alienation and suddenly understood that he had embarked on the road to death. . . . In fact, it was the loss of everything that brought him to the bottom line of his identity. He hit the bedrock of his sonship.

This is what happened to me. I had circled back on the road to home and found that I could not cross the threshold of my father's house. The legacy of my dutiful sibling was a barrier whose gates would never really open. In a line that pierced my heart, Nouwen wrote, "I am the prodigal son every time I search for unconditional love where it cannot be found."

Despite parallels between my story and the Gospel parable, I had not thought of myself as a prodigal son, because unlike the wretched man of the parable, I had not squandered my inheritance in wild living in the world. But now I saw that I was, in fact, a prodigal, in the sense that I had looked for unconditional love in the wrong place. My father, for all his strength and virtue, and for all the love that he had for me, could not offer me that love without conditions. Nor could my sister.

It hit me that I had made myself a prodigal son by searching for unconditional love and security in a place where it could not exist. Only God the Father could offer what I wanted and needed. Suddenly it was clear: I had made family and place, and above all Daddy, into my gods.

I was not only a prodigal but also, in a sense, a heretic, an idol worshiper. My decades-long dream of coming back to take my rightful place among my family in our ancestral home had been revealed as an illusion by my homecoming. That fantasy was as much a Medusa to me now as Farinata's Florence had been to him.

Reading Dante had unearthed the torment that had dogged me throughout my religious life. I had never believed that God loved me. Oh, I knew on an abstract level that he loved me, because he is God, and God is supposed to love his creatures. It's his duty. But I knew that I disappointed him. I was not the son he really wanted.

When I was a Protestant, I didn't believe that God loved me. When I was a Catholic, I didn't believe it. And now that I was Orthodox, I still didn't believe it. Not really. To affirm it in your mind, as I did, is not the same thing as taking it into your heart.

At last I knew why this had been impossible for me. As my father was on earth, so was my Father in heaven. He was so good, strong, and wise that his judgment on my worth (as I perceived it) must be true. If only I could make myself perfect, maybe he would accept me.

There it was. The lie, unveiled. I had enthroned family and place—and their personification, my father—in my heart in the place of God. This was the greatest sin that led me to the dark wood in the middle of the journey of my life. It was *my* sin, not the sins of others. I had to own it and repent of it. This sinful disposition, the refusal to believe that God the Father loved and affirmed me, formed an impassable barrier around my heart, one I had spent a lifetime reinforcing. Tearing down that wall would require nothing less than divine intervention.

But at least now I knew what I was dealing with.

HOW TO QUIT BEING AN IDOL WORSHIPER

To be a heretic in Dante's era was to disbelieve in Catholic orthodoxy. Today, a broader, more secular definition is to believe that partial truths are whole truths. It takes steady, unflinching examination of our own consciences to uncover idol-making heresies—that is, beliefs that hold relative goods to be absolute.

Search your heart for things you have set up as idols—especially good things, like family, spouse, country, religion, or a worthy cause. To hold on to the things of this world, even the good things, as if they always will exist, and always should exist, is, in biblical terms to worship creation, not the Creator. Or as Taoist philosophy teaches, any specific thing that can be identified as the Tao (the Path of Life) is not the Tao. Cast down your idols—that is, all those finite things you worship, and you will live.

12

IS LIFE EVER NOT
WORTH LIVING?

I made my house into my gallows.

[*Inferno* XIII:151]

Suicide Poses the Most Fundamental Question

After my breakthrough in the Circle of the Heretics, I was more excited than I had been in ages. A crack had appeared in the doorway and a shaft of sunlight had muscled its way in, opening a lane to the land of the living. I was sure I was on to something big, and I couldn't stop talking about it.

Julie tried to be enthusiastic, but I know a forced smile when I see it.

"I'm sorry, I know I annoy you with this Dante stuff."

"No, I'm glad for you," she said unconvincingly. "It's just that this is really hard. I'm trying to be excited for your progress, but when you've got three kids to home-school, laundry to do, kids to take to 4-H and tennis, the library, the chickens, and I don't even know what else, it's really hard to give a damn about hell."

"That's a good line."

"Shut up."

Julie headed out the front door to pick up Lucas and Nora from whatever they were doing that afternoon. I didn't know. I hardly ever did. I was preoccupied with being sick, and with Dante. Julie knew that conquering this disease depended on my escaping the labyrinth of my family issues, and she knew that the *Commedia* was helping. But to her, my pilgrimage through hell with Dante sometimes felt like me going off on a hike with my new best friend, leaving her behind to do the drudge work of parenting.

After she left that afternoon, I was feeling uncharacteristically alert, so I opened my *Inferno,* ran my fingers over its pages, and moved on to the next ring of the pit: the Circle of the Suicides.

On the way, Virgil explains to Dante the geography of the Inferno. The highly structured hell of Dante's imagination is not the way Christianity sees the abode of the damned. Dante invented it as a way of examining the nature of sin and how it manifests itself in the world. As a good medieval Catholic, Dante certainly believed in the existence of hell, but its architecture is entirely his own creation and should not be taken as a theological text. And even for those who don't believe in a literal hell, the poet's imaginative framework provides a useful template for the examination of the conscience.

The organizing principle of hell is to sort sinners by how they used their free will. All sinners are in hell for misusing their power to choose and refusing to recognize that there was anything wrong with what they were doing.

But not all sins are the same. In the *Commedia*, the outer circles of hell—that is, those farthest away from the center of the earth, where Satan dwells—exist to punish sins of incontinence. This is where the souls of those whose bodily passions overcame them (or, in the case of the heretical tombmates Farinata and Cavalcante, those who professed that there is no soul, only the body).

Farther down the circles of the incontinent lies the section of hell where those who gave in to violence live. Here dwell those who were violent against themselves, violent against their neighbor, or violent against God. In Dante's model, sins of violence are worse than sins of incontinence, because violence also involves the intellect, which is the part of the human person most like God.

Yet the worst sins, which we will encounter as we near the heart of hell, are sins of fraud, which are entirely about corrupting the intellect, the image of God within us. These are sins that strike at the essence of what separates man from beast: our reason. Worse, fraud "severs the bond of love" that unites people in society, Virgil teaches, and makes living peaceably together impossible. This is why traitors are in the deepest pit.

Virgil tells the pilgrim:

Every evil deed despised in Heaven
has as its end injustice. Each such end
harms someone else through either force or fraud.

[*Inferno* XI:22–24]

What does it mean to say that every sin is rooted in injustice? A just order is an order in which everything is where it is supposed to be, doing what it is supposed to be doing. To sin is to introduce disharmony into the system. As the pilgrim will learn in greater detail later in his journey, the entire universe runs on the power of love. Sin, therefore, can be thought of as being like a blood clot that disrupts the smooth flow of love. The popular conception of sin is that it breaks a rule or a law, and that is true, or at least not false. But that doesn't account for the depths of Dante's vision. For him, *sin is a metaphysical phenomenon.* Sin is not an abstract idea but something that is woven into the fabric of reality.

The worst sins, in Dante's reckoning, are those that make peaceful, fruitful life in community impossible, because they sunder social bonds and defeat the possibility of justice. All the problems of divided Florence, divided Italy, and indeed our own strife-filled world begin with individuals choosing something other than unity with the love of God as their goal in life. In the *Commedia*, to put anything above God is ultimately to worship the self.

For Dante, suicide is in most cases profoundly immoral, primarily because it is a rejection of the gift of life, which is God's to give and to withdraw. Yet suicide is a matter of utmost gravity even for those who don't believe in God. "There is only one really serious philosophical question, and that is suicide," said Albert Camus. "Judging whether life is or is not worth living amounts to answering the fundamental question of philosophy."

Why do people kill themselves? For some, it is an act of insanity. For others, self-sacrifice can be a noble act; Dante places in purgatory the virtuous Roman statesman Cato the Younger, who committed suicide as a protest against Caesar's corruption, and therefore in the interest of the greater good. But the suicides in hell have earned their place there by rejecting life simply because they cannot live it on their own selfish terms.

Dante and Virgil cross a boiling river of blood, where the souls of those damned for violence against others bob and wail. They come ashore in another dark wood, the realm of the suicides. When Dante plucks a twig from a tall bush, the stem runs dark with blood.

"Why do you tear me?" the bush wails. "Are you completely without pity?"

The talking shrub is Pier della Vigne, once one of the most powerful men in the Holy Roman Empire. As chancellor to Emperor Frederick II, Pier brags that he once "held both keys to Frederick's heart." Pier fell victim to intriguers at the imperial court, who fingered him as a plotter against the emperor. Frederick had his chancellor arrested, blinded, and imprisoned. Unable to endure his fall from power and prestige, Pier killed himself in prison.

In hell, the man who destroyed the body, the roots of his own earthly existence, lives for eternity as a plant—burdened by consciousness, but unable to move.

A noted poet of the thirteenth century, Pier puts his rhetorical gifts to work making himself out to be a noble, tragic figure.

My mind, in scornful temper,
hoping by dying to escape from scorn,
made me, though just, against myself unjust.

By this tree's new-sprung roots I give my oath:
not once did I break faith
with my true lord, a man so worthy of honor.

[*Inferno* XIII:70–75]

This is the source of Pier's fatal error: he put his ultimate faith in a mere mortal, and found the meaning of his life in serving another man. In the misery of his exile, Pier concluded that life without Frederick was not worth living, and so he killed himself. Pier loved life when things were going well for him, but when fortune turned against him, he threw it all away.

Surely Dante faced the same temptation to end everything after his unjust exile from Florence. Indeed, I suspect that the poet's making the suicide a part of a dark wood telegraphs to the reader that the despondent poet was contemplating killing himself when Virgil appeared to rescue him from such a death.

Some woods are much darker than others; however deep my own despair was for a time, the thought of suicide never remotely occurred to me. Yet what I was enduring with my depression and physical illness was not living, or at least not a life that I could long sustain. Something had to give, and I was responsible for making sure it did.

Pier's florid tale made me wonder about whether my own highly developed sense of rhetoric was unwittingly feeding my self-pity. I could not deny that there was a part of me that took perverse pleasure in the dramatic qualities of this family saga. As miserable as all this was making me, I had to face the possibility that there was a nasty little Pier della Vigne inside me who enjoyed aestheticizing the misery and seeing myself and others tangled up in this plot line as characters in a novel.

I had both Pier and Farinata in mind as I drove out to the mission that weekend for Saturday night vespers and confession. The foolish Pier was a weak man, a sycophant whose life meant nothing apart from the emperor's service. The pilgrim Dante seems to sympathize with Pier—his moral awakening is a work in progress—but Dante the poet knows that

Pier's flowery speech is nothing but an elaborate rationalization for a squalid act of cowardice.

"We are all unreliable narrators of our own lives, none of us authorities on the things we know most intimately," said the classicist James J. O'Donnell in his biography of St. Augustine. None of the sinners in *Inferno* can be trusted to tell the truth about themselves—and this is part of their damnable condition. As I moved deeper into Dante's tale, it occurred to me that the story I told myself about myself and the people in my life might not be true, or at least not true in the way I thought. Dante's storytelling invited me to try to stand outside myself and see my world and the choices I had made in a new light.

I knew my confession was going to take a while, so I waited in the fellowship hall for everyone else to go before me. Finally it was my turn. The interior of the church was so comforting in the last hour of a summer afternoon. The walls and ceiling, painted cerulean to recall the veil of the Virgin, glowed faintly. The saints looked on silently from their icons on the walls, a cloud of witnesses floating in blue-green planes. The room still smelled of frankincense and beeswax from vespers. I crossed the nave, stood next to Father Matthew, kissed the Gospel book and a cross, then opened my heart.

"I had a real breakthrough this week," I said. "Dante showed me something important. I think it might be the key to this thing."

"Tell me." Father Matthew never hurries anybody. He wants you to unburden your soul.

Standing next to him at the icon stand, I told him about Farinata and how his overwhelming devotion to family and place led him to damnation. I told Father Matthew about Cavalcante, Farinata's tombmate, and how all he wanted to know from the pilgrim was how his son, a prominent Florentine poet, was doing.

"I saw my dad in these guys," I said. "I've always seen him as sort of the king of West Feliciana Parish. He knows everything about this place."

"Yeah, Mr. Ray seems like the kind of man you would go to if you needed to know how to do anything around here," Father Matthew said.

"Exactly. And I respect him so much for that," I said. "The problem is he defined his own character by his devotion to the land, and to his family as well."

I told Father Matthew about a back-porch confession Daddy made to me shortly after my return. It was the most astonishing moment of humble self-revelation I had ever witnessed in him. My father, the embodiment of loyalty to family and place, told me one Sunday that his great regret in life was that he gave up his liberty to stay in West Feliciana and serve his mother, father, and extended family. No matter what they needed done, they could always call on good ol' Ray. Now that they were all long dead, he told me, he had realized that they'd taken the gifts of loving service for granted and had never really loved him. They were all a pack of users—takers, never givers, he said.

Now that I was home for good, he told me I had done the right thing by leaving long ago. What a reversal of our fateful conversation nearly twenty years earlier! And yet, it changed nothing between us.

"He's so, so bitter," I told Father Matthew.

"Because he thought he did everything right, showing them love the only way he knew how, and they didn't love him back?"

"You've got it," I said. "He knows he made a mistake there, making a god of his family, but he still does it. He doesn't see how that affects me and our relationship."

"You are here to confess your own sins, not your father's."

"I know, I'm sorry. But I'm getting to my own sins."

I explained how much I had revered Daddy as a child, and grew up listening to his stories about the family and the land. "When I'm gone," he would tell Ruthie and me, "this land will all be yours to pass on to your children." This was a sacred trust. This was the right order of things.

"And you didn't want it, but Ruthie did."

"Well, I wanted it, but not in the way he wanted me to want it. I wasn't made for this place. I was weird by his standards. I think he saw every deviation from himself in me as a rejection of everything he stood for, of everything he had to give me."

"I can see that."

The root of the problem, I explained, was that my dad couldn't see me as *me*. I could not live here without being crushed by his will. I wanted the good things of family, but the price was too high.

"And this is your sin how?"

"You remember me telling you a while back that I have a lot of trouble believing that God loves me? That I felt like I could never make him happy enough to deserve his love? This is where it comes from. I didn't understand it until Dante made me think about it, but without meaning to, I made gods of family and place. I made them into my idols. I set them up in my heart where God ought to be."

Father Matthew looked at me, his brow creased.

"There's more," I said, then told him the story of Pier della Vigne. "Don't worry," I hastened to add, "I'm not a potential suicide. It's that there's a part of me that can't deal with life without my father's approval. Isn't that stupid?" I asked.

"It's not stupid."

"Well, I feel stupid. I'm forty-six years old, and I am stuck in this damn ditch, where I have been since childhood. I couldn't take it when I was younger, and ran away. I'm tired of running. I've got to face down this dragon and kill it. I don't know what to do now, but I want to confess that I have worshiped idols, and I am sorry. I put other things before God. I want to lay those idols at the foot of the Cross and be done with them."

Father Matthew said nothing. He bowed his head again and reached down to lift his stole, which was my signal to kneel. He put his stole over my head, pronounced the words of absolution, made the sign of the cross over my head, then unveiled me. I kissed his right hand, stood up, and walked out of the church feeling light.

A few nights later, I was lying in bed in the dark, with Julie asleep next to me. I was saying my five hundred Jesus Prayers, frustrated because I had put it off till the last moments of the day, and struggling through my fatigue to focus on it. By the time I arrived at the fourth cycle around my prayer rope—that is, after three hundred prayers—I was on autopilot.

And then something strange happened. The words *God loves me* appeared not in my head but in my heart. It was the strangest thing—like someone was standing at my bedside, placing them into my chest. Not *God loves you*, but *God loves me*.

Just like that: *God loves me*. Like it was the most natural thing in the world. There it sat in my heart, like a pearl. It scared me at first, this mystical experience, because I feared it might go away. I finished my prayers, smiling in the darkness, because the words remained there, radiating. I fell asleep with the words repeating in my mind: *God loves me. God loves me.*

When I awakened the next morning, the first thing I noticed was a feeling in my chest. It was as if someone had laid a cornerstone in my heart, and chiseled into the stone were those three blessed words. All morning, I could physically feel them in my chest, humming along like a happy little pacemaker. I refused my usual impulse to analyze what happened; I chose to accept it as a gift.

To this day, the words remain there, as if they were written on my heart. God loves me, and he had established a beachhead within my soul. It was a small patch of ground, but it was real and firm, and now it was where I stood. And Dante Alighieri had led me to it.

HOW TO FIND A REASON TO LIVE

Living to serve others is usually a virtue. But if the worth of your life depends on the judgment of others—your parents, your spouse, your children, your employer, anybody—then it becomes a vice. When you cannot live without the approval of others, you grant them power that they do not have a right to have, and may not even want. Worse, you expect more of them than they can give.

If you are a religious believer, you know by faith that only God has perfect judgment—and that God alone loves you perfectly. He has given you the gift of life; what you do with it in service to him and his will for your life is your gift in return. Write this on your heart: *God loves me*. Believe it. Live it.

13

THE GREAT AND THE GOOD

"O my dear father," I said, "if you'll but listen,
I will tell you exactly what I saw . . ."

[*Purgatorio* XV:124–125]

What Sons Do—and Do Not—
Owe Their Father Figures

"**I** have a sense," my writer friend Tony Woodlief once told a counselor, "that I'm supposed to do something great."

"Oh yeah," said the counselor, smiling. "Everyone has that feeling about himself. This is America."

Believe in yourself. That's the fundamental lesson of the cultural catechism by which our society instructs the young. It starts with Disney films, continues with egotistical coddling from helicopter parents, and is confirmed by a consumerist, individualist culture that teaches us we are the center of the universe. In every time and place, making money, achieving worldly success, and satisfying our own desires have always been important goals. It's part of the human condition. Even Dante had to deal with it. But in the past, religious and civic values functioned as a counterweight to the soul's natural egotism.

Today, social science shows that the millennial generation is one of the most self-centered in American history. I'm not blaming them, exactly; their parents and their culture formed their outlook. Christian

Smith, a leading sociologist of religion, has found that the de facto religion of the young is a narcissistic, do-it-yourself creed he calls "moralistic therapeutic deism." Smith's work has shown that many young adult Americans are adrift on a sea of moral relativism, with no idea where to turn for moral guidance and trustworthy insight.

"Having freed people from the formative influences and obligations of town, church, extended family, and conventional morality," Smith writes, "American individualism has exposed those people to the more powerful influences and manipulations of mass consumer capitalism."

People today think of themselves as free—but free for what? Surveying the most up-to-date sociological research on Americans born in the 1980s and 1990s, psychology professor Jean M. Twenge concludes, "This generation is more confident, more assertive, more entitled—and more miserable." In her 2007 book, *Generation Me*, Twenge says that focusing on the self was more or less tolerated by past generations, but the millennials are the first generation in which it was actively encouraged.

"GenMe is not as much self-absorbed as self-important," Twenge writes. "They take it for granted that they're unique, special individuals, so they don't need to think about it."

Eventually the truth will catch up with them. A young pastor friend in Washington, D.C., tells me that that the biggest problem he faces in dealing with his congregation of young, highly educated, high-achieving professionals is an overwhelming sense of dread and anxiety about their own worth and direction in life. He said that they really want to be good, but what this culture has taught them about what it means to be good— *achieve, achieve, achieve!*—is leading them into a dark wood.

One autumn day, I sat at a communal table in a trattoria in Florence talking to an expatriate American businessman who was in from Shanghai on vacation. He asked what I was doing in Tuscany, and I told him I was researching a book about Dante. Over wine, we talked about our paths in life. When I told him that I had left Philadelphia for a tiny town in south Louisiana, he looked shocked.

"How can you stand to live in—?" He stopped himself before finishing the sentence, but it was clear what he meant: *How can you bear living in the middle of nowhere?*

I told him about my sister, Ruthie, and what I called her "little way." Her death had revealed to me how much meaning and worth one can have living a quiet, modest life in an out-of-the-way place, as long as one fulfills one's calling with a heart full of love and gratitude. It reset my parameters for what constitutes greatness, I told him. A big part of this, I explained, was how watching Ruthie die with such grace deepened my commitment to faith and helped me see the world and my place in it with a more spiritual vision than I had before.

The man, who looked to be about forty years old, told me that he had graduated from a posh New England prep school and gone on to Harvard. He had been working overseas in a high-paying job for years but was burning out. Earlier that day he had been hunting truffles in the Tuscan countryside, then had gone shopping in upscale boutiques. Because the man's life so far had been one of stellar achievement, he had the money to take luxury vacations all the time. And yet he sat there at our table in Florence with a long face, telling a stranger from back home about the futility and unhappiness of his life.

At the same time, it was plain that he could not imagine any alternative. Everything in this man's experience and every mentor to whom he had listened told him he had done the right thing. Like the Washington pastor's congregation, this businessman had been "good," according to the standards of contemporary American culture, but he was miserable— and could see no way out.

If these worldly high achievers had a patron in the afterlife, it would be Brunetto Latini, a distinguished Florentine poet and civic leader who had been a mentor to Dante. In *Inferno*, the pilgrim Dante is shocked to find this esteemed father figure suffering in a flame-lashed desert with the sodomites.

Now, there is nothing more politically incorrect today than the word "sodomites" to describe gay people, but it was a standard term in Dante's era, and the one he uses in the *Commedia*. Before you write off this canto as the work of a bigoted Catholic of the Middle Ages, consider what the sin of sodomy meant to Dante in a philosophical sense. This canto, you'll find, makes a point not about sex—it hardly comes up—but about the way we approach the things we make.

It's pointless to try to make Dante into a modern liberal on the question of homosexuality. Some academics have tried, but the scholarly consensus is that the poet really did believe that homosexuality was a mortal sin. The reason Dante believed that is key to understanding this canto's lesson about the meaning of our creative work. You do not have to accept the poet's judgment on homosexuality to profit from his experience in this imaginative encounter with an indisputably great man from his past.

Dante and Virgil are now in the circle of hell reserved for the violent. In Dante's reckoning, sodomy, even consensual sodomy, is violence against nature, which is to say an attack on the God-given means for creating new life. That the sodomites live running forever in a scorched desert discloses the nature of the sin: all that passionate heat, resulting in sterility. In Dante's view, homosexuals take the generative act—sex, I mean—and use it not for the potential creation of new life, which is its prime function, but rather to serve their own disordered desires.

Sodomy—I will use Dante's term—was common in Florence of the High Middle Ages and Renaissance. It became so common that Florence developed an international reputation for being a center of Renaissance gay life, and the city government established an office for the prosecution of gay sex. As far back as Dante's day, it was by no means out of the ordinary for men to have sexual relationships with men, in particular younger men who were socially subordinate to them. This did not prevent those men from marrying, fathering children, and fulfilling their social roles as family patriarchs. There was no such thing as gay identity as we know it in modern times. Homosexuality was not something you were, but rather something you did.

Here, among the sodomites, the pilgrim Dante has one of the most moving encounters of his entire journey. Walking with Virgil along a dike rising above the sulfurous plain, Dante feels one of the sodomites below tug at the hem of his garment. He looks down and sees a charred but familiar face.

"Are you here, Ser Brunetto?" the shocked pilgrim asks. The way Dante addresses Brunetto shows his esteem for the man. He uses the formal "you" in Italian, as well as "Ser," a title of respect. As well he should, for Brunetto Latini was one of the great Italians of the High Middle Ages, a diplomat, statesman, and man of letters. We do not know if Dante studied under Brunetto, but any man with the talents and aspirations of young Alighieri would naturally look up to Brunetto as a model.

In their encounter on the burning plain, Brunetto calls Dante "son." The love the old master and his younger devotee feel for each other is palpable. This episode reminds us again that serious, damnable vice can exist within an otherwise noble character.

Brunetto asks Dante what brings him into hell. The pilgrim responds:

> *"In the sunlit life above," I answered,*
> *"in a valley there, I lost my way*
> *before I reached the zenith of my days.*

> *"Only yesterday morning did I leave it,*
> *but had turned back when he appeared,*
> *and now along this road he leads me home."*

> [*Inferno* XV:49–54]

Brunetto doesn't seem to understand, and responds with encouragement.

> *And he to me: "By following your star*
> *You cannot fail to reach a glorious port,*
> *if I saw clearly in the happy life.*

"Had I not died too soon,
seeing that heaven favors you,
I would have lent you comfort in your work."

[*Inferno* XV:55–60]

The pilgrim, deeply moved by these words, responds:

"If all my prayers were answered,"
I said to him, "You would not yet
Be banished from mankind."

[*Inferno* XV:79–87]

The exchange between the fatherly Brunetto and his younger charge is so loving we almost forget that Brunetto is in hell. What's going on here? If Brunetto is damned for sexual immorality, why are he and Dante talking about the secret to worldly success?

This is a moment when the difference between Dante, the author of the *Commedia*, and the character called Dante becomes clear. Chastened by the wisdom of experience, the poet here is showing us the trap old Brunetto unwittingly lays for his younger, fictional self. In the *Commedia*, the stars symbolize God's watchful presence. And travelers navigate by the stars. Brunetto misleads him in two crucial ways: by counseling that the purpose of writing is to win worldly fame and by instructing the pilgrim that he should plot his course through life not by following the divine plan but by seeking his own interests.

Brunetto is in hell for sodomy, but Dante indicates here that his sexual sin symbolizes a deeper malady of the spirit, one that rendered Brunetto's writing sterile. Brunetto is a vain man, a writer and public intellectual who thought the way to pursue immortality was to serve his own cause in his work—and a spiritually blind teacher who, one suspects, sees Dante's progress as an artist chiefly as a means to hitch himself to a rising star. For the damned, it is always about themselves.

Brunetto's sodomy symbolizes a misuse of his God-given generative powers—that is, Brunetto's misuse of his creative abilities as a writer and artist. To create only for the sake of magnifying your own fame and success in the world is, spiritually speaking, a sterile act. As far as we know, the poet Dante never faced the temptation to have sex with men, but as we see here, his beloved mentor Brunetto attempts to seduce Dante into a kind of artistic and intellectual sodomy.

How much happier would young people be if they began their careers thinking not of the fame, fortune, and glory they will receive from professional accomplishment but rather of the good they can do for others.

Dante Alighieri's early verse was brilliant, but he might today be as forgotten as Brunetto Latini if he had not written the *Commedia*, which he composed for transcendent ends. Few if any of us will accomplish a feat as immortal as writing the *Commedia*, but what good we may do in this world, and what glory may remain after we leave it, will come only if we serve something greater than ourselves.

In my own writing career, I found early success writing reviews and criticism. Nurtured on the biting sarcasm of the 1980s magazine *Spy*, I developed a knack for turning a stiletto phrase that knifed my targets. As a television critic and later as a film reviewer, I enjoyed penning vicious takedowns of bad programs and movies.

But I was doing it to boost my own ego. It was fun to make people laugh at the expense of others, and I had a true gift for witty condemnation. Walking back to my office at the *New York Post* after screening a lousy movie, I amused myself by sharpening the insults I planned to flourish in my next performance on the page.

What changed me was becoming a father. I became more sensitive to violence in film after I left professional movie reviewing. Changing beats at the newspaper coincided with the birth of my first child, Matthew. One chilly autumn afternoon, I sat with baby Matt, then only two months old, in my Brooklyn living room and settled in to watch Martin Scorsese's *Goodfellas*. The Mafia film had been one of my favorite movies when it came out in 1990, and now, nine years later, I relished the chance to see it again.

I lasted about forty minutes before turning the television off in disgust. I could not take the graphic violence. It had not much bothered me before. But Matt had changed me. The act of cradling that helpless infant had taught me a lesson about the preciousness of life. No sermons, op-eds, books, or magazine essays had changed my views about excessive violence. The vulnerability of my newborn son taught me how fragile life was. This time I didn't need my wife to tell me to turn away from an image for the sake of my conscience.

After that, my own writing took a slow turn away from gratuitous viciousness, though I'm sure it will always be a temptation of mine. I'm not saying that sharp criticism is never justified. The late Roger Ebert wrote scathingly about movies he hated, but he always wrote with a passion that came from caring about cinema, not from self-aggrandizement. Ebert had integrity; every word he wrote about the movies arose from a devotion to art.

When I wrote *Little Way*, the letters and emails I received from readers thanking me for the witness I bore to my sister's life moved me profoundly. My correspondents brought me to tears more than once with tales of how Ruthie's story had changed their own lives for the better, as it had mine. Driving home from Uncle Jimmy's funeral, I told my mother that from then on I wanted to write books that built people up and gave them reason to hope.

"I hope you do," she said. "It has been the most wonderful thing to see how Ruthie's story has changed lives. That story you told about the couple living in Florida who moved back to Louisiana after reading *Little Way* touches my heart. I know Ruthie would love it."

There is enough of that smarty-pants *Spy* reader in me to wince at the idea of writing hopeful books, but I really do want to live up to that ideal. Raising Matthew, Lucas, and Nora has made me want to devote my most serious writing to building a better world for them. And believing, as a Christian, that I will be accountable to God for how I used the talent he gave me has on many occasions given me pause before I've indulged in verbal cruelty for the sake of cleverness (and driven me to the confessional when I have crossed the line).

There's another aspect to this meeting with Brunetto, one that spoke to me as I sought a way out of my own dark wood. Brunetto's best-known work was a medieval encyclopedia titled *Treasure*. His parting words to Dante were "Let my *Treasure*, in which I still live on, be in your mind—I ask for nothing more." The Dante scholar Giuseppe Mazzotta says that Brunetto's biggest mistake here is to believe that the life of his literary "son" is the same thing as his own.

"He never faces the difference between Dante and himself," Mazzotta writes in his book *Reading Dante*. "He refuses to see that Dante's life can have its own development and its own destiny, a destiny which he cannot understand at all."

This hit me hard. I knew that my own dad had never understood why I wanted to be a writer. Neither he nor my sister grasped how I could make money with words. It seemed to them that I was getting away with something. My father didn't really begrudge me my professional success; he just didn't understand it. I think that in his eyes, my decision not to follow in his footsteps by staying in Starhill and living the life he wanted me to live was a selfish mistake.

That's why Dante's relationship to Brunetto resonated with me. It tracks with how I looked up to my own father and sought his approval, even after I left for high school and college and rebelled against him and his view of the world. I wanted to be my own man, but I also wanted to make my father proud of his son. He taught me by example the finer qualities of manhood: taking care of your wife and children, being honest and upright in your dealings with others, working hard, helping your neighbor, standing up for the little guy, striving to do what is right and shun what is wrong, and living by a code of honor.

If Daddy had not been so extraordinarily good at embodying those virtues, much of what is good in me would not exist. When the pilgrim Dante pays grateful tribute to the older man, he speaks for my sentiment toward my own father.

> *"For I remember well and now lament*
> *the cherished, kind, paternal image of You*
> *when, there in the world, from time to time,*

"You taught me how man makes himself immortal.
And how much gratitude I owe for that
my tongue, while I still live, must give report."

[*Inferno* XV:82–87]

When Brunetto showers the pilgrim with compliments and advice, who can doubt that he sincerely wants his boy to do well? The problem is that Brunetto is not aware of the limits of his own vision. He did not "see clearly" in the past life, as he reckons; he only saw Dante as an instrument of his own will. And at this stage of his journey, the pilgrim is not morally aware enough to discern that Brunetto, the father figure who taught him so much, is not a reliable guide to his own destiny. The pilgrim is so moved by seeing his early mentor that he seems to forget the man is among the damned. Dante is beginning to see the world through spiritually renewed eyes, but Brunetto, in the eternal desert of hell, will always view things through the eyes of worldly glory. Brunetto thinks he sees clearly, but he is not the sort of man to question his own perception or the story that taught him what to look for in life.

This is a subtle point but an important one. The journey through hell is important to teach the pilgrim how sin works and how he fell victim to it. In the *Commedia*, all sin comes from a perversion of love. In this case, the love and respect that Dante and Brunetto share threaten to mislead the younger man. Dante is at risk of misusing his creative gift and failing to achieve the purpose for which God created him.

This was me. As long as I still believed in my heart that Daddy saw clearly and rightly how I should live my life, I would be at risk. I would be at risk of misusing the gifts, creative and otherwise, that God gave me. I would be at risk of shortchanging my wife and children. And if I remained ill, I would be at risk of seriously damaging my health forever, even fatally.

None of this was my father's fault. I was a middle-aged man. There were no excuses for remaining stuck in childhood. Filial respect and gratitude had nothing to do with it. I saw that now.

Walking with Dante as he spoke with Ser Brunetto, I better under-stood the dynamic between my father and me. Like my own father, Bru-netto was a man of immense talent and character, and an inspiration to Dante, who thought of himself as Brunetto's son. Like my own father, Brunetto wanted Dante to succeed in the world, to make his mark; Dante understood this as a gesture of kindness, and deferred respectfully to the older man's wisdom.

And like my own father, Brunetto could not imagine a future for his "son" separate from his will and from his affection for the boy. Had the pilgrim Dante yoked himself to the advice of the admirable older poet, he might have found some worldly success, but he would have stifled his own fecundity as a writer.

Besides, all the damned ended up in hell because they egotistically preferred their own wills to the will of God. I certainly would not pass that kind of judgment on my father, but the Brunetto incident forced me to reflect on how Daddy's unhappiness with me derived precisely from the fact that I, who bore his name, was not a replica of him.

Reading this canto, I realized that as much as my father and I loved each other, we navigated by different lights and always would. If I was to escape this desert, I would have to keep walking. The only way out was going to be by keeping my eyes focused not on my indomitable father, not on my confused and ailing self, but on God and God alone. There was a reason he led me back to Starhill, and I had to keep on going to find out what it was.

HOW TO FIND A MENTOR
WORTH FOLLOWING

Everyone thinks they are destined for greatness. It's true, but it isn't greatness as most people think about it. Greatness is a measure of the excellence of your character, not the breadth of your ego. The tragedy of your life would not be failing to become rich, famous, or professionally accomplished; it would be in missing out on the opportunity to be and to do good. Whom do you look up to in life as a measure of greatness? Who are your heroes, your mentors? Ask yourself: do they see clearly what true greatness is? Are their lives and philosophies examples of love, service, and humility? If not—if they don't see that you can be, like Brunetto, a best-selling author and a respected statesman, and still fail at life—then they do not have your best interests at heart. Follow leaders who can show you how to be not merely successful, but truly great.

14

SINS OF THE FATHERS

Ravenous wolves in shepherds' clothing
can be seen, from here above, in every pasture.
O God our defender, why do you not act?

[*Paradiso* XXVII:55–57]

On the Difference Between Religion and God

I taly in the late thirteenth and fourteenth centuries was a place of constant turmoil and warfare. Peace, stability, and good government were hard to come by, because you did not know whom you could trust. Trust was the most precious commodity.

In the *Commedia*, the fraudulent—those who use their intellects to deceive others deliberately—are the worst category of sinner. I was surprised by this. Fraud is worse than murder? Dante makes a case that's plausible, if not necessarily convincing.

First, the calculating nature of fraud befouls the part of our humanity that is most like God: our intellect. Beasts can have voracious appetites, and beasts can do violence, but only man, gifted with reason, can commit fraud. Second, the willingness of the fraudulent to lie to get what they want, and to sever all bonds of obligation for the sake of self-advancement, undermines the basis for all human society.

Trust is the absence of fear. When you cannot trust, daily life is fraught with paranoia. It makes growth in love all but impossible, because to open yourself to love and its works is to make yourself vulnerable. If the instinct for self-preservation requires you to fear and mistrust others, love doesn't have a chance, and neither does the common good.

Fraud killed my faith in the Roman Catholic Church. It was matched only by the ongoing family crisis as the most painful experience of my life. Both events were so devastating because they made me doubt something that was at the core of my identity, even my sense of reality.

I emerged from that brutal loss wiser, and I regained my love and respect for Catholicism—though I did not return to Rome, and am happy and grateful to be Orthodox. Still, I learned a harsh lesson about the nature of fraud and the danger of placing your trust in anything but God and God alone.

Salvation for Sale

In his sojourn among the fraudulent, the pilgrim Dante walks among the simonists. Simony—usually, the selling of church offices—was widespread in the Church of Dante's day. Given the secular power of the Church in the High Middle Ages, bishops had the opportunity to grow rich and powerful. Rome sometimes sold bishoprics to the highest bidder, and the Church was riddled with priests and monks, from the simplest village padre to the pope himself, who turned the Church into an exchange for worldly wealth and power. Pontiffs thought nothing of placing cities such as Florence under interdict—that is, forbidding them the sacraments—until the cities yielded to papal political desires. When one believes that one's eternal life depends on access to baptism, confession, and communion, a pope holding souls hostage to a power grab is a grave scandal and a terrible sin.

Boniface VIII, the Roman pontiff at the time of Dante's exile, ruled the Church (and parts of Italy) like a greedy corporate chief and ruthless warlord. A skilled political intriguer who was a consummate Machiavellian two centuries before Machiavelli was born, Boniface helped engineer Dante's exile through fraud and betrayal.

Far from being militantly anticlerical, Dante Alighieri was a faithful

Catholic who devoted a surprising portion of the *Commedia* to prophetic denunciations of clerical corruption, precisely because he loved the Church and believed that Jesus Christ founded it as the ordinary way for mankind to find salvation. If humanity could not trust the Church, how could they believe the Gospel?

In all three books of the *Commedia*, Dante excoriates bishops, priests, and monks for betraying Christ with their worldliness. In Paradiso, Dante has St. Peter, the martyred first pope, rebuking his successors for their greed.

"The Bride of Christ was not nurtured with my blood—
Nor that of Linus and of Cletus—
To serve the cause of gaining gold."

[*Paradiso* XXVII:'40–42]

Dante's St. Peter goes on to condemn the contemporary popes for waging war against other Christians. Later, Beatrice, the pilgrim's heavenly guide, blasts both churchmen and the laity for their unseriousness about faith.

"Christ did not say to His first congregation:
'Go preach idle nonsense to the world,'
but gave to them a sound foundation.

"And that alone resounded from their lips,
so that, in their warfare to ignite the faith,
they used the Gospel as their shield and lance.

"Now preachers ply their trade with buffoonery and jokes,
their cowls inflating if they get a laugh,
and the people ask for nothing more."

[*Paradiso* XXIX:109–117]

These imaginative discourses deriding decadence in the church are seven centuries old, but for many of us Christians today, are as fresh as last Sunday's services.

The *contrapasso* Dante conceived for simonists in his *Inferno* is almost comic in its acute diagnosis of the nature of clerical fraud: they are stuffed head down in a hole with only their legs extended. Because baptismal fonts in Dante's Florence were cylindrical, the poet intends the punishment to be a satanic parody of baptism. The image also recalls the Florentine punishment for assassins: burial upside down in the earth, with soil shoveled in to suffocate the killer. Thus do churchmen who murder the sense of the sacred within the community receive God's justice.

Spying a simonist whose legs burn hotter than most, Dante descends into a ditch to speak with him. The man in the hole cries out, "Is that you already? Are you here already, Boniface?" This is Pope Nicholas III, predecessor of the sitting pope, who, in the poet's judgment, is bound for hell.

Outraged by Nicholas's befouling of the Church, the pilgrim lectures the damned pope with unrestrained fury. "Stay then, for you are justly punished," Dante thunders. If it weren't for his respect for the papal office, the pilgrim says,

> *"I would resort to even harsher words*
> *because your avarice afflicts the world,*
> *trampling down the good and raising up the wicked."*

> [*Inferno* XIX:100–102]

Notice that *because.* As head of the Church, the institution that proclaims truth in faith and morals, Pope Nicholas rewarded evil and punished the righteous. If the people cannot trust the institutional Church to uphold righteousness, they are sheep without a shepherd.

After Dante finishes his rebuke, Virgil is so pleased that he takes the pilgrim in his arms and carries him over the arched bridge to the next ditch. Why is the master so happy? Because he sees that Dante is finally waking up to the reality of sin and its effects. If the masses come to believe that the Church is nothing more than a racket, their eternal salvation will be in danger, to say nothing of the peace and good order of society.

How I Let Scandal Steal My Faith

In early 2002, a Kansas father named Horace Patterson told me about the suicide of his adult son, a former altar boy who had been molested by their parish priest. After the man's suicide, his parents discovered that the local diocese had known about this priest's pedophilia for many years, but had kept assigning him to parishes and lying to the people in them.

By the time the official investigation ended, at least seventeen victims of Father Robert Larson had been identified. Five of them had committed suicide. In 2001, Father Larson spent five years in prison for his crimes. He died in 2014.

Horace recalled to me in a phone interview the day he received the news of his son's death. "I sat outside for two hours, crying and waiting for the family to come home to tell them," he told me.

Something inside me broke during that conversation. At the time I was a relatively new father; Matthew was not yet three. I imagined myself in Horace's chair on that hateful day. Images I conjured lodged in my heart like shrapnel. I could not enter a church for mass without feeling them.

In only my first six months of writing about the scandal, I received a staggering education in the grotesque reality behind the Church's façade. There was the cardinal whispered by many credible sources to be a serial sex abuser and who used back channels to try to have me taken off my investigation. There was the priesthood candidate I interviewed who told lurid stories of seminaries like brothels. There was the former priest who resigned his priesthood in his sexually corrupt diocese after the bishop covered up a sexual harassment investigation in the seminary.

Over the next few years, I heard stories like this again and again. It was like acid dripping onto the bonds of faith and reason that bound me to the Church. Over time, it reduced me to an anxious spiritual wreck who expected priests and bishops to lie as a matter of course. In mass, I could not look at my children without thinking that the Catholic bishops would be willing to sacrifice them for the sake of defending their privileges and the Church's image.

In our Dallas parish, the scandal seemed very far away, even though the *Dallas Morning News* was publishing stories exposing church corruption locally and nationally. The parish hummed along, oblivious to it all, like a sacrament factory. The absence of a sense of crisis in parish life deepened Julie's and my disillusionment.

One Sunday, listening to the priest's greeting-card homily and silently fuming, I realized that I did not trust that man to be a spiritual father to me. He was pleasant and he was popular, but he was not serious. Judging by his homilies, this priest thought his role was to anesthetize his flock, not heal us.

It wasn't just him. In my years worshiping in Catholic parishes throughout the country, this kind of clerical mediocrity was normal, but I found it tolerable. Dealing with it during the scandal, however, compelled me to face how little trust I had in most priests as spiritual leaders. I thought: *They want to tell me that everything is fine within the Church and that everything is fine within me, when I know that both are lies.*

We found a parish with more robust pastoral leadership. It was thirty miles away, but it was worth it to be part of a congregation in which the priests were pastorally serious and theologically orthodox. Finally, a safe harbor.

And then we caught one of the priests in a lie. Unknown to most of the congregation, this priest had been suspended from a ministry in Pennsylvania after a formal complaint of sexual abuse and had returned to his hometown, Dallas. He was a charmer and had somehow talked his way into our parish. The pastor, an older man, bought the same tale he told us: that theological liberals in his Pennsylvania diocese had driven him out for his fidelity to Catholic teaching. The pastor quietly put him to work in the parish without telling the diocesan bishop, a violation of Church policy. There seemed no end to the layers of fraud in the Church.

Julie and I had grown fond of the smooth-talking priest and were planning to invite him to dinner. When I discovered the con man's lie and found out his real story, I told Julie. That was the end for her. She broke down, sobbing, "We can never trust any of them again!"

Julie was right. If she and I, who knew so much about the scandals and were on guard to the point of paranoia, could have been fooled by this liar, possibly putting the safety of our children at risk, it was over for us as Catholics. We began by not trusting the bishops; we ended by not trusting ourselves. The dam cracked; the fear, wrath, and anxiety came barreling through the breach, washing away the last of our will to believe. By that time, we were Catholics in name only.

We no longer believed that our salvation depended on remaining in communion with the Roman Catholic Church. In fact, we intuited that our salvation might well depend on breaking that communion. We were in danger of losing the ability to believe in Christianity at all.

Julie and I began taking the kids to an Orthodox church because, from a Catholic point of view, Orthodox Christianity has valid sacraments. It was not possible for us to receive them unless we converted to Orthodoxy, but at least we could be present around the Eucharist in a beautiful liturgy. Eventually the grandeur of the liturgy and the kindness of the congregation won our hearts, and we converted.

But my relationship to the institutional church had shifted radically. And I carried with me into Orthodoxy a severely impaired ability to trust anyone in religious authority.

It bothers me that my Orthodox conversion was not intellectually clean. I did not rationally consider the arguments for Orthodoxy over Catholicism and make my decision coolly and deliberately. I grabbed hold of Orthodoxy as the only thing that would keep me from drowning in a tempest of rage and despair. Today, as I approach a decade in Orthodoxy, I am grateful for my faith, as messy as my entry into it was, and am firmly committed to it.

And I am grateful that the spiritual healing I have received through Orthodoxy has helped me love the Catholic Church once again—and so has Dante. Though the *Commedia* is a devastating indictment of the medieval Church's wickedness, it is a far more powerful witness to its

spiritual greatness. The same Catholic Church that gave the world Boniface VIII also gave it Dante Alighieri. So much the better for the world.

Spiritual Pride Goes Before a Spiritual Fall

Last fall, after my friend and I visited Dante's tomb in Ravenna, we made
a pilgrimage to a monastery in Norcia, the Italian birthplace of St. Benedict, my patron. I stood in the church listening to those monks—most of
them young Americans—chant the traditional Latin mass, and I thanked
God for them. Their path is no longer mine, but we are brothers walking
our separate ways to the same destination.

Later, talking with some of the monks in the monastery brewery, I
noticed that these men radiate a peace that is almost luminous. A Texas-
born novice, noticing the prayer rope wrapped around my wrist, pulled
one out of the pocket of his habit.

"Stick with the Jesus Prayer," he said, smiling.

The ragged, desperate path I took into the Orthodox Church taught
me an important lesson in humility. I had built my Catholicism on my
own intellectual pride, not on the true conversion of my heart. I thought
of myself as having joined the intellectual A-team of Christianity, and
even of being on the right side of history. *How lovely it is that I am a
Catholic,* I once thought, *and how marvelous that I am a Catholic with all
these other Catholics, heirs to the tradition that built Chartres, established
the monasteries, birthed the* Summa, *produced Palestrina, and generated
so much that is precious in our civilization.*

Oh sure, the Church was a mess; everybody knew that, and I took
perverse pleasure in griping with my Catholic friends about the woebegone
liturgies, the spiritual shallowness, and the lack of conviction among the
clergy and laity. More critically, I knew that the Church had done evil in
the past, and I could accept that as an abstract concept while still affirming
my belief. Incredible as it seems now, it never seriously occurred to me that
churchmen were as capable today of working evil as they had ever been.

Only too late did I understand that my mistake was idealizing, even
idolizing, these men and the Church they led.

Clerical corruption exists in Orthodoxy too, of course, and I once allowed myself to be drawn into a bruising spat with cutthroat church politicians that left me even more cynical about institutional religion than I had been before. Yet from that, and from my bitter Catholic experience, I learned that focusing on the failures of the bishops and clergy and allowing my rage at injustice within the Church to direct my thoughts and actions was leading me down a road to spiritual ruin.

It was a fragile, fearful Christian who fell into the spiritual care of Father Matthew in the autumn of 2012.

"I knew you had been badly hurt by the Church, and that I had to be careful how I dealt with you," Father Matthew told me two years later. "I knew that I had to earn your trust before you would listen to anything I had to say about how to deal with your family issues."

I was never a molestation victim, nor, to my knowledge, was I close to any. Why had I been so spiritually ravaged by the Church? This was a mystery that I could not penetrate. During my crisis years as a Catholic, I had a few close friends who were both stalwart believers and utterly undeceived about Church corruption. They hated it too, but they had not come undone like I had. What made the difference? I could not fathom it.

But now, in the *Commedia*, I saw that Dante was one of those Catholics. He seemed to grasp the meaning of Church corruption to the marrow—and yet he believed. The poet was able to stare down the evil of the clergy, including its Supreme Pastors, condemn them as devils, and yet affirm the goodness of God through the Church, despite its rotten state. This astounded me.

That Dante accomplished this comforted me, because it showed me that it was possible to be clear-eyed and outspoken about the wickedness of the men who run the Church, yet iron-willed in one's commitment to God within that Church.

I had failed at this. Dante had not. He was my hero. Whatever he knew that gave him such strength, I needed to learn it to protect myself as an Orthodox Christian if my faith was ever put to the test again.

But for me, there was more to this canto than the grievances of a pious Catholic against bad Popes and priests. Dante lost his mother when he was a small boy, and his father sometime between the ages of sixteen and eighteen. Having been orphaned before reaching manhood must have been a devastating emotional blow to young Dante.

In fact, Dante's father, Alighiero Alighieri, died when he was around the same age I was when I lost my own father as a mentor. Though he never mentions Alighiero in the *Commedia*, Dante filled the poem with father figures: Virgil, of course, then Brunetto Latini, and finally, in *Paradiso*, his noble ancestor Cacciaguida. We also see throughout the poem the dark father: Boniface VIII, who, as spiritual patriarch of Western Christians and an Italian warlord responsible for Dante's exile, was a cruel parody of a just and loving father.

Reading the *Commedia*, I could see that in my teens and twenties, when I was wending a path toward Catholicism, I had regarded the Church as a new father, a father I knew how to please because the rules were clear. If I partook of the sacraments, joined the life of the Church, and made my way toward holiness, I would make God the Father happy and win his affirmation. That was the theory, anyway.

It worked, mostly. I became a much happier and more confident person, and trusted deeply in the authority of the Church—especially because Pope John Paul II, who impressed me as strong, merciful, and just, was its patriarch. Still, as I have said, accepting that God loved me was something I did only on the level of theory. In my heart, contrary to the teachings of the Church, I believed that he loved me as a matter of divine duty but didn't approve of me. I would have to prove my love for him.

And so when we all learned how so many priests used their roles as fathers to abuse the children in their spiritual care, the disclosures affected me with an intensity I did not fully understand, not even years after I left the Roman church spiritually broken.

Reading Dante forced a revelation. Yes, the collapse of my Catholic faith had been about fear, injustice, hypocrisy, and the obliteration of trust. But more than that, it had been about fatherhood and sonship.

In the poem, the pilgrim Dante stood over the pope, symbol of a spiritual father, and summoned the courage to rebuke him for his failures.

But the fact that Dante kept his faith when his spiritual fathers failed indicated an inner spiritual strength that I did not have.

What did this have to say to me in my own struggle with the legacy of my childhood, my unsettled relationship with Daddy, and my quest for spiritual and emotional wholeness? I was not quite sure, but if my lessons from the Circle of Lust and the Circle of Heretics were any indication, it was about my sentimental idealism. If I expected more of women and more of family and place than they could deliver, it's probably true that I had unrealistic expectations of the patriarchs in my life, both clerical and familial.

HOW TO BE FAITHFUL DESPITE THE CHURCH

God speaks to us through religion and religious leaders, but they are not the voice of God. It's a paradox, but one necessary to master if you're going to hold on to your faith in spite of the failures of religious leaders. If your faith cannot survive learning that a pastor, rabbi, or other religious authority is corrupt, then your faith is not strong enough. They are only human beings; even the greatest among them is flawed, just as you are. Cultivate the habit of prayer and serving God by doing good works; this strengthens your own spirituality and gives you a firm foundation from which to speak out against injustice in religious institutions. You can't control the behavior of your religious leaders, but you can control your response to it.

Be grateful for holiness when you find it among churchmen, but do not expect it. As Flannery O'Connor wrote, "All human nature vigorously resists grace because grace changes us and the change is painful. Priests resist it as well as others." To combat the temptation to idealize the clergy, practice thinking of them not as saints but as fellow sinners. Tolkien's advice about viewing your partner in love as a "companion in shipwreck" is a useful point of view to adopt toward the Church and its clergy.

15

THE END OF ALL OUR EXPLORING

Not tenderness for a son, nor filial duty
toward my agèd father, nor the love I owed
Penelope that would have made her glad,

could overcome the fervor that was mine
to gain experience of the world . . .

[*Inferno* XXVI:94–98]

A Seeker Charts a Course Through Life

I had been on the road with Dante for a month or so, and my progress was plain to me though not to my wife. She was trying to be supportive, but my struggles were taking a toll on her. Not only was I pretty much dead weight around the house, but my weakness and frequent long naps left Julie feeling abandoned. She was carrying a heavy burden, one exacerbated by her fear that I would never again be healthy and might even have some grave illness that would end my life prematurely, as had happened to my sister.

Now, for the first time since we arrived in Louisiana and I fell ill, I felt that I was gaining traction. I tried to share my discoveries in Dante with Julie, not only because she is my best friend but also because I wanted to encourage her to hope that this crisis was heading toward resolution.

She tried to fake it out of politeness, but she didn't want to hear it.

One afternoon, making jam after a particularly stressful day, she said to me, "I feel like I'm the only one in our life who can never fall apart, no matter what."

I brought my concerns about Julie to Father Matthew.

"Ever heard the term 'compassion fatigue'?" Father Matthew said. "I learned about it when I was a hospital chaplain. Long-term chronic illness is one of the most stressful things there is. Being a caregiver for a sick husband and three home-schooled kids? Wow. God bless her.

"Not having a spouse there just to vent to, to spend time with, to help—it's not anything anyone would want to endure," Father Matthew said. "Just be patient and loving, and do whatever you can to help out. Chronic illness is something that affects the whole family. Try to be sensitive to what she's dealing with."

On the drive home I thought about how hard this failed homecoming had been on Julie too. After all, she had wanted to move here as much as I did. She had wanted to give all she had to Ruthie's motherless children, because they were family. But the door remained closed, and there was nothing we could do about it.

Should the Captain of His Soul Go Down With the Ship?

It was mid-September, and I was approaching the end of *Inferno*. Dante and Virgil arrive at the ditch in which the false counselors dwell. In life they used their authority to intentionally mislead others for their own benefit. Here the pilgrim Dante encounters his darkest self in the person of the mythical voyager Ulysses, known to the Greeks as Odysseus.

In Dante's version of the Ulysses myth, the clever, silver-tongued captain used his intelligence and his oratorical skills to persuade his exhausted crew, recently returned to their homes and families after many years at war, to leave home and follow him on an exploratory journey beyond the known world. Why? To satisfy his curiosity about the world. In his encounter with Dante, Ulysses says that he allowed no duty, not even to his wife, children, and aged parents, to stand between himself and fulfilling his quest for knowledge.

Ulysses sets sail for the West in a single ship with a faithful crew. As they approach the Straits of Gibraltar, Ulysses knows that he and his men have reached a boundary that their religion commands may not be crossed. And so the captain makes a speech to his weary crew:

> "O brothers," I said, "who, in the course
> of a hundred thousand perils, at last
> have reached the west, to such brief wakefulness
>
> "of our senses as remains to us,
> do not deny yourselves the chance to know—
> following the sun—the world where no one lives.
>
> "Consider how your souls were sown:
> you were not made to live like brutes or beasts,
> but to pursue virtue and knowledge."

[Inferno XXVI:112–120]

Inflamed with the craving to know the unknown, the men rowed toward the setting sun, into the open ocean. For five months they rowed. At last in the moonlight they caught sight of a distant mountain, higher than any the bold explorers had ever seen. Suddenly a tempest blew up. The boat sank; the captain and his crew drowned. Ulysses was damned for all eternity as one who gave false counsel.

To us, Ulysses appears as a hero, a man who risked, and lost, his life for the sake of expanding humankind's knowledge of the world. To have died on a quest in pursuit of virtue and knowledge is a profoundly honorable thing, is it not? Why does the poet put him in hell?

In the *Commedia*, recall, sin consists not only in loving and desiring bad things but also in loving and desiring good things in the wrong way.

For Dante, there is no more passionate love than the love of knowledge, the desire for understanding. Yet the love of knowledge for its own sake, like its unrestrained pursuit, corrupts and destroys. This has been a fundamental truth proclaimed by religion and wisdom traditions from ancient days. Consider Adam and Eve transgressing a divinely set boundary by eating the fruit of the Tree of Knowledge of Good and Evil. Think of Prometheus stealing fire from the Greek gods.

We in the West tragically lost this ancient wisdom in the nineteenth century with the advent of the Romantic era. The Romantic hero was the individual who defied custom and authority and forged his own path. We still believe it today, in part because the pursuit of knowledge, especially when it requires the courage to stand up to traditional authority, really can be a good.

What we have forgotten is that the quest for knowledge is not an ultimate good but only a conditional one. Chasing knowledge for its own sake can be heroic, but it can also be an excuse for serving the ego. If we have gotten this far with Dante, we know that the damned often cloak their sin in a veil of virtue. So it is with Ulysses, whose blind ambition to know caused him to throw off his obligations to his home and his family, and to deceive his men into doing the same to serve him. His insatiable curiosity caused him to refuse the warning of the gods to go no farther. Ulysses was a false counselor, because he used his wit to persuade others to do something evil by convincing them it was good.

Vainglorious Ulysses had, in effect, taken Brunetto Latini's advice to follow his own star on a voyage of discovery across the great sea of the unknown. His port of glory was first the floor of the ocean and then a gutter in hell. Dante, a trailblazing intellectual driven by the fire in his mind, sees his own potential fate in that of Ulysses. He reflects on this encounter with an empathy that seems almost brokenhearted:

I grieved then and now I grieve again
As my thoughts turn to what I saw,
And more than is my way, I curb my powers

lest they run on where virtue fail to guide them,
so that, if friendly star or something better still
has granted me its boon, I don't misuse the gift.

[*Inferno* XXVI:19–24]

This is the turning point in the pilgrim's journey through hell. It is when he finally sees where pride can take him. That he grieves over Ulysses's fate tells us how much of himself he saw in the condemned sailor. Ulysses's fault was not in pursuing knowledge; his fault was doing so without being guided by morality or divine decree. The misuse of his eloquence, his intelligence, and his courage cast him into hell.

That the pilgrim does not pity the damned Ulysses himself, as he did Francesca and Brunetto, tells us how much he has grown in his awareness of the seriousness of sin. Chastened by the example of Ulysses, the pilgrim consciously affirms that he is not free to use his intellectual and artistic gifts without limits. There are legitimate boundaries beyond which he cannot go without facing disaster.

I put *Inferno* down and stared at the blank ceiling of the guest bedroom, where I was reading and resting. Was I Ulysses? Daddy and Ruthie undoubtedly thought so. For them, to make my home beyond the borders of West Feliciana Parish was a transgression of the limits set by familial obligations. It was a refusal to pay what I rightly owed. It was ingratitude. It was disloyalty. It was the most selfish thing I could have done.

But I was not Ulysses, not in my own estimation. True, I had ventured and settled far beyond my ancestral home, both literally and symbolically, by exploring different forms of Christianity, different culinary traditions, different ways of educating my children, and other ways of living that were alien to the family back home. Ruthie, far more than our father, had taken every instance of difference between us as a personal insult.

Twice I had come back to Louisiana, hoping to build a life there. Twice my hopeful expectation of reconciliation and harmony had been dashed by the unwillingness of Daddy and other family members to compromise.

Were they right? I did not believe they were. But deep down, even after the revelation at Farinata's tomb, I clung to the fear that they were. By this point in my own journey through the *Inferno*, I was familiar with how blind we are to our own sins. Therefore, an examination of my conscience compelled me to consider the possibility that my Starhill family saw some flaw within me that I did not.

After all, nearly all the sinners in hell convinced themselves in the mortal life that the evil that they did was good, or at least understandable. Of no figure is this more true than Ulysses, and about no character in the *Inferno* is the damnable sin harder for us to understand. As the Dante biographer A. N. Wilson writes of Ulysses, "He is so noble to the end, and his quest, to pursue knowledge wherever the quest may take him, is the ideal of Modern Man." More prosaically, the path I took out into the world to explore my own calling was a totally normal one in American life, even in some ways an admirable one.

But there are a lot of things many Americans today find admirable, or at least normal, that I don't accept. They usually have to do with a refusal to live for anything higher than satisfying one's own desires. Had I been guilty of this in my own life's odyssey? It was undeniable that by moving away from Louisiana I had put my own desires ahead of the wishes of my family and the bonds of obligation linking us. What I wasn't quite sure of now was the extent to which my desires and their expectations were just.

I walked out of the bedroom and into the kitchen. Julie was loading the dishwasher.

"So, I know you don't really like to talk about Dante," I said, "but I need to discuss this canto I just read with you."

"Honey, it's not that I don't like to talk about Dante," she said, turning off the faucet. "It's that you are so deeply into it that I don't have the time to follow. I don't know what to say to you most of the time."

"Okay. I'm sorry."

"No, don't be sorry. Tell me, what is it?"

So I told her about Ulysses, and why he went to hell. I told her I couldn't shake the idea that I might be the Ulysses of my family, and that

I had deceived myself into thinking that I was right to leave in the first place. "I don't think that's true," I said, "but the belief that it might be so is a thorn in my side. And maybe this hell I'm in now with my sickness is punishment for my self-delusion."

"Rodgie, believe me, the problem is not that you left. The problem is that you are *you*," she said. "They are never going to accept you. You can't change that. But you have got to understand that that does not make you bad."

"I believe you," I told her, "But I know how selfish I can be—"

"No comment."

"So noted. Anyway, I know how selfish I can be, and I don't want to be that guy. The thing is, I'm so emotionally involved with all this that I can't tell who is being more selfish: me or them."

Julie shook her head to indicate that she was not following me.

"I mean, I don't know which one of us is expecting more from the other than they have a right to expect," I said. "Maybe we both are."

Dante was helping me work this out, I told her, and so were Mike and Father Matthew. Things were starting to make sense to me. "Please have faith," I said, "and be patient. There is going to be an end to all this."

"Good. Keep working at it," she said. "But I want you to remember something. You have a family right here in this house who loves you, and who would love to have their husband and father back. And there's a church out in Starhill that wants you and needs you. Why aren't all of us enough?"

"I'm sorry. I know you're mad at me about all this."

"Sweetie, I'm *not* mad," she said, throwing the dish towel onto the counter. "I'm just really, really tired, and I'm tired of the place in your mind that your family takes up. I'm jealous of it. We moved here for them. It didn't work out. But we've got a lot of good things going on in this town."

"I'm sorry I moved us here," I said.

"No, I'm glad we moved here," she said. "This is a great town. I just wish you could get out of your head and join us here."

A Dream Journey Reveals My Destination

Feeling an attack of fatigue coming on, I returned to the alcove bed—the kids were now calling it the "man cave"—and fell asleep. I had an intense dream, one so vivid it was almost like a hallucination. I wrote down the details as soon as I woke up later that evening.

I am leading a group of tourists who have come to West Feliciana toward the woods where I grew up hunting with my father and the men of our community. Daddy and the other hunters have gone ahead of us, and I can hear the hounds baying in the distance.

I feel like a fraud, leading this group. I don't want to go into the woods, which are thick, dark, and impenetrable. We pass through fields—fields I remember from my childhood—leading down to the Mississippi River.

Our group comes upon a neatly graded gravel road that heads down the slope to the river's edge. The path is straight and almost shimmers in the sunlight. There are a number of buildings—inns, restaurants, and houses— built along the road. My first thought on seeing this is, They've ruined it!

But on second glance, I change my mind. This isn't a series of strip malls but actually a charming, bustling neighborhood. This is a sign of civilization.

Not knowing what else to do, I lead the tourists into a hunting lodge, and we take our seats at an empty restaurant. I could get used to this, I think, then wonder how I am going to break it to the tourists in my group that my father and the hunters are too far ahead and that we are going to stay here in the lodge.

When I thought about this dream, the symbolism struck me as clear: for me, staying on the straight path meant not following Daddy. He fit naturally into his world, but for me it was and is a dark wood. The dream told me it is possible for me to settle on the border of my father's realm, but that to try to enter into it would be a disaster.

The message was also clear: attempting that imaginative journey to my father's realm, as I had been trying to do all my life, was the act of a Ulysses, full of hubris and heedless of natural limits. So yes, I was in fact Ulysses—not because I had left Starhill, and not because I had come back to Starhill, but because I identified my own destination as my father's and tried to follow him there. That was how I had lost the straight path divine providence had laid out for me.

The only way to recover it was to let Daddy go into the woods with his men and his hounds and to stay behind in the lodge, taking care of those for whom I was responsible and finding my place within that harmony. After all, hunters need a place to stay when they come out of the woods. Maybe it was my place to provide one for them. The Mississippi River at the end of the golden road was eternity, and that lodge was to be my resting place along that straight path.

That dream was an important turning point in my healing. Much later, long after I had left my own dark wood, I read Richard Lansing's translation of Dante's *Convivio*, a short philosophical work he wrote just prior to beginning the *Commedia*. This passage from Book IV of *Convivio* brought the dream to mind:

> Now since God is the cause of our souls and has created them like himself (as it is written, "Let us make man in our own image and likeness"), the soul desires above all else to return to him. And just as the pilgrim who walks along a road on which he has never traveled before believes that every house which he sees from afar is an inn, and finding it not so fixes his expectations on the next one, and so moves from house to house until he comes to the inn, so our soul, as soon as it enters upon this new and never traveled road of life, fixes its eyes on the goal of its supreme good, and therefore believes that everything it sees which seems to possess some good in it is that supreme good.

Because a partial good can never be the ultimate good, the traveler's philosophical error forces him to keep seeking, in vain, his destination. This is how we lose the straight path through life, says Dante.

"A wise traveler reaches his goal and rests," he continues. "The wanderer never reaches it, but with great lethargy of mind forever directs his hungry eyes before him."

This was the message of my Ulysses dream, and this is the message of the *Commedia*. The search was over; to keep going now was pure egotism. For me, my home with Julie and our children, and St. John the Theologian, our country mission church, are the inns God gave me on the straight path to eternal bliss. I must learn to rest there. As long as my imagination chases my father through the woods, and my heart plays the part of the lonely hunter, I will never find peace.

HOW TO SEEK AND TO FIND

"Intellectual curiosity is a desire like any other," said the poet W. H. Auden, warning that we risk disaster by giving full rein to this craving. To believe that because something *can* be known or experienced, it *should* be known or experienced is a characteristic vice of our time.

Ulysses not only deceived his faithful crew, who paid with their lives, but he also deceived himself. What do you seek? Why do you seek it? Do you expect to find anything, or is the journey itself your real destination? When you follow your bliss, who pays the price of your peregrinations?

Think hard about these questions, and be ruthless with yourself in answering them. What you call a courageous quest might in truth be a cowardly flight from your true destiny. And cultivate respect for limits, which, when doing what they are supposed to do, function not as barriers but as guardrails.

16

OUT OF EGYPT

"Hold on tight, for by such rungs as these,"
said my master, panting like a man exhausted,
"must we depart from so much evil."

[*Inferno* XXXIV:82–84]

The Hard Road to Freedom

I did not have the chance to get to know my other guide, therapist Mike Holmes, as well as I did Father Matthew. We met weekly in his office on Baton Rouge's south side, and as you would expect, I did all the talking. Mike was surprisingly easy to talk to. He was around my age, was married with kids, and had an engaging, open manner. I felt like I was talking to a buddy, not a therapist; I never felt like I was being handled. And though he was an ordained Southern Baptist pastor as well as a licensed therapist and would bring our shared Christian faith into our conversations, Mike never preached at me.

What he told me in our first meeting in the summer of 2013 guided our entire relationship the seven months we saw each other: that I could not control other people, but I could control my reaction to them. Mike helped me to see that I was not powerless in the face of my emotions and anxieties. When he pointed out things that I already knew about myself and my relationships, for some reason I felt that having a trained professional with no subjective investment in the family system made these insights more credible.

And he made fruitful connections that I could not. One week I briefed him on a trip I had made to Wisconsin a few days earlier, to lecture at a small Lutheran college about *Little Way*. After my talk, I met a transgendered man and his wife in the audience. They had read my book, loved it, and wanted to hear me speak. But they had been afraid to come because they knew I was a Christian, and a conservative one. The couple feared judgment and rejection, but they had come anyway, on the advice of a friend.

"It's funny, Mike," I told him. "These are not the kind of people I hang out with, but they really impressed me. They were kind and spiritually serious. I enjoyed talking with them. Even though we are so different, we made a connection. I've been thinking about that all week. There was something really human that passed between us, and it kind of knocked me back."

"Now that's interesting," Mike said. "You saw that couple as different, maybe even strange by your standards, but you saw them as real people. Let's take that thought and apply it to your family. Can you see them as different, and extend to them the same grace?"

This is what Mike did all the time. It was Dante's strategy too. I could hardly walk through a canto at Dante's side without seeing some aspect of myself, and my agonized situation with my family, in the lives of the personalities I met there. Many weeks I would begin a session with Mike by saying, "So I was reading in Dante this week . . ."

Making Hell out of Heaven on Earth

Mike and I missed a few appointments, so when I showed up at his office one late September morning, I announced that I had big news.

"Let's hear it," Mike said.

"I am an idol worshiper," I said wryly.

He smiled and cocked his head, as if to say, *Um, what?*

"Since we last met, I discovered that I am an idol worshiper," I said in a mock-serious tone. "Or was one. It's a Dante thing."

Intrigued, Mike signaled for me to go on.

I told him about the encounter with Farinata, and the revelation from it that the real gods of my father and me, despite our professed Christianity, are family and place. "It's what we serve, whether we mean to or not," I explained.

"How does this change the way you see your family?" Mike asked.

"I'm not sure, to be honest," I said. "It's opening my mind to a more nuanced view of the situation, I can say that much. I see my dad and me trapped by the same vision, if that makes any sense. Ruthie was too."

"Trapped?"

"Yeah. It's like the family and place thing cast a spell over all of us," I said. "It's helpful for me to see them as good people who are just as captive to that false image as I was."

Our conversation moved into the consequences of human fallibility. We are always let down by those we love, Mike said. It's in our nature. He reminded me of instances from our past discussions in which I conceded having failed Julie and the children in various ways.

"That's a great thing I've learned from Orthodoxy," I said. "There's a lot of emphasis on forgiveness, on asking for it and extending it. Julie and I do that in our family a lot."

"Why can't you do it in your Starhill family?" Mike asked.

"Because nobody can admit fault," I said. "It's not something my family does. They never fail; they only are failed."

As I said that I felt a plume of anxiety arise within me and mushroom out to my shoulders and down my arms. I took a sip from the large plastic tumbler of ice water I kept with me at all times, since the Epstein-Barr virus left me perpetually thirsty. Then I changed the subject, telling Mike that I had been struck by the way the pilgrim Dante treated an evil pope he meets in hell. I envied the poet's faith, I said. Mike asked why.

"Because he didn't allow the sins of men to shake it," I said. "I know a few Catholics like that. I know a lot more Catholics, and other kinds of Christians, who will not confront the shadow side of Church life, because they're afraid of what they'll see there."

"That happens."

"Dante wasn't like that. He spoke out against corruption in the Church, but he never lost sight of the truth and beauty in the Church."

I told Mike about how seeing the Chartres cathedral at seventeen had been the start of my lifelong quest for God.

"If I remember correctly from *Little Way*, you went back there after Ruthie died," he said.

"I did. I went by myself. It wasn't the same. I mean, it was still an incredible experience, but I couldn't see it with the same eyes as before. Funny, but the first time I saw Chartres, I was not a Catholic, and the second time I saw Chartres, I was not a Catholic. But in the time between, I had been a Catholic."

"Was that hard for you, the second time?"

"Oh, yeah. I was quite melancholy about it. I wanted so badly to see Chartres again as I had seen it before. I wanted that same feeling of connection, of being a part of something so much bigger than myself."

Later that morning, sitting in Starbucks with a cup of coffee, I couldn't shake the thought that those two visits to Chartres—one as a youth, the other as a man in middle age—had something to tell me about my relationship to Starhill. Both were places that had once meant a lot to me, but which I had returned to in the past couple of years and been disappointed by.

What was the nature of that disappointment? With Starhill, it was discovering that my dream of harmonizing with family and place was a false ideal. I wanted to go home again, but that home did not exist, not as I thought it did. Finding that out had just about wrecked me.

In the same way, the splendor of the cathedral in Chartres had been dimmed for me by the passage of time and my disillusionment with the Catholic Church. I thought about how the Catholic Church raised that cathedral in Chartres in the first half of the thirteenth century and consecrated it in 1260—five years before Dante's birth. During that period, the Catholic Church led several crusades, including one that sacked the city of Constantinople, laying the groundwork for the devastating schism between the Eastern and Western churches. Rome established the Inquisition and massacred thousands of Cathar heretics in France's Languedoc region.

The Church corruption Dante lived through was incomparably greater than anything I had seen—but so too was the spiritual intensity and aesthetic glory of the Church. And this surely had a lot to do with why Dante could express his rage at injustice within the Church without losing his faith: his vision kept both realities—the good and the evil—in focus. One did not cancel out the other.

In the same way, all that is best in my family cannot be easily separated from the worst. The Ruthie who trash-talked me behind my back for leaving home and getting above myself is the same Ruthie whose love of our Louisiana home and its people inspired me to return. The father whose steadfast refusal to recognize the limits and the harm of the family code and its ideology of family and place is the same father who made a good, loving home for Mama, Ruthie, and me.

Come to think of it, he's the same father who lent a hand to poor country people trying to bring running water into their homes. He's the same father who would leave home in the middle of the night to fix his brother's broken water well, and who kept Loisie and Mossie's porch filled with firewood every winter. He's the father who helped found the Starhill Volunteer Fire Department and who served as its first chief because it was a way to serve his neighbors.

That counted for a lot. If there had not been profound goodness in both my father and my sister, family and place would not have been so alluring to me and would not have drawn me back—twice. And if those things had not been real, I would not have seen all those men and women of our parish coming out to help my Starhill family during Ruthie's illness and after her death. The book I wrote about that time in our family's life is as true an image of my family as Chartres was of the medieval Catholic Church.

But both were partial truths, and I wanted them to be whole truths. Dante was showing me that this is foolishness. What I expected, it was becoming clear, was a return to the innocence and wonder of childhood. I wanted to regain that sense of primal unity with my family, where things were rightly ordered by my father, and to climb into Daddy's lap with Ruthie at day's end and feel loved and secure. I wanted to return to the sacred grove surrounding Aunt Lois and Aunt Hilda's cabin, where I first learned to love faraway places and beautiful things.

I desired to recover that first love for the Church—not just for the Catholic Church, but for the history, the certainty, and the grandeur of institutional Christianity. I ached to see once more a Chartres in which there was nowhere that was not beautiful and filled with the clarifying, warming light of God, a light that had once led me out of a dark wood of my own making.

These things I wanted were good things, but it was immature to desire them as a grown man. In the end, I longed for Utopia, a childish thing to do.

Icon or Idol? It's All in How You See It

The coffee shop was alive with the burble of conversation and the hiss of the espresso machine, but I could barely hear it. Something was happening within me. I pulled out of my book bag an English version of Dante's first book, *Vita Nuova*, a gift from its translator, Andrew Frisardi. Something I had read there about the difference between idols and icons aided my understanding earlier in the journey. I found the passage again and read:

> An icon is an image for contemplating a reality that transcends the specific image; the image leads the mind, through the senses, to direct communion with the intelligibles. An idol is an image to which we are attached for the sake of the image per se. Obviously one and the same object can be an idol or an icon—our approach to it is what makes the difference.

This insight had clarified earlier to me the nature of my disordered relationship with family and place. Now it expanded my understanding of my basic condition. It wasn't simply that I saw family, place, and religion as idols—that is, as ends in themselves—but that my distorted vision prevented me from seeing them as they really were: as icons, damaged though they may be, through which the light of God shone. They were not ends, but imperfect means to the perfect end: God.

Here were the means of escaping the dark wood: reorienting my inner vision to see the world around me as an icon, not an idol. I had to judge all things by the degree to which the light of God shines through them, and to which they serve as a sign pointing toward God.

And I had to turn myself into an icon. That is to say, as long as I sought my ultimate good through increasing my pleasure and decreasing my pain, I would be serving the idol I had made of my own ego, not serving God.

I was not yet certain what that would entail, but I knew I could do it. Mike had told me on our first day together that gaining control over my thoughts, my will, and my inner vision was the goal of our therapy, and I believed him. But how was I going to make this change?

Now that we were reaching the end of the inferno stage of Dante's pilgrimage (and mine), I knew some things I had not known when I set out with my poet guides.

I knew now that we condemn ourselves to misery not so much because of what we hate but because of what we love and the way we love. This gave me a new way to think of sin and brokenness, both in myself and in others.

It had never made sense that my father and my sister didn't love me; they plainly did. What I could now see is that the way they loved me required perfect reciprocity. And to have moved away from our family and its land was, to them, a failure of reciprocity; it was a rejection of their love.

They were wrong. But this was how they saw the world. The fact that they were such good, decent, even noble people only left me confused and uncertain of myself. Coming to understand this about them didn't make it right, but it did help me to make sense of the situation.

But in my way, I was guilty of the same thing. Because of my wounded pride, because of my aggrieved sense of justice, because of my considerable ego, I found it hard to love them unconditionally.

Brunetto Latini's fate taught me that my father shared with Dante's tragic Tuscan mentor a pride in the accomplishments of his son (or in

Dante's case, "son"), but he also shared an inability to view his son as distinct from his own personality and will. My relationship with my dad never became what it could have been because he could not accept the conditions under which our father-son relationship could be fruitful.

But I was guilty of the same thing. I accepted his flawed judgment in spite of myself and still craved his approval.

I knew that in the wake of Ruthie's death, a shattering loss that contained within it the possibility for renewed family life, my Starhill kin were Farinata and Cavalcante. My folks and Ruthie's family refused to see that things had changed. All the old alliances and old certainties had to be reaffirmed by force of will.

But wasn't this true for me as well? Though I desperately wanted things to change (so much that I had been willing to move home), it turned out that I might be as fixated on and as paralyzed by the past as they were.

I knew too that just as Dante had been able to criticize the behavior of his spiritual father the pope without losing his faith in the papacy or the Church, I had to find a way to be able to separate the things I did not like in the way my dad treated me from who he was as my father, to whom respect and honor was rightly due.

I also knew that I wasn't Ulysses. There was nothing wrong with wanting to go into the world and try my vocation as a writer. My Louisiana family had expected more from me than they had a right to expect. But there was more Ulysses in me than there ought to have been. I was being unfaithful to my duties to my wife and children, and to my church family because I could not shake my lifelong compulsion to keep rowing hard toward a port that could never be reached.

All these things I knew because, as had happened with Dante the pilgrim, my walk through my own inferno compelled me to examine my life and myself with a searching eye and to discard illusions that kept me a prisoner of the dark wood. Dante taught me to see the nature of my condition more clearly. I knew now where I was, how I had arrived there, and the way back to the straight path. The mission now was to take it.

"It is time for us to leave, for we have seen it all," says Virgil to Dante.

They are standing at the frozen floor of the pit in the center of the earth, at the point in all the universe farthest from God. On that spot is the fallen archangel Lucifer, towering like a monstrous colossus over his kingdom of death, immobilized to the waist in a vast ice-bound lake called Cocytus. All mortal men who choose themselves over God ultimately choose Lucifer, says Dante. And what a three-faced horror he is!

> *Beneath each face two mighty wings emerged,*
>   *such as befit so vast a bird:*
> *I never saw such massive sails at sea.*
>
> *They were featherless and fashioned*
> *like a bat's wings. When he flapped them,*
> *he sent forth three separate winds,*
>
> *The sources of the ice upon Cocytus.*
> *Out of six eyes he wept and his three chins*
> *dripped tears and drooled blood-red saliva.*
> *With his teeth, just like a hackle*
> *pounding flax, he champed a sinner*
> *In each mouth, tormenting three at once.*

[*Inferno* XXXIV:46–57]

The Beast's legs are as big as redwood trees, and covered with ice-encrusted hair. In the final verses of *Inferno*, Dante and Virgil climb down the enormous flanks of the Beast and keep going until they emerge on the other side of the world, into the light of a new day. It is near sunrise on Easter Sunday morning. Dante can see a few stars remaining in the dawn sky above.

The pilgrim has descended into the deepest recesses of sin, laid his hands on the personification of evil, and been restored to consciousness of his own true condition. Like the Hebrew slaves of the biblical exodus,

Dante obeyed the call to leave Egypt and march toward freedom. But Egypt had not yet left him—nor had it gone out of me.

The story of how this happened is the next part of our journey.

HOW TO RECKON HONESTLY WITH YOURSELF

The journey through hell has been about examining our own faults, and discovering the reality of sin's hold on our hearts. The first part of saving your life is coming to understand how you endangered it by loving wrongly, and living under the rule of your passions.

Loving wrongly can lead us to make idols—that is, to treat things as sacred, which though good are not sacred. Things like romantic love, food and drink, work, family, patriotism, art, scholarship, science, sports, literature, even religion—all these things can be idols if we allow our passion for them to rule us like gods.

Whatever idol you worship—and all of us, religious or not, are tempted by idolatry—the ultimate idol you worship is yourself. No discerning reader gets out of Dante's inferno without having had at least one soul-shaking encounter with their ugliest self. And here's the hard but necessary truth: it's nobody's fault but your own.

And you cannot free yourself from the black hole of sin without help from God, or a Higher Power. This is the core truth at the heart of every twelve-step program, because it recognizes a spiritual reality: by itself, human will cannot conquer the Medusa-like power of the passions. The only way to conquer the passions is to first admit your powerlessness over them.

This isn't about gaining self-confidence, feeling better about yourself, or discovering inner peace, though you will be given all those things in time. This is really about deciding for light or darkness, slavery or freedom, life or death.

You are free to choose. But choose you must.

PART III

PURGATORIO, OR
HOW TO BE HEALED

17

STAND UP AND WALK

Now I shall sing the second kingdom,
There where the soul of man is cleansed,
Made worthy to ascend to Heaven.

[Purgatorio I:4–6]

Climbing the Holy Mountain,
One Step at a Time

o you believe in purgatory? Unless you are a Roman Catholic,
probably not. Like Protestants, Orthodox Christians do not
believe in purgatory, the realm of the afterlife that, in Roman
Catholic teaching since the High Middle Ages, is the temporary abode
of the saved who are not yet pure enough to stand in the presence of
God. They suffer, but do so happily because they know the asceticism
imposed on them in purgatory has meaning: it is preparing them for
unity with God.

If Dante's *Inferno* is about recognizing the harsh reality of your sinfulness, his *Purgatorio* is about learning how to overcome the sinful tendencies that drag us down and prevent us from living a life of spiritual
health and wholeness. *Purgatorio* is an allegory of our lives on earth and
the struggles we face to purify our hearts and strengthen them in love
and virtue.

Though purgatory is not an Orthodox teaching, practicing asceticism in the mortal life is central to the Orthodox spirituality. Every Sunday, we in the little St. John's flock park our cars under the oaks, make our way into the church, say our prayers and make our bows in front of the icons, then begin the liturgy with chanted prayers, psalms, and Scripture readings. And every Sunday, no matter how much his sermon celebrates joy and gladness, Father Matthew is going to talk about the ascetic life. Feasting and fasting are both needed to maintain balance in our lives. Teachings about asceticism are not just for Lent but rather are part of the weekly ritual of life in our congregation.

One Sunday in autumn, Father Matthew opened with the Gospel story of the rich young ruler who came to Jesus asking what he needed to do to be saved. Jesus told him to keep the law; the rich young ruler said he had done so. Then Jesus told him to sell all he had, give the money to the poor, and follow him. The Bible tells us the rich young ruler went away sad, because he would not take that radical step.

"We are all like that man," said Father Matthew. "We may not be rich in material wealth, but we are all rich in passions."

In Orthodoxy, the term "passions" refers to sinful desires. Both Orthodoxy and Dante teach that these desires are not to be exterminated but rather mastered and changed by grace into something holy.

Our passions may be the love of good food, Father Matthew preached, or a passion for our career. It may be a destructive passion—say, a passion for strong drink—or it may even be a passion that is normally a good thing, like a devotion to serving others.

"But I tell you, brothers and sisters, whatever your passions are, you will not be spiritually healed unless you set them aside and follow Christ above all things," he said. "Notice that Jesus does not tell the rich young ruler to read a book to figure out what to do. He says, 'Follow me.'"

The decision to put God first, the priest said, is not a one-time decision, but a decision that must be renewed every day, sometimes every hour.

"We know it is possible to do that," he said. "Look around you: we have the saints to show us how." Father Matthew swept his hand around the nave, drawing attention to the icons adorning the walls. These are painted images, in rich golds, deep reds, and austere blues, depicting Jesus, the Virgin Mary, and saints from every age of the Church, as well as scenes from the Bible. In our mission parish, we have an icon of St. John the Baptist dressed in the skins of a wild animal. There is St. Patrick, the fifth-century evangelizer of Ireland, and Nicholas, the holy fourth-century bishop whose generosity gave rise to the legend of Santa Claus.

There are also more modern saints. Our church's icon of St. Seraphim of Sarov, a nineteenth-century Russian hermit and miracle worker, shows him bent over, walking with a cane. The monk was attacked in his forest hermitage by robbers who beat him and left him for dead. He survived and forgave his attackers, asking the authorities not to punish them. There on our walls is an image of St. Xenia, an eighteenth-century woman widowed when young, who gave away all her possessions and lived among the poor of St. Petersburg, acquiring a reputation for great holiness. And there is an icon of St. John Maximovich, a Russian bishop who led a flock sent into diaspora by the Bolshevik Revolution, and who had acquired a reputation as a great mystic by the time of his death in 1966 in San Francisco.

I looked around at these icons as Father Matthew preached and thought about how these saints are now honored because they had done what the *Commedia* teaches us to do: cleanse our souls and empty out our egos so that the light and love of God can shine through us and illuminate the world. My faith tradition teaches us to contemplate the stories of these saints' lives and to mimic them in our own circumstances.

"The Church is a spiritual hospital, brothers and sisters, and Jesus is the Great Physician," Father Matthew said. "Grace is the medicine that will heal us. Prayer and fasting open our souls to grace."

That sermon sliced right to the heart of *Purgatorio*. Everyone in purgatory is saved from hell and destined for heaven because before death they called on the mercy of God. But they must have their fierce attachments to particular passions burned away before they can enter fully into the presence of the All-Holy. In this life, that can be accomplished only through ascetic struggle: that is, by practicing the habit of denying yourself your cravings for the sake of something higher.

Purgatorio is not about coming to believe the truth; it is about living out the truth in your daily life. To put it in secular terms, *Purgatorio* teaches us how to overcome destructive habits of thought and action that trap us in our own personal dark wood and will destroy our lives if we do not act against them. Dante's way will be familiar to readers familiar with twelve-step programs, which map out the road to liberation from the slavery of addiction like this:

1. Confront the depths and realities of your brokenness, and take responsibility for it.
2. Recognize your need for deliverance from your addiction.
3. Accept that you cannot overcome addiction on your own, and call on the help of a Higher Power.

In Christian teaching, salvation was accomplished for humankind by Jesus Christ in his death and resurrection. Yet God, in his love for us, will not force us to accept it. We still have to say yes to his saving grace—and say yes again and again, aligning our wills ever more closely with his, cooperating with him to cleanse our hearts of the desires that draw us away from him.

Everyone who has tried to quit smoking, lose weight, or do anything else difficult to change their lives knows that you do it only by renewing that decision day after day. We face down cravings for the old life and, with the grace of God and the strength of our own free will, deny them. In time, the hold of these cravings fades, and we grow into freedom and wholeness. *Purgatorio*, then, is the story of how we recover from our addiction to passions, learn to love rightly, and create within ourselves the space for God's grace to transform us.

The Lesson of the Reed

Purgatorio begins on Easter Sunday morning, with Dante and Virgil landing on a beach at the base of Mount Purgatory. Cato the Younger, the old man who guards the mountain, tells Virgil how to prepare the pilgrim for the ascent.

"Go then, make sure you gird him
with a straight reed and bathe his face,
to wipe all traces of defilement from it,

"for it would not be fitting to appear,
his eyes still dimmed by any mist,
before the minister, the first from paradise.

"This little island, at its lowest point,
there where the waves beat down on it,
grows reeds in soft and pliant mud.

"There no other plant can leaf,
or harden to endure,
without succumbing to the battering waves."

[*Purgatorio* I:92–105]

The reed is a Christian symbol of humility, without which Dante cannot climb higher. After whipping Christ and crowning him with thorns, the Roman soldiers gave Christ a reed as a pathetic scepter for a mock ruler. In Christian iconography, the reed is a sign of Jesus's willingness to suffer humiliation to fulfill the will of his Father.

In *Purgatorio*, the reed, found at the lowest point of the island, stands for the humility that is the absolute requirement for advancement in the spiritual life. There are no quick fixes to our problems, no easy cleanups to the messes we have made in our lives. You can't get to paradise without the long, hard slog up the mountain. Nobody can get to heaven without first dying to the passions.

We must take on the qualities of the reed—whose lowliness and ability to absorb the blows of life without breaking are the source of its enduring strength—if we are to reach the summit in triumph. The reed embodies the Taoist principle of *wu-wei*, or "non-doing," which instructs one to go along with the flow of events when action cannot change them, and to overcome adversity through patient endurance.

Dante and Virgil stand on the shore, wondering about their next move. Suddenly they spy a bright light approaching over the sea. This, says Virgil, is an angel of the Lord, so intensely luminous that the pilgrim cannot bear the sight.

The angel pilots a boat filled with over one hundred of the recently deceased, the saved bound for purgatory and, at the end of their journey, paradise. What a different picture this image of transport is from Charon's ferry across the Styx into hell. Those passengers cursed God, each other, and every living thing. By contrast, these shades "together with one voice" sing Psalm 114, a short hymn celebrating the deliverance of the people of Israel from Egyptian captivity.

For Dante, hell is analogous to Egypt in the Exodus story. Purgatory, it follows, stands for the forty years the ancient Israelites spent wandering in the desert. They could not enter the promised land until the ways of slavery had been purged from their hearts.

Throughout the journey up the mountain, the pilgrim Dante will be conscious of the temptation to return to the security of Egyptian slavery. Freedom and responsibility are hard. In the story from the Hebrew Bible, the Israelites became impatient with God and used the gold they brought with them out of Egypt to make an idol, a golden calf. This happens to us every time we look back on the past and prefer the pain we know from the old life to the possibility of liberty and new life.

The pilgrim Dante faces the temptation to return to the old life as soon as the new arrivals disembark. In the crowd, Dante sees someone he recognizes: Casella, a musician he knew back in Italy. Purgatory, as we shall see, is a place of happy reunions. Exhausted from the rigors of the journey, Dante asks his old friend to sing some of the love songs that used to make him feel so good.

And so Casella does, singing some of Dante's own poetry. The crowd falls under its spell, forgetting all their cares.

Suddenly Cato the Younger appears and tears into them.

"What carelessness, what delay is this?
Hurry to the mountain and there shed the slough
that lets not God be known to you."

[*Purgatorio* II:121–123]

The penitents scatter and begin the walk up the mountain. It's not that music and poetry are bad; it's that they are bad at this moment, because they distract the people from their mission. "All our troubles, if we carefully seek out their source, derive in some way from not knowing how to make a proper use of time," says Dante in his *Convivio*.

'Do You Want to Be Healed?'

Good things embraced at the wrong time can bring us harm. If the pilgrim Dante stays on the beach listening to the old sweet songs of home, his mind dwelling on the old life, he might never be able to reach paradise.

For me, this is an ever-present temptation. I can find every reason to avoid doing the work I need to do when something more pleasant beckons. Dante tells us here that our newfound freedom is at risk when we prefer to dally and procrastinate, even when we distract ourselves with good things, rather than get on with the mission given to us.

Besides, it is all too easy to fall back into bad habits. This happened to me in late September, shortly after I began *Purgatorio*. Since beginning therapy and the *Commedia* in the summer, I had been making progress in mastering my emotional responses to my family's challenges, but lately I had hit a wall.

I saw my parents once or twice each week, usually on the way back to St. Francisville after Matt's classes in Baton Rouge, as the route took us near their Starhill house. I made it my habit to bring them fresh bread or a dessert as a treat from the city. Most afternoons I would find them sitting on their front porch, smoking and entertaining visitors, or inside watching Fox News. I would sit for a while and talk, but found that I was once again short-tempered in the face of their usual quirks.

Mama has always had a habit of telling the same stories over and over. It's not early Alzheimer's; it's just one of those things she does. Everybody accommodates it. It's no big thing, really, but I let it become a big thing to me.

"Hannah called the other day to say she can't come up this weekend because—"

"I know, Mama. You told me yesterday."

"Oh. She's doing fine at her job. They might promote her. She said that—"

"Mama, I *know*. We had this entire discussion last night, don't you remember?"

"Well," she said frostily, "I was just trying to make conversation."

There was another, more serious reason it was hard to make conversation. Since we had been back, I noticed both of my folks had a habit of forgetting things we had talked about, including things they had said, and recasting previous conversations in a significantly different way. They had long had a weakness for shaping facts to suit their preferred narrative, not understanding what they were doing. It was, I concluded, a coping mechanism. Before she became ill, I would complain about this to Ruthie from time to time in our phone calls. "Oh, don't let it bother you," she would say. "That's just Mama and Daddy. Just let them talk and move on."

Ruthie had an enviable ability to just let them talk and move on. Not me. After her cancer diagnosis, I would often phone her after a call from my parents reporting Ruthie's latest news, only to discover that they had garbled the information.

"If you want to know what's going on with me, you call me," Ruthie said. "You know they're going to get things wrong and believe what they want to believe."

After my return home, conversations with my parents about family matters sometimes unhorsed me. When I would sit on their couch and discuss a prickly situation, inevitably either my mother or my father would make a statement that would directly contradict some fact or opinion they had offered previously, sometimes even just the day before.

"Wait a minute," I would say, and point out that they had claimed something different just the other day.

But they would look at me like I was the crazy one.

It wasn't that they were trying to be manipulative. It was rather that in their grief, they were letting their emotional needs dictate the family's story, which necessitated pretending that everything was fine. Once I was having lunch with my mother in the Magnolia Café in St. Francisville. We started arguing over something rude and hurtful that Claire and Rebekah had done. Mama went to elaborate lengths to defend their behavior, which, however unintentional on the girls' part, had been indefensible to me.

After I challenged her on every point, she lost her cool. She set her iced tea glass down hard and looked at me with fire in her eyes.

"I'm not going to do anything to alienate those girls!" she said, inadvertently revealing a key truth about the dynamic within my family. For my folks, the need for family stability trumped everything, and the cornerstone of a stable family was to do and believe whatever was necessary to make sure the girls gave the appearance that everything was fine.

These were traumatized children, and I didn't blame them for the decisions they made. They were part of a family system where the default position in a crisis was to deny pain and push on. Their cancer-stricken mother had told her friends that she insisted on saying everything was fine because she feared her world would fall apart if she believed otherwise. This was my family's way. Take those girls to grief counseling? No. That was not what our people did.

Our people also did not respond to crises by allowing new information to alter their views. Rather, they doubled down on what they already believed, and fit the facts around whichever story gave them comfort.

It's a very human way to respond, but it was excruciating for me. Everyone in the family was expected to serve the narrative, no matter who got trampled. It had always been like that with us, but Ruthie's death made it much worse. In Dantean terms, the family was having its Casella moment, dallying on the beach in therapeutic distraction when it needed to be moving on toward the hard road of true healing.

"Maybe it has to do with the anniversary of Ruthie's death," I told Mike. "We just passed the two-year mark. But it seems like my folks are really on edge. I know I am. Every conversation is tense. We never talk about any big issues, but I check on them every day, and even small talk is hard."

"Do you think they see it the same way?" Mike asked.

"I have no idea," I said. "Aside from Hannah, nobody can talk about what's really going on. Everything has to always be 'fine,' even when it's not fine. My mom and dad see me as the villain, I think, because I won't play along with the script." By now I was clenching and unclenching my fists.

Mike told me that in the last two sessions with me, he had seen me losing ground in the struggle for freedom and falling back into familiar patterns. "I think you have made real progress in gaining an understanding of how the dynamics work in your family, and within yourself," he said. "But you need to be clear about something. Understanding is not enough; you have to *act* on that understanding."

I threw up my hands. "That's hard to do when the ground is always shifting underneath your feet, and you can never trust that people are being straight with you, or with themselves."

"Let me remind you again that you don't have it in your power to change them. You can only change yourself," he said. Then he leaned in. "Let me ask you something, Rod. Do you want to be healed?"

"Of course I do."

"It's the same question that Jesus asked the lame man by the pool of Bethesda," Mike said. "He could have healed the man without asking, but Jesus wanted the lame man to put his desire into words."

Mike explained that when a person has been suffering for a long time, he tends to build his life around his pain. He may think he wants healing, but in truth he is afraid of it. Jesus's poolside question cut through the man's potential evasions, forcing him to see the choice in front of him.

"You have healing open to you, Rod, if you want it," Mike continued. "But you have to want it bad enough to stand up and walk."

True healing, he explained, required me to step away from the distracting family drama and to get moving toward real life. Nobody could make this decision for me.

Sleepwalking Through Real Life

Joyful things were happening all around me, if only I would open my eyes, Julie kept telling me. For example, she and I liked throwing small dinner parties, though we had done that far less often recently because of my illness. One of the happiest memories of that fall was a long, cheerfully boozy evening with our friends James and Ashley. We sat by candlelight at our table, ate chicken in red wine vinegar sauce that I had prepared from a recipe in a French cookbook, downed three bottles of wine, and laughed till just about midnight. Later that fall, James and Ashley had our family out to dine under a canopy of stars at their farmhouse. These were wonderful friends who made our lives here richer.

Julie reminded me that the virus had gone into remission when we were in Paris the previous October but had come roaring back after our return to Louisiana.

"See, it really is all in your head," she said. "I know the virus is not imaginary, but if you can conquer this stress, you can beat this thing. You've got to push back hard against it."

She was right. This was not a matter of contemplation, not any longer. This was a matter of action. Did I desire to get better, or did I just want to talk about getting better? The lesson was clear: if I wanted to be healed, I had to get up and walk—even if it meant going up a mountain or spending forty years in the desert.

This is what *purgatorio* is for. There is no easy way. There is no other way at all. None of my guides—not Dante, not Mike, not Father Matthew—was telling me what I wanted to hear. They were telling me what I needed to hear to save my life.

HOW TO STOP WASTING TIME
AND START BECOMING GREAT

Inferno was for learning about the nature of our sins; purgatorio is for learning how to overcome our tendencies to fall victim to them. Understanding our dilemma is important, but it's not enough. What we *do* with that understanding makes the difference between life and death.

Humility is the foundation of all spiritual progress. Humility builds resilience. Stop thinking of yourself as at the center of your world and you will find it becomes easier to endure life's setbacks. Plus, you will in time become more grateful, more merciful, and more loving.

Do you really want to be healed? Then act like it. Stop wasting time talking about being sick. Choose to live. Do your exercises. Take your medicine. Get up, and get moving.

18

THE WILL TO LOVE

And I: "The profound mysteries
that here so richly manifest themselves to me,
to our eyes below are so concealed

that they exist there through belief alone,
on which is based our hope to rise above."

[*Paradiso* XXIV:70–74]

You Cannot Think Your Way to the Mountaintop

As they begin their ascent of Mount Purgatory, Virgil lectures Dante about the pointlessness of asking questions that cannot be answered:

"Foolish is he who hopes that with our reason
we can trace the infinite path
taken by one Substance in three Persons.

"Be content, then, all you mortals, with the quia,
for could you, on your own, have understood,
there was no need for Mary to give birth."

[*Purgatorio* III:34–39]

He is talking about Trinitarian theology, but his general point is that some things are known only to God. We have to accept them on faith; this is what he means when he speaks of the *quia*, a Latin term used in Scholastic philosophy; it can be loosely translated here as "just because." If we could know all that God knows, we would be one with him, says Virgil, and would not have needed Jesus to bridge the chasm between heaven and earth.

This is a strong warning about the limits of intellection. In lines suffused with personal mourning, Virgil recalls Aristotle, Plato, and "many others"—like himself—who tried to approach God by their reason alone, and whose failure condemns them to "eternal grief."

Knowledge in this sense does not mean simply propositional knowledge—that is, facts and ideas. The intellect, in the sense Dante means, refers to one's entire capacity to know things, including through intuition. In Christianity, the Fall—Adam and Eve's catastrophic decision to eat of the fruit so they could know what God knew—caused a radical break between God and humanity, one that human beings cannot repair on their own. Given our finitude and brokenness, and God's infinitude and perfection, we cannot hope to know God and his reality without divine assistance.

That's what Virgil is getting at here. Thinking we can know everything there is to know, that the depths of reality can be fully plumbed with the unaided intellect, is to condemn oneself to hopeless longing for an unattainable sense of certainty. Similarly, thinking that the solution to our problems can be found through using reason and logic alone—the default position of bookish people like me—may prevent us from seeing the true nature of our struggles. Do not expect reason and logic to comprehend matters of faith and will. If a man is unwilling to consider an argument, a proposition, or a possibility, reason is powerless to affect his mind.

We see this in the gentle foothills of Mount Purgatory, called Ante-Purgatory, when Dante and Virgil enter the camp of the late repentant. These are souls who called on God's mercy only at the end of their lives.

They found salvation but are so spiritually feeble that they must rest a while before attempting the climb.

The first group they meet are the contumacious, whose late repentance was caused by their stubbornness. It wasn't an intellectual discovery that saved the contumacious but an act of the will. What kept them from hell was not want of a reasonable argument for God's existence but a refusal to admit that they were sinners. I was once there, telling myself that I was a principled skeptic, when in truth I did not *want* to believe in God. Doing so would require me to admit that I wasn't the center of the universe.

Matters of the will can only be dealt with by the will. Heart has to speak to heart. Reason can be an aid to conversion and repentance, but it can always be refused.

One of the contumacious is Manfred, the son of Emperor Frederick II. Manfred ran afoul of the pope, was excommunicated, and died on the field of battle. In his dying breath, Manfred, exiled from the communion of the faithful, wept and begged for divine mercy.

> "Horrible were my sins
> but Infinite Goodness with wide-open arms
> receives whoever turns to it. . . .
>
> "By such a curse as [the Church's] none is so lost
> that the eternal Love cannot return
> as long as hope maintains a thread of green."
>
> [*Purgatorio* III:121–123, 133–135]

When I first read those lines, coming so soon after the horrors of the inferno, Manfred's testimony nearly moved me to tears. All it took to save him was a single act of humility, a minor turn of the will that opened the floodgates of mercy. The "thread of green" is hope that faith will deliver him. Even the most fragile faith serves as a lifeline pulling a lost soul out of the jaws of hell into eternal life. That thin green reed, symbolizing hope and humility, is like the thread that led the mythical Greek hero Theseus out of the labyrinth.

In the next passage of their pilgrimage, Dante and Virgil meet the shades of those who died violently and unexpectedly. They did not have time to prepare their souls to meet their Maker, but they repented in their final seconds; that was enough for divine mercy to snatch them from the jaws of the inferno. Any step away from one's ego, no matter how tiny, can make all the difference in eternity.

Buonconte da Montefeltro is one of these penitents. He was a prominent Ghibelline leader who bled to death from wounds suffered in a decisive battle against the Guelphs—a battle in which Dante fought on the side of the Guelphs. Here on the holy mountain two enemies who last met on the field of battle can greet each other as brothers.

"I was of Montefeltro," the penitent says. "I am Buonconte." In Dante's world, a man's identity was inextricably tied to his city and its factions. Here in purgatory, all that has fallen away. Farinata is in hell, falsely fixated on his grandiose status in the previous life, not noticing that none of that matters now. Buonconte is different—and so, now, is Dante.

Though the battle that killed Buonconte was a Guelph victory that solidified the Guelphs' hold on Florence, by the time he composed the *Purgatorio*, Dante the exiled poet knew all too well how fleeting earthly victories are. And having everything he had taken from him in political strife, Dante Alighieri surely must now have had more empathy for the losers in Italy's endless wars.

Rather than bicker as he did with Farinata, Dante simply listens to this great Ghibelline's awful story of what happened to his body.

"*The rain fell and the overflow that earth*
could not absorb rushed to the gullies

"*and, gathering in surging torrents, poured*
headlong down the seaward stream
with so much rage nothing could hold it back.

"At its mouth the blood-red Archiano found
my frozen corpse and swept it down the Arno,
undoing at my chest the cross

"my arms had made when I was overcome by pain.
it spun me past its banks and to the bottom,
then covered and enclosed me with its spoils."

[*Purgatorio* V:119–129]

This is a shocking description of nature's remorseless processes unmaking our once-dignified bodies. Reading this, I thought of what cancer had done to my once-beautiful sister. I thought about how much I had taken good health for granted until I came down with Epstein-Barr. And I thought of how Daddy, in his prime a man of magnificent vigor, had been slowly crushed over the past decade by aging.

Now he was too weak to do any physical labor. His back, battered by roping calves and riding bulls in the rodeo as a young man, reproached him constantly. In the past year, he had gone from using a cane to depending on a walker to go even as far as his front porch. This proud man, who for decades used his strong back and limbs to work his land, hunt in its forests, and help his friends and neighbors, was now condemned to spend most of every day imprisoned in his armchair, passing his time watching television.

Purgatory is a land where everyone has suffered death and received mercy. In this place, humility and gratitude compel them to live out the poet W. H. Auden's command: "You shall love your crooked neighbour / With your crooked heart."

In the next canto, Virgil and Dante stop to ask a shade for directions. When the shade asks where they are from, Virgil says, "Mantua." He can't get another word out before the shade leaps forward, saying, "O Mantuan, I am Sordello of your city."

This man, Sordello, doesn't know he's speaking to the immortal Virgil. All he knows is that he's meeting someone from back home, and that's enough to call forth his brotherly affection. The souls in purgatory want to establish camaraderie and connection—unlike the damned, and unlike the Italians of Dante's world.

Sordello's warm greeting sets Dante off on a long, scathing denunciation of the spiteful and warring people of his homeland, "gnawing on each other." He rips the Florentines in particular for making a mockery of virtue. They honor love and justice with their tongues, while in their hearts they do all they can to gain advantage over one another.

In purgatory, memories of the past only matter insofar as they act as a spur to repentance, to casting aside egotism and learning to share the pilgrimage up the mountain joyfully with others. This is how the past becomes a blessing. In my very southern family, though, the past is a self-chosen burden.

The South: More Stoic Than Christian

Back in the fall of 2012, when Father Matthew and his wife, Anna, first came to town to talk to us about starting a mission, a local clergyman told him that the greatest challenge he would face in West Feliciana Parish would not be hostility to religion, it would be the unwillingness of people to leave their family's church, no matter how unhappy they were there.

"You're right about that," I added, laughing. "The real religion of our parish is ancestor worship."

It was a joke, of course, but there is a lot of truth in the jibe. In the South, loyalty to tradition dies hard. After Father Matthew had been living here a year or so, I asked him what characteristic of the South stood out most clearly to him. He didn't hesitate one bit, saying, "The way you all hold a grudge."

I was taken aback by the swiftness of his answer, but the more I thought about it, the more sense it made. In the most rural corner of West Feliciana, there are two tiny Methodist churches, a short distance down a blacktop road from each other. They have the same pastor, who preaches at one and then the other each Sunday.

Why two churches? The split goes back to a Civil War–era dispute between two Methodist families. Despite the passage of 150 years, the two congregations stand apart on tradition and principle. And nobody thinks a thing is wrong with it.

That's an extreme example, perhaps, but a somewhat more relaxed version the honor code is pervasive in southern life today. I spent my twenties and thirties living outside of the South and often felt my southern roots tugging at me over what you might call questions of honor. There were certain ways that honorable people behaved, period. In the South, when a mother tells her misbehaving child, "You ought to be ashamed of yourself," it's a rebuke that stings.

Though I sometimes chafed under the honor code and sometimes laughed at it, to a great extent I still live by it. What moderated its hold over me was my practice of the Christian faith—or, to be precise, the discovery that authentic Christianity called me to something more than the southern civil religion of good manners, personal rectitude, and stiff-upper-lip fatalism that I had grown up with.

Christianity is a religion whose founder was a god who chose to be despised, brutalized, and killed for the sake of humankind. To enter into the story of Jesus of Nazareth is to see that humility is more important than pride, and that love is more important than justice.

No contemporary Americans are better able to understand the honor culture of Dante's Florence than southerners, where vestiges of that aristocratic ethic still thrive. Discovering that the hundred-year civil war between Guelph and Ghibelline began over a debt of honor did not surprise me at all. The aristocratic ethic of chivalry that dominated late medieval Europe was celebrated by the antebellum South, and though weakened by modernity, it remains alive today.

The poet may plainly decry the destruction of communal life caused by status conflicts among the Tuscan grandees, but he does not denounce chivalry. In fact, one of his most celebrated characters in the *Commedia* is Cacciaguida, an ancestor who distinguished himself as a Crusader. Dante honors him as a father figure whose nobility elevates his character above the moneyed rabble of contemporary Florence. Despite its worst aspects, Dante sees something worth venerating in the culture of honor.

So do I. The Catholic novelist Walker Percy complained that the traditional South was more Stoic than Christian, but he did not wholly reject the morality of Stoic honor culture. Percy believed, rather, that its laudable emphasis on strong personal character should be improved and fulfilled by the Christian sense of charity and universal brotherhood. Stoicism's moral courage in the face of suffering, in Percy's view, must be perfected by Christianity's teaching that suffering opens the door for grace to transform us in love.

I believe these things too. So, yes, I roll my eyes at the moonlight-and-magnolias excess of Deep South romanticism, and yes, I find some southern traditionalism confining. But as I have aged, I have grown to understand and to respect many aspects of Daddy and Ruthie's tenaciously held position. Truth is, the things I admire and value most about their way of life—the deep community bonds, the strong sense of family, and the rich particularism of Louisiana life—are made possible largely because southerners esteem tradition more devoutly than most other Americans.

They understand that once you start questioning a tradition and examining it with reason, you have begun to undermine it, whether you intend to or not. Once you ask, "Should I keep going to my family's church?" you are halfway out the door.

Decades ago, when I told my father I was leaving Methodism, he was nonplussed.

"But the Drehers have always been Methodist," he said.

"Daddy, Methodism didn't even exist in America when the first Dreher came here from Germany," I said. "He was probably either Lutheran or a Catholic."

My father just stared at me.

"I can tell you the theological reasons why I can't be Methodist anymore, if you want to talk about it," I said.

He did not. *The Drehers have always been Methodist.* There was nothing more to say.

I did not realize it at the time, but to my father, I wasn't rejecting Methodism; I was rejecting the Drehers. It was a matter of disloyalty to the family, and though he was too polite to say so, in his Stoic eyes I had behaved selfishly and dishonorably.

Reading the *Commedia* and confronting the good and the bad in medieval Italy's honor culture, I began to appreciate the perceived threat I posed to what Daddy and Ruthie saw as the best things in life, the beliefs and practices that made life worth living. After all, if I could leave the family's ancestral home, abandon the family religion, and be disloyal to the family's ways of cooking, raising kids, spending leisure time, and so forth, maybe future generations would too. And then, chaos. We would forget who we are. Our descendants would lose access to the most important truths and experiences about life. The seeker must be stigmatized so that others do not sail beyond the boundaries set by the community.

This is a truth that many modern people like me find inconvenient. We want the benefits of community, but without giving up individuality and mobility. We want the benefits of religion, but without having to submit to its disciplines. We want traditions, but only the ones we like. This doesn't work.

But it doesn't work either to believe that it is sensible or even possible to stop change. "If we want things to stay as they are, things will have to change," says a Sicilian aristocrat in *The Leopard*, a historical novel about tradition in a time of revolutionary upheaval.

The practical wisdom in that paradoxical line is that a society must discern what it must let go of to preserve things that are more important to it. Virgil told Dante that divine mysteries must be accepted on faith. Unless tradition is our god, it must be subject to reason at some point.

There is another line in the book that captures the tragic flaw of traditional societies: "The Sicilians never want to improve for the simple reason that they think themselves perfect; their vanity is stronger than their misery."

Change as a Means of Conservation

After my sister died and I returned, my Starhill family was pinned tight between these two sentiments of vanity and misery. Ruthie's death brought tremendous change to us, though we did not want it. She was to have been the matriarch who anchored the family in Starhill into the next generation. It was stunning to me to think of Starhill without someone from our family there. On reflection, I realized how much my own sense of liberty depended on the security of knowing that there was always going to be someone from our family tending its roots. Doing my part to keep family tradition going in my sister's absence was part of the reason I came home.

My family's traditions had long been a source of life and wisdom and stability over time. My pride would not let me release my grip on that family tradition, no matter that it was tearing down the very thing it intended to protect. I was used to playing this role of perpetually aggrieved outsider; and like Manfred, I was stubbornly holding on to that custom and my grudges, no matter how miserable it made me (and my wife).

"The kids and I are your family too, you know," Julie said to me one day. "Why don't you spend more time thinking about people who want a relationship with you instead of obsessing over people who really don't?"

She was right, I realized, as I thought about the relationships I had established in the area, and the new life emerging from them.

I had been part of the founding of a mission church that is both from the most traditional branch of Christianity and also radical by the standards of our place. And it was alive and growing! This is one of the threads of green that Manfred spoke of.

My kids were a delight. Matt was over the moon with his love of astronomy and had already rocketed farther into its deep reaches than most fourteen-year-olds. My college buddy Keith Comeaux, the director of the Mars Rover mission at the Jet Propulsion Laboratory in Pasadena, offered to show Matt around, so I took him to California as a birthday present that summer. Watching him talk with scientists there, I was dazzled by the scope of his knowledge and hungered to be more involved in his life.

Lucas was beginning to discover his musical gifts, and his beautiful devotion to family—shades of his aunt Ruthie, I thought—made me sorrowful that I was not more engaged with him. For her part, Nora was a devout reader, and had discovered a complicated passion for hot tea, of all things. She was turning into a fellow Francophile and gourmand. "When I get to be a grown-up, you will find me sitting on airplanes reading books," she told me. How could I be in such darkness with those three lights in my life?

We had come back to Louisiana for my folks and for my sister's family, but we also had a number of cousins who lived in and around Starhill, the sons and daughters of my dad's uncle Murphy. I barely knew the younger generation, who had just been coming into the world when I moved away. Now most of them had children of their own. They welcomed us with open arms, and we spent hours out by pool at the home of my cousin Andy and his wife, Nancy, and at holiday gatherings of the whole Dreher clan.

I also enjoyed rediscovering my cousins Amy and Lisa from my mom's side of the family. I had been out of touch since I'd moved away in the 1980s. It was a pleasure to renew that friendship as adults.

West Feliciana is plantation country, and its traditional spring festival celebrates the parish's antebellum history. During my illness and my subsequent Dante pilgrimage, friends and I came up with the idea for a more contemporary cultural event later in the year, and decided to start a literary festival in honor of my hero Walker Percy. The Walker Percy Weekend, as we called it, drew hundreds of people from all over the United States for two days of books, bourbon, boiled crawfish, and *laissez les bon temps rouler*. This was another of Manfred's green threads.

How many more were there to be woven into a new life for me in this old place? If I was going to have a future here, I was going to have to let go of the past. There was no reason to keep hanging on.

But then, as Virgil could have told me, this was no longer a matter of reason.

HOW TO LIVE WITH MYSTERY AND GRACE

You must accept that there are some things that cannot be known, and must be taken on faith. To believe otherwise is to condemn yourself to a fruitless search for a certainty that does not exist. Certainty provides psychological comfort, but it may exact a very high price on you and those around you. Let it go. Life is not a problem to be solved, but a mystery to be lived.

On the holy mountain, distinctions that separate people on earth no longer matter. True honor is found in humility, companionship, and helping others bear their suffering. If you want to be happy and move forward spiritually, stop seeing yourself as better or more deserving than others. Ask your neighbor what you can do to help them, and do it.

The world is always passing away. Traditions can guide us to truth and goodness, but when they cease to serve life, they become monstrous. The art of successful living requires discerning what things need to change to preserve the things that really matter.

19

THE GHOST IN YOU

Surely we should help them wash away the stains
they carried with them, so that pure and light
they may approach the star-hung spheres.

[*Purgatorio* XI:34–36]

The Ties That Bind Us Beyond the Grave

U nlike the damned, the souls in purgatory are eager for camaraderie and connection. Former enemies meet as friends:
Buonconte and Dante, veterans of opposing armies in the Battle
of Campaldino. King Ottokar of Bohemia comforts the mournful
Emperor Rudolf, a rival who killed him in the mortal life. Death does not
separate these men; to the contrary, dying in the mercy of God brings
them together in love.

In the Christian tradition, death does not truly separate the living
and those who die in God's favor. But mortals often forget this truth, as
Dante discovers on his ascent. Many of the shades he meets ask the pilgrim to carry a message back to their family and friends on earth: *pray*
for me.

In Catholic teaching, the prayers of the living help the souls of the
faithful departed move more quickly toward God. Dante incorporates
that belief into the *Commedia*. The larger lesson in this is that those who

still abide in God—this, of course, excludes the damned—are part of the same community and have responsibility for one another's welfare.

Christianity calls this the communion of saints. Twenty years ago, the communion of saints became real to me in an unusual way. It's why I do not fail to heed Dante's direction in *Purgatorio* to remember the dead in my prayers.

My paternal grandfather, Murphy Dreher Sr., died in 1994, at the age of ninety. We called him Dede (pronounced "deedee"). In his final years, my father discovered that someone close to Dede was robbing him blind. Daddy confronted his father and the embezzler with the irrefutable evidence, but Dede, whose mind had grown feeble with age, couldn't accept the facts. My father had a tape recorder hidden in his shirt pocket during this meeting. He played for me the recording of the embezzler confessing to the act and daring my father to do something about it. Dede took the thief's side.

Daddy was crushed. It was his duty to look out for his father's best interests, but his father had made that impossible. Still, Daddy continued to serve his elderly father, driving him to the hospital for all his appointments. When Dede finally died, with my father holding his hand, my sister, Ruthie, and I were relieved; we feared that our dad, in his anxiety and grief over his father's disavowal, would go to his grave before Dede.

I flew home for the funeral. We buried Dede in the Starhill cemetery on a Tuesday morning, and I returned with my parents to their house. Exhausted by the events of the previous days, Daddy and Mama lay down for a nap. I sat working at a desk in my old bedroom.

Suddenly I heard three sharp raps on the window. I spun around and walked to it, but nothing was there. My parents live in the country, with no neighbors close by, and there are no trees or bushes by that window. There wasn't a soul in the yard.

Maybe it was a bird crashing into the window, I thought, though I knew better than to think the same bird would whack the window three times.

The next morning at breakfast, Daddy looked worried.

"The strangest thing happened last night," he said. "You and Mama were sleeping, but I couldn't get to sleep to save my soul. I was sitting in my chair in the living room reading when I heard this knocking on the living room windows. It was after midnight. I went to the back door and looked out, but nothing was there."

"The dogs didn't bark?" I asked.

"Nope, not a sound. I sat back down in my chair, then I heard the door to our bedroom open and close," he continued. "I looked down the hallway and there was somebody standing there in white. I thought it was your mother. 'Dorothy, is that you, honey?' I said. I didn't get an answer."

"What did you do?" I said.

"Well, I got out of my chair and went down the hallway. Nobody was there. I opened up the bedroom door and there was your mother, sleeping just as soundly as she had been when I left her."

"Lord have mercy, Daddy, that's some story," I said. "Do you have any idea what it might have been?"

He did not. But it was plainly weighing on his mind. I told him about the rapping on the window. That unsettled him.

"Do you remember that story I did for the paper a couple of years ago, about that Catholic priest down in Bayou Pigeon who's an exorcist? The old man who goes around to haunted houses with his helpers and gets rid of ghosts?"

Daddy nodded.

"I don't want to be freaky about this, but would you mind if I called him and asked him to come up and bless the house, just in case?"

"But we're not Catholic," Daddy said.

"Doesn't matter. He'll come. I'll call after breakfast."

Later that morning, I phoned Father Mario Termini at his rectory on the bayou. I told him about my grandfather's death and about the strange occurrences. He said he would come with Shelby and Florence, two Cajun grandmothers who help him in cases like this.

I had met them two years earlier on their mission to a poltergeist-infested house on the north shore of Lake Pontchartrain. Shelby, who was about my mother's age, had a powerful gift of spiritual discernment. I had seen her work. She was a large lady, but I had watched as an invisible force lifted her and threw her backward over a chair.

"We'll be there tomorrow after lunchtime," Father Termini said. "When we come in, don't tell Shelby that your grandfather died. We don't want to lead her in any direction."

At breakfast the next morning, my father was a nervous wreck.

"Last night, I was laying in bed asleep, when I felt the softest pressure on my back," he said. "I woke up and realized I wasn't dreaming. It felt like a baby's arm, but bigger, the size of a man's," he said. "Then I felt fingers wrapping around my shoulders."

"Oh, my God!" I exlaimed.

"I was wide awake by then," my dad said. "I pushed myself up fast, and I felt whatever it was let go. Then I heard this sound like a hiss and a pop, and it was gone."

Later that morning, my parents were working together on a computer in a small detached office in their yard when my mother saw someone walk past the window. "Ray, get the door," she said. Daddy opened the door, but no one was there.

After lunch, the dogs barked. The crew from Bayou Pigeon had arrived. I greeted them. Father Termini, a short, intense older man whose head was ringed by close-cropped white hair, stepped into the kitchen and took my mother's hand. Behind him came Florence, a stout older woman with a sweet, grandmotherly face and a warm manner. And then there was tall, broad-shouldered Shelby, wearing a plain cotton dress, looking timidly downward, clutching a rosary in her hand.

I introduced them all to my parents and led them to the living room. The three visitors sat together on the sofa. Shelby whispered something in Father's ear.

"That porch swing you have in your kitchen—Shelby dreamed about it last night," the priest said. "All I told her was that we had a job to go to on Thursday. When I picked her up today, she said she had dreamed that we were going to see some people in the hills, and they had a porch swing in their kitchen."

Father Termini asked my folks for permission to pray a rosary, which they granted. I had been a Catholic convert for a year at that point, so I joined them. After we finished, Shelby asked my mother if it was all right to walk around the house. "Please, go wherever you want," Mama said.

I followed her into my bedroom, where I had first heard the banging. Shelby stopped cold, and said, "There's something in that closet."

I called my mother into the room. We began to root through the closet, which was used for storage.

"It's still there," she said, after a minute. The air conditioning was going full blast, but Shelby's face was beet red, and pearls of sweat were beginning to necklace her.

"Are you okay, Shelby?" I asked.

"I can't stay in this room," she said. "Keep looking in that closet."

Mama stayed in the room digging in the closet for anything that might be suspicious. I followed Shelby into my parents' bedroom. She meandered slowly, poking through their closets, to no effect. When she rounded the far side of the bed, approaching a bedside table with a number of framed photographs on it, Shelby began to shake. She held on to a bedpost to steady herself, then stepped to the table.

I stood by her side as she handled each framed photograph individually. Most of them she returned to the table, but three she dropped onto the bed as if she had picked up a hot skillet with bare hands.

"What's the meaning of these pictures?" she asked me.

I glanced at them. "My grandfather died late last week. We buried him a couple of days ago. Those pictures are of women who were close to him. That one's my grandmother, who died in 1976. That other one's his mother, Florence. And that last one is his grandmother."

"Don't you have a picture of him in a frame?" Shelby asked.

"We did. I don't know what happened to it."

"Find it," said Father Termini, from across the room. "I think it's important."

We all returned to the living room, sat down, and began to pray quietly. Suddenly my mother, who was still in my bedroom searching the closet, shouted. I ran to see what was the matter, and met her in the hallway. She was crying.

She was holding our framed portrait of Dede. "It was in the closet, behind a board," she said.

I rushed it to Shelby, who put it on her lap, laid her hand on it, and bowed her head. A moment later she whispered something to the priest. Father Termini leveled his gaze on my father.

"It's him," said the priest. "And he says he can't move on unless you help him get forgiveness."

My father froze.

"Daddy," I said, "tell him about what happened between you and Dede!"

And so he did, revealing everything about the pain of his father's rejection and his fidelity to the old man in spite of it all. After he finished, Father Termini said quietly to my father, "Do you forgive him?"

"I do," said my father, nearly breathless.

Father Termini blessed the house, and a week later he had a mass for the repose of Dede's soul. There were no more ghostly visitations at our house.

I believe that upon his death, my grandfather saw how much his son had loved him, and how his son suffered and sacrificed for his sake. And Dede was remorseful. His sorrow was so great that he could not advance spiritually. He could not let go of this world without his son's forgiveness.

Can I explain this theologically? No, not really. But I believe I saw the power of a living man's forgiveness free the soul of a dead man trapped by guilt and let him move on to the next life.

That encounter with the ghost of my grandfather has remained strong with me over the years. Though I don't believe in the Catholic doctrine of purgatory, I believe, with other Orthodox Christians, that an intermediate state for some souls may exist. I believe that my sister, Ruthie, is in heaven, but I pray for her anyway, and I ask her to pray for me.

In Philadelphia, a few days before we loaded the truck and moved south, Julie and I lay in bed talking about how worried we were that we would not be able to connect with Ruthie's children. Just before daylight the next morning, I had an intense dream. In it, I was standing in our second-floor living room amid the half-packed boxes when I heard the door downstairs open and someone walking up the stairs.

It was Ruthie, wearing a snow-white angora sweater with a thick collar close around her neck. She was carrying a pan of muffins and smiling.

"I thought you were dead!" I said.

"Oh, I am," she said sweetly. "I just wanted to tell you that everything is going to be all right."

"Thank you for saying that. Will you stay for a while?"

"No, I need to get on back."

Then I woke up. The dream had been so realistic that I wasn't sure it had been a dream at all. Whether it was an expression of my imagination or a real visitation, I have no idea, but I will say this: when I was home in Louisiana, I learned from an old friend of Ruthie's who had survived cancer that shortly after my sister's death, the friend awakened in the middle of the night and saw Ruthie standing at the foot of her bed, smiling, wearing the same snow-white angora sweater.

Ruthie never owned a sweater like that.

In any case, it is an ancient tradition of the Christian church to pray for God's mercy on the souls of the dead. Whether or not there is a spiritual abode like Dante's purgatory, it is good to affirm with our prayers that those who have passed into the next life are still with us, still part of us. We remain one in the bond of love.

Driving my dad back from a doctor's appointment in Baton Rouge after we'd moved back to Louisiana, I was eager to tell him about my reading in the *Commedia* and how it was helping me with my own struggles. The spiritual bonds we have with our families and with others are so strong that they even last beyond the grave, I told him.

"Don't you remember the story about what happened with Dede and his ghost?" I said.

"Oh, I do," he replied. "How could I forget something like that?" Then he began to speak about that grim time in his life, and how twenty years on, the memory of his father's unjust treatment of him still caused him pain.

"Daddy," I said quietly, staring straight ahead at the road, "I feel the same way about the way y'all have acted toward me since we came back here."

Silence.

We drove on, together, but apart.

HOW TO MAKE PEACE WITH THE DEAD

Whether or not you believe the souls of the once-living carry on in another realm or that our prayers can help them, the spiritual bonds between the dead and us are real. They linger in our memories, both individual and collective, and affect the way we live. They haunt us, and will not be quiet until we deal with them. Our own spiritual progress may depend on making peace with the dead, literally or symbolically, and forgiving them for the wrongs they did to us in life.

Letting them move on toward eternal peace, and allowing ourselves to progress toward love and healing, requires severing unhealthy attachments. Forgiveness is the key that opens the door to freedom—for us, and maybe for them too. Whose memory among the dead haunts you today? Say a prayer, silently or aloud, forgiving them and releasing them of their debt to you. And continue to pray for their peace, because in so doing, the soul you will bring the most peace to is your own.

20

PRIDE

---

*Your renown is but the hue of grass, which comes
and goes, and the same sun that makes it spring
green from the ground will wither it.*

[Purgatorio XI:115–117]

Defeating the Purest of the Passions

At last, the pilgrim and the master leave the foothills of the holy
mountain and arrive at the gates of purgatory.

*I now saw . . . a gate, with three steps leading
up to it, each one of a different color.
The keeper of that gate as yet said not a word.*

*And, when my eyes could make him out more clearly,
I saw that he was seated above the topmost step,
his face so bright I could not bear to look.*

*In his hand he held a naked sword,
which so reflected his bright rays
I often had to turn my eager eyes away.*

[Purgatorio IX:76–84]

The figure Dante writes about is an angel guarding the great gate. The first of these steps is of white marble, the second is a dark purple, and the third appears "as flaming red blood that spurts out from a vein." These steps represent the three stages of purging sin: contrition, confession, and penance.

In *Inferno* Dante and Virgil stood in terror before the red-hot iron gates of Dis. It took divine intervention in the form of an angel to force open the portal to the infernal city. Here in purgatory, all that is required is that the penitent pilgrim prostrate himself before the angel and beg for God's mercy.

Opening the gates to the Kingdom of God with the keys entrusted to him by St. Peter, the angel sternly admonishes, "Enter, but I warn you he who looks back must then return outside." This is a powerful caution not to dwell on your past sins, lest they cast a Medusa-like spell and cause you to lose your spiritual progress.

Pride is purgatory's first terrace because it is the root of all sin and is therefore the hardest tendency to purge. Dante and Virgil enter the terrace on a narrow path, with the sheer face of the mountain to one side. The bank is made of white marble and has been engraved by the very finger of God. The divine artworks are so realistic that in Dante's eyes they come to life.

The images—bas-relief scenes from the Bible and classical myth and history—illustrate the virtue of humility, which the purgation on that terrace will teach the penitents. The first image depicts the Virgin Mary humbly saying yes to the Holy Spirit when the Archangel Gabriel brings news that she has miraculously conceived the messiah. Through the doorway of her humility came the salvation of the world.

The second shows King David, hitching up his robes and dancing among the people with joyful abandon before the Ark of the Covenant, showing himself to be "at once more and less than king." That's a deftly ironic line: David behaved in a way beneath the dignity of a monarch, but showed himself to be greater than a monarch by humbling himself before the Lord in worshipful ecstasy.

The third panel tells a story told of the Roman emperor Trajan, who stooped to fulfill a poor widow's request for justice. The idea is that Trajan, who was in full regalia and on an imperial mission, put the needs of his humble subject ahead of his own.

These living images inaugurate a lesson that the penitent pilgrim Dante must learn on each terrace. The terrace begins with three successive scenes of the virtue the pilgrim will encounter on that level, as an inspiration. Then he meets penitents working out their penances. Finally he leaves the terrace with an experience of three scenes of the vice now purged, to discourage him from returning to it.

These emotionally gripping scenes rendered with supernatural artistry reveal the power of great art to transform us. The poet Dante is showing us how stories and images prepare our imaginations for moral instruction by engaging our emotions.

Research psychologists Keith Oatley and Maja Djikic have shown that people are more likely to be open to new ideas when those ideas are presented to them in the form of a story. But they also found that a work of nonfiction is more effective than fiction if the reader perceives it to have high artistic quality.

On our side porch overlooking the yard, I read this canto with a smile of recognition. That was precisely what Dante had been doing to me! The farther along I went on this journey, the more the people the pilgrim met stayed on my mind.

Pushing a grocery cart through the supermarket, I would daydream about Manfred falling to the ground, mortally wounded, weeping and begging for mercy with his final breaths. As I drove past the dreary chemical plants in north Baton Rouge, my mind lingered on doomed, glamorous Francesca. Sitting in an Adirondack chair with a cold beer at a backyard cookout, I gazed at the Spanish moss draping the live oaks and thought about Dante at the philosopher's garden party in limbo, the second circle of the inferno. The poet's images proved to be stowaways who showed themselves at the oddest times.

Without quite realizing what was happening to me, I gave myself over completely to Dante, absorbing the personalities of his figures and identifying with them as I considered how my life and my sins were like theirs. Brunetto Latini, that marvelous egotist, reminded me of a favorite professor, charming and vain. Put him in an ice cream suit and give him a bourbon-filled julep cup and Farinata, a bastard of peacock magnificence, could hold court on the front porch of a Feliciana plantation manse. All of these people, these medieval Tuscans the wayfaring poet met on the road, were so alien yet so familiar. At times I felt like the pilgrim standing before the bas-reliefs on the holy mountain, not entirely sure if these figures were living or dead.

I was astonished by the power these fictional characters had over my moral imagination. These weren't principles, these weren't arguments; these were people who displayed the whole panoply of human nature, from its most corrupt to its most pure.

I could have read the same lessons they were teaching me in a self-help book, but they likely wouldn't have taken root within me. Likewise, I suspect that if I had not been able to relate the advice of my confessor and my therapist to figures in the *Commedia*, I would have had a much more difficult time putting their advice to work in my life.

The Liberating Power of Beauty

As I first discovered thirty years ago in the nave of the Chartres cathedral, the shock of beauty catapults us out of the everydayness of our lives and gives us a new way to see ourselves and the possibilities before us. Though the encounter with beauty might make us suffer, in the end, it is through that pain that we are set free.

The words and the images in Dante's great poem worked a conversion within me. Their beauty and truth cracked the stone in my chest and made me confront the nature of my condition.

There is no lesson in the *Commedia* that I had not read or heard before, but Dante incarnated that wisdom in verses that pierced the rocky soil of my heart and planted seeds of truth there, seeds that neither my anxiety, nor my insecurity, nor my anger, nor my weakness, could dislodge.

At some point on this literary pilgrimage, a shift within me took place, one so subtle I had not noticed it. I ceased to be a reader observing a character called Dante and his adventures, and began to identify with the pilgrim in a way I never had before, nor had done with any literary character. The *Commedia* had become the book of my life.

Once you have seen yourself in Farinata, in Pier della Vigne, in Brunetto, and in Ulysses, once you have stood with Dante and Virgil on the beach listening to Casella's song, wanting to abandon the hard road ahead and rest for a while, they become part of you. In their fates you observe—no, you *feel*—the logic of your own trajectory through life revealing itself to you. And if you take these words and images into your heart, you gather within yourself the will to change the direction of your own story.

Like the pilgrim character, I began to experience the drama of every station along the way of this journey as a chance to work out my own future—not just an opportunity but also a command. Dante's passage through the afterlife tells us that our passage through this life is consequential and must not be taken lightly. "We tell ourselves stories in order to live," said the essayist Joan Didion, and the stories I told myself now were Dante's. He was helping me work out my own destiny, inviting me to be the hero of my own life.

During this time, a Christian friend said to me, "It's like *The Divine Comedy* is your Bible." He didn't mean it kindly, but he was making a quintessentially Dantean point. The *Commedia* was speaking to me more powerfully than Scripture, and in so doing was leading me closer to the God of the Bible than anything I had ever read. If we believe that God is everywhere present and fills all things, then we should not be surprised when he uses whatever he can to bring us back to himself.

In *Purgatorio*, the virtues and the vices on the wall carvings include Bible stories as well as events from history and mythology. They all testify to truth. Farther up the mountain, Dante and Virgil meet the shade of Statius, a first-century Roman poet, who thanks the master for writing the *Aeneid*, a pre-Christian poem that led to Statius's own conversion to Christianity.

After they pass the wall carvings, Dante turns to see a group of shades struggling in his direction. These are the prideful, carrying heavy rocks on their backs, nearly crushed by their burdens as they stagger along, beating their breasts as a sign of penitence. Their bodies are bent toward the ground. They thought, in their pride, that they were above everything, but now the weight of their prideful disposition forces them to bend their stiff necks, making them face the dust from which they came.

Shaken by the sight, Dante addresses the reader directly.

O vainglorious Christians, miserable wretches!
Sick in the visions engendered in your minds,
you put your trust in backward steps.

Do you not see that we are born as worms,
though able to transform into angelic butterflies
that unimpeded soar to justice?

[*Purgatorio* X:121–126]

The ascetic labors of these penitents are a shock to us, but they are part of the transition process. What Dante says here is that our defective inner vision leads us to take the wrong road and to put our trust in things that pull us back. We must understand that however miserable and grubby we may be, God did not make us to live this way, but rather created us to be transformed into someone beautiful and light, someone whose spirit soars.

Suffering comes to everyone. It's the human condition. What you do with that suffering determines whether or not you remain an earthbound caterpillar or metamorphose into a butterfly.

Reflecting on what he has seen, the pilgrim muses on the power of art to affect our inner vision. To encounter a terrible thing depicted in art can cause real distress or evoke other emotions appropriate to the intention of the artist. This is how the pilgrim's moral and spiritual transformation takes place—and this is what the *Commedia* brings about in the reader who gives himself to Dante.

When Dante first sees the bas-reliefs on the mountainside, Virgil stands at his shoulder, "on that side of him where we have our hearts." The key to our transformation is the heart, not the reasoning mind, because it is the heart, symbolically speaking, that controls the will. Art, at its best, works below and above the level of rationality. The image, whether painted, sculpted, or presented in the written word, holds the power to alter a man's destiny.

As he watches the prideful pass by, Dante speaks to the shade of Omberto, an Italian nobleman whose illustrious family's arrogance started a war that proved the ruin of them all. He says:

". . . *Pride has undone*
not only me but all my kinsmen,
whom it has dragged into calamity."

[*Purgatorio* XI:67–69]

Those lines electrified me. They could be the epitaph for my family, I realized, if we didn't find a way to untangle this knot that binds us.

The next penitent Dante meets on this terrace is an artist named Oderisi of Gubbio, a painter who had been one of the greats of his day. He confesses to the pilgrim that in the mortal life "an overwhelming need to excel at any cost held fast my heart." The only thing that saved him, Oderisi says, was turning to God before the end.

In contrast to Brunetto Latini, who told the pilgrim Dante to focus on writing for fame, Oderisi tells the pilgrim that artistic greatness is fleeting.

"*Worldly fame is nothing but a gust of wind,*
first blowing from one quarter, then another,
changing name with every new direction."

[*Purgatorio* XI:100–102]

The painter warns Dante that his rising star too shall fade, and that the esteem of the world is a ruse and a snare. His lesson is meant to teach us to rightly order our talent and accomplishment by standards higher than those of popular success. Fame, or at least taking inordinate pride in our talent and deeds, is a phantom, and if we make its pursuit our god, as Brunetto did, we risk hell.

What does God see when he looks at us and our stewardship of the gifts he has given us? Have we made good use of them? Have we used them to serve him and the good, or have we used them to serve ourselves and our own egos? Or have we made our personal fame—to be the best artist, the greatest deal maker, the top athlete, the most powerful politician—our goal?

It's harder than we think to know for sure. Everybody can look at a man like Donald Trump and know that there goes an avatar of pride. But pride is insidious; when we look at a man like Trump and think, "Thank you, Lord, that you haven't made me like him," are we not guilty of spiritual pride?

Oderisi's words made me reflect on my own vocation as a writer. All writers want audiences, and all of us want to make money. These are not bad things if they are the fruit of having written in service to the truth. But if they are only to serve your own reputation, you abuse your gift and corrupt your craft. The remembrance of bitchy slanders I wrote early in my career as a film critic, when I wanted to impress the world with my caustic wit, pains me to this day. More seriously, the older Dante surely grieved over those like his fictional Francesca, misled by the idolatrous love poetry he wrote as a young man.

The poet Dante knows, of course, from bitter experience that you can be rich, famous, and powerful one day and be a tramp and a beggar the next. This is the hard truth behind the advice he has Oderisi deliver to his fictional self. A chastened Dante replies, "Your true words pierce my heart with fit humility and ease a heavy swelling there."

This is a major turning point for the pilgrim. As he parts with Oderisi, Dante is startled by how easy and light his steps are. Virgil instructs him to keep his eyes cast downward to the earth, where the pilgrim sees more extraordinary carvings by the hand of God, this time depicting the terrible fates of biblical and mythological figures, all destroyed by pride. The holy mountain will not let a pilgrim, even a successfully penitent one, pass without a final reminder of what he has been delivered from by his repentance.

I had thought myself a victim of my family's pride, but I could not leave this terrace without facing the fact that I was also now a victim of my own. My vanity was offended by my family's inability to give me the love I thought I deserved. My pride was a weight I carried on my bent back day after day, and it wearied my body so greatly that sometimes I could scarcely leave the house.

HOW TO LET GO OF YOUR EGO

To live is to suffer. To become fully human is to overcome suffering by allowing it to give us wings. Stop thinking about how your struggles are weighing you down, and start thinking, with humility, about how they can lift you up, and make you more compassionate and merciful. Changing your attitude can turn a burden into a blessing.

Art is a doorway to truth. It speaks to us primarily through the heart, and opens the portal to truths difficult to access with the intellect alone. Beauty can shock us into recognizing truths to which we have closed our minds. Don't be afraid of art and beauty. All truth is God's truth, all beauty shows the way to him.

Pride is a terrible weight, one that keeps us chained to the earth. Consider that the sins you find most offensive in others may be your own sins as well. Self-knowledge begins with the realization that the things you refuse to accept in others are often aspects of your own character, from which you must repent. Healing begins when you lay down the burden of your prideful ego, and drag your own shadow into the light.

21

E N V Y

My blood was so consumed by envy
that, had I seen a man take joy in life,
you would have seen my skin turn livid.

[*Purgatorio* XIV:82–84]

When You Want Them to Hurt Like You Do

Duruing my long illness, I still visited my folks, usually two or
three times each week. Sometimes I would bring the kids, who
loved being around them. Mama and Daddy were visibly concerned about my health and often asked how I was feeling. If I was having
a good day, I told them so; if not, I told them that too.

"You got to get that ol' stress off of you," my father would inevitably say.

And I would answer, "I know. I'm trying."

They were nervous; they had lost one child to illness, and they could
not bear to think about losing another. I never told them about the lym-
phoma risk, but the fact that this illness had been with me for well over a
year was on their minds a lot.

Once my mother said, "I know what this is. You're still mourning
Ruthie."

"For God's sake, no, I'm not," I said.

They looked shocked and hurt.

"No, I don't mean it like that," I said. "Of course I'm sorry she's not here. But that's not what this is about."

I didn't go any further; I knew it would do no good. How many times had I had this conversation with them?

"We've got to find a doctor who can help you get over this stuff," Daddy said once, rocking on the front porch.

"I've told you, there's no cure for this," I replied. "The only way to make it go away is to get rid of all this stress."

"Baby, where is this stress coming from?" he said, raising his voice in frustration.

"From all this mess in the family," I said.

"This is just killing me, seeing you like this," Mama said between drags on her Marlboro. I knew she meant it.

"We can't stand to see our boy sick," Daddy said. He meant it too.

There had been versions of this conversation spoken on the back porch too, in the living room, and around their kitchen table. We rehearsed it in the car when I would drive one or both of them on short trips. We had it over shrimp po'boys at the Cajun roadhouse on the other side of the river. We practiced it on the phone.

They could not make a connection between the words coming out of my mouth and any course of action they might undertake to help solve the problem. And I resented it. Boy, did I resent it. Yet the concern in their uncomprehending eyes was genuine; they were not indifferent to my suffering. It was all very confusing, as if we were on the same planet but in different worlds.

"Maybe she envied you," people would say to me about Ruthie. "Maybe she wanted to leave home and see the world but didn't feel like she could. If you were gone, somebody had to be home with your folks."

No way, not Ruthie. She was a country girl to the marrow and wanted to be nowhere in the world more than at home in West Feliciana Parish. She wouldn't have traded places with me for anything.

And then I walked with Dante along the terrace of envy, and I discovered that I was wrong.

When I think of envy, I imagine people wanting what others have.

By that measure, my sister was not envious of me. But as I learned by reading the *Commedia*, that's not the way medieval people thought of envy. To them, envy was resenting others for what they have. From what our parents told me about Ruthie, that was how she saw me. This is what it meant to be a "user" in my family's parlance: someone who gets what he has at the expense of others.

And Dante, confronting the envious penitents, sees a sight that renders his eyes "overwhelmed by grief." There, huddled together against the side of the mountain out of fear of falling off the edge, sits a knot of shades, their eyes sewn shut with wire, "as is done to the untrained falcon because it won't be calmed."

In the mortal life, the envious cast their eyes with malice on others and wished them harm, or at least spited their good fortune. In so doing, they weakened the bonds of community. In purgatory, they are temporarily blinded and are forced to take hold of their neighbors, depending on them for safety and help in not falling off the mountain ledge. Tears of repentance seep from under the eyelids they cannot open.

The eyes of the envious are deprived of vision so they can learn to depend on their neighbor more and to "see" their neighbor with the inner eye of compassion and solidarity in shared suffering and shared protection from danger. When the wires come out of their eyelids, they will see with different eyes, with a vision that has been purified from the distorting lens of the self.

In the *Commedia*, Dante writes about the public consequences of the private sin of envy. The pilgrim meets penitents from Italy who lament the unraveling of the social fabric in their valley back home. The worldview of the people in that valley has become so corrupted by envy that either they cannot see virtue or they see virtue as vice. And their children and children's children were suffering for it.

This is how a community that ought to be a source of human flourishing becomes corrupted. This is how our families fall apart over the generations. It doesn't begin with envy alone, but it does begin with sins—lust, pride, wrath, and so on—that people do not confront when they emerge within their own hearts, and which therefore cloud their moral vision.

When we sin today, when we give it a foothold in our own hearts, or in our families or communities, we risk afflicting our own descendants with the consequences of our vice, down the generations.

Here's the thing that caught me by surprise on the Terrace of Envy: discovering that I am tempted by the same sin. On the worst days of my fatigue and depression, when I would lie in bed all afternoon, feeling that my body was buried under cold, wet blankets, I would feel sorry for myself and envy the family members who had lived in Starhill all along. We wanted so badly to be a part of their lives, but that door had all but closed.

Dante would not accept my self-pity. If I begrudged them pleasure and happiness in a life they had decided shouldn't have me and my family in it, how was I any different from Ruthie? Was I not also guilty of envy?

Yes, as a matter of fact, I was. Besides, what kind of small-minded egotist was I to hold a grudge against my folks and the Lemings? Ruthie— my parents' daughter, Mike's wife, the girls' mother—had wasted away to nothing before their eyes over nineteen excruciating months, then died, leaving a blast crater in their lives. And I was resentful because they wouldn't pay attention to my family and me?

After vespers one warm October night, I took my spiteful passions to Father Matthew in confession.

"I know my anger is wrong, and that's why I'm in confession," I said. "I realized, reading Dante this week, that I resented all of them for being happy without us. I know it's not right, but I can't get out from under this anger."

I explained that I felt like I was living the prodigal son parable, but in this telling, the father is not running out to welcome the long-lost son but rather taking the side of the bitter older brother and not letting the younger one come through the gate.

"That's tough," Father Matthew said. "So what do you want?"

"I want justice. It's not fair, the way they do me."

"You want justice?" he said, chuckling. "What is justice? You have no right to expect justice. It's nice if you get it, but if you don't, that doesn't release you from the commandment to love. The elder brother in the prodigal son story stood on justice, but his father stood on love."

"Okay, but I think that if I do that, they're going to win."

"Win? This is a contest, Benedict?" he said. "I don't know about you, but from where I sit, it doesn't look to me like you're winning much of anything by hanging on to all of this."

"I know," I sighed. "All I can do is lay this at the foot of the Cross and ask for God's help."

After we put the kids to bed that night, Julie wanted to watch a movie. I told her to go ahead without me, that I didn't feel up to it. Truth was, I had too much on my mind from my confession, thinking about my own envy.

I had hurt my sister by moving away when we were young. She, like our father, felt the sting of rejection, and to protect herself and her sense of moral order, she interpreted my subsequent success and happiness as a sign of my low character.

And there I was, tempted to do the same thing to those in my family. I was wrong. My envy at their happiness was the result of my pride—and I had to lay both those burdens down if I wanted to be healed.

It hurt to think about letting go of my own expectation of justice. I had to prepare myself for the likelihood that my sister's husband and children would find satisfaction in a life without my family and me in it—and I had to love them enough to be genuinely happy for them. I had expected my parents and my sister to do that for me when I moved away to Washington, hadn't I?

I could hear Father Matthew's voice in my ear: "Love is more important than justice." I had no right to withhold from my Starhill family today what I had expected them to give me all the years that I was away.

If I did not do this, if I did not throw off my pride and bridle my envy, if instead I dwelled on the pain, the rejection, and the sense of injustice I felt, I was going to remain compromised by illness and depression. I was going to continue bringing misery on Julie and our children, and mark myself out as a hypocritical Christian. Indeed, I would become the embittered and envious elder brother of the biblical parable.

And I would miss out on the blessings I had been given in this new life back in my hometown: a renewed relationship with a constellation of cousins I had never known well, a great church where I was growing spiritually as I never had before, warm nights under the stars drinking wine with new friends, the soaring pleasures of a rich writing and reading life, and the joy of watching my children flourish.

In conversation with Dante, Virgil sums up the tragedy of humankind trapped by envy, blind to the blessings of life because they can only see what others unjustly have:

> "The heavens call to you and wheel about you,
> revealing their eternal splendors,
> but your eyes are fixed upon the earth.
> For that, He, seeing all, does smite you."

> [*Purgatorio* XIV:148–151]

Dante Alighieri did his best work after he accepted that he would probably always be an exile, and after he gave up on the possibility of getting justice in this life. He lifted his eyes from the earth of Florence and Tuscany and set them on the heavens, the abode of God. There was a lesson in that for me.

HOW TO WANT THE BEST FOR OTHERS

You are the greatest victim of your envy. Envy never lets you rest. It feeds off your insecurity, off a nagging feeling that others are getting away with something at your expense. Envy tears you apart, and robs you—and those you infect with it—of the possibility of a peaceful life. Jaundiced eyes see justice as everyone being equally miserable.

Envy is a poison; love is its antidote. Love does not expect or demand justice. Love sets no conditions. Love does not regard the good of others as coming at one's own expense, but rather rejoices in their good fortune. To see with the eyes of love is to cease to count the blessings of others, and instead to focus on your own. The love that can transform your envy into a desire for the good of others—that kind of love is blind.

22

WRATH

Gloom of hell or of a night deprived
of all the stars, beneath a barren sky
which everywhere was overcast with clouds,

had never put so dark a veil across my eyes
or been so harsh and stinging to my sight
as was the smoke that covered us

so that I could not keep my eyelids open.

[*Purgatorio* XVI:1–7]

A Fire With Heat, but No Light

Early in my *Commedia* pilgrimage, watching the pilgrim spar verbally with Farinata in the Circle of the Heretics was the first occasion on which I knew that the poet Dante had my number. In a single canto, Dante diagnosed the spiritual and psychological cause of my malaise: having made idols of family and place.

Now, on purgatory's Terrace of Wrath, I was staggered as he both explained why I could not free myself from the clutches of my sins—especially pride and envy—and taught me how to break their death grip. It happened like this.

As the pilgrim approaches the Terrace of Wrath, he is overcome by

ecstatic visions showing figures from the Bible and classical culture deflect-
ing anger with love. The last of the three visions features St. Stephen, the
first martyr, begging God to forgive the mob that stoned him to death.

Virgil, noticing that the pilgrim's pace has slowed down, asks him
what's wrong. Dante explains that he is so enraptured by the visions that
he can barely walk. Virgil acknowledges this, and continues:

> *"These things were shown so you would not refuse*
> *to open your heart to the waters of peace*
> *that pour from the eternal fountain."*

> [*Purgatorio* XV:130–132]

When you have epiphanies with great personal relevance, the master
continues, you must remember that these experiences come to you for a
reason. They exist not for themselves, but rather to spur your repentance
and "to put fresh vigor in your step" in the pilgrimage to unity with God.

I needed to hear these words. Every day I spent with the *Commedia*
dazzled me with new insights and awe at the poet's artistry. Yet Virgil
reminded me that art is *for* something; if I treasured the poem for its own
sake, I would misuse it. This work of art is meant to change my life, to
bring me closer to God, to heal me.

Suddenly a cloud of choking black smoke envelops Dante and the
master. This is wrath, and it renders the pilgrim blind, unable to see a
thing beyond anger. I stood there on the mountainside with Dante and
felt the heat from the smoke. I felt it sting my eyes and burn my nostrils.
I remembered working as a reporter down at Ground Zero days after the
Twin Towers fell, and how something poisonous in the smoke rising from
the pit made my head ache in the same place every time I went near the
hole.

In the heart of that darkness, at the midpoint of the entire *Commedia*, Dante meets a man who gives him the secret of deliverance. He is
Marco the Lombard, a nobleman who agrees with the pilgrim that the

world is in a terrible state. Dante begs Marco to tell him why this is so, so
that he can return to earth and tell all the others.

Here is Marco's reply. For me, this discourse is the crown jewel in a
poem heavy laden with treasure:

First he heaved a heavy sigh, which grief wrung
To a groan, and then began: "Brother,
The world is blind and indeed you come from it.

"You who are still alive assign each cause
only to the heavens, as though they drew
all things along upon their necessary paths.

"If that were so, free choice would be denied you,
and there would be no justice when one feels
joy for doing good or misery for evil.

"Yes, the heavens give motion to your inclinations.
I don't say all of them, but, even if I did,
You still possess a light to winnow good from evil,

"and you have free will. Should it bear the strain
in its first struggles with the heavens,
then, rightly nurtured, it will conquer all.

"To a greater power and a better nature you, free,
are subject, and these create the mind in you
that the heavens have not in their charge.

"Therefore, if the world around you goes astray,
in you is the cause and in you let it be sought."

[Purgatorio XVI:64–83]

Marco's words hit me like a bolt of lightning. The Lombard whose wrath had blinded him in the mortal life delivered the same message that Mike Holmes had on the first day of my therapy: *You can't change the world, but you can change the way you react to it.*

I had understood Mike's words, but their meaning had not sunk in. Now, standing within a black cloud of wrath, spite stinging my eyes, I heard the same message from the penitent Marco—and I got it.

That cloud had descended upon me the moment Hannah told me the ugly truth about our family on the Boulevard St-Germain, and it had never left. It was as hot as the fires of Dis. It was as heavy as the boulder of pride. It was as tormenting as the swarm of stinging wasps leaving the faces of the sinners in hell's vestibule dripping with blood.

Marco helped me feel its malignant power. And he told me how to dispel it: stop blaming my family, my dead sister, my nature, or anything else for my sickness and depression. *In me is the cause, and in me let it be sought.*

My wrath at my family was keeping me from seeing the love that is truly there, however bent and tangled by our fallen human nature. My sin of wrath would only let me see their sins against me. I could not open their eyes—but I could open my own.

It was a matter of deciding to do it. It was a matter of will. All these things I had seen on the journey, all I had learned about myself and others—it was all useless unless I did something with these insights.

This was a breakthrough! "Julie, listen to this," I said, turning to my wife in the bed. But she was asleep, and she was still dozing when I left early the next morning to drop Matthew off and head on to Mike's office for my weekly appointment.

"I had a real eureka moment last night." I told Mike as I sat down.

Mike listened to my story with a broad smile illuminating his face.

"You get it now," he said, beaming. "We have been trying to get to this moment from the beginning. You have power over the images you want to let into your mind. You control them; they don't control you. You have the freedom to choose whether or not to let those emotions in."

I considered this, and then told Mike that throughout the *Commedia,* the poet Dante is completely frank about the terrible situation in Florence and in Italy. He is perfectly clear about the corruption in the Church and in the state. Nothing escapes his sight.

"He decided that his wrath was keeping him from doing what he needed to do to get back on the straight path," I said. "Virgil told him to use good memories, peaceful memories, to fight off the ones that provoked him to wrath."

"That's good," Mike said. "Now, read me that line again about free will."

"'And you have free will,'" I began. "'Should it bear the strain in its first struggles with the heavens, then, rightly nurtured, it will conquer all.'"

"What is that telling us?" Mike said. "It's saying that if you can use your will to hold out against your sin nature, the thing that makes you fall back on all those old hurts and right back into anger, you can overcome this."

"And I am responsible for my own healing, right?" I said.

"Right. Again, though, the question is this: do you want to be healed?"

All those sinful dispositions, pride and envy and wrath, had trapped me in the brambles of a dark and scary wood. The more I flailed in anger, the more tightly I was bound.

I couldn't live like this. But could I really change? Dante was showing me the way out. So was my priest. So was my therapist. And ultimately, through them all, so was God.

Now I saw the way forward. Could I take the straight path, even if it went up a rocky mountain? Yes.

HOW TO QUIT BEING SO ANGRY

It is normal to be angry when somebody hurts or offends you, or behaves unjustly. Wrath becomes a sin when it overtakes your reason and becomes an obsession. It is a fire that will not cease to burn until it has destroyed you. However, you are not powerless in the face of it. You have free will, and can refuse anger—indeed, you can refuse any temptation. Nothing is fated. But you have to be willing to fight the only fight you can be certain of winning: the fight on the battlefield of your own heart. The more you resist wrath, the easier it becomes. When tempted by anger, focus your mind on stories of love given in return for hatred. These images, Dante says "must unlock compassion."

You cannot control others, but you can control your own reactions to them, and cease to be a pawn of your own passions. This does not mean looking the other way in the face of injustice, it means refusing to allow it to steal your peace. "Acquire the Holy Spirit, and thousands around you will be saved," said St. Seraphim of Sarov. By conquering your rebel heart, and delivering yourself from wrath, the world you save might be your own.

23

SLOTH

And he: "A love of good that falls short
of its duty is here restored, here in this place.
Here the slackened oar is pulled with greater force."

[*Purgatorio* XVII:85–87]

When You Don't Care Enough to Do Your Very Best

Whether I could muster and maintain the will to resist temptations to pride, envy, and wrath depended on how well I mastered the lessons of the mountain's next level: the Terrace of Sloth.

Sloth means laziness, but it also means apathy, or a sense of dejection that causes you to lose interest in the world beyond yourself. Before reading the *Commedia*, my idea of slothfulness was the sluggard who won't get off the couch and mow the lawn, or the teenager who would rather play video games than do his homework. It's far more complicated than that, says Dante, who approaches the subject through a discussion with Virgil about love.

A certain unhealthy indifference to the world beyond yourself is an effect of depression. That's a medical condition that is not the same thing as sloth, which requires a moral choice. My doctor had told me that I was depressed.

But that did not let me off the hook for sloth, because in my case the separation was not as clean as I thought. Some people become depressed because of biochemical factors beyond their control. Others slip into depression because a natural sadness—the death of a loved one, the end of a marriage, the loss of a job—overcomes their ability to cope with it.

My depression was a reaction to a tormenting situation over which I thought I had no power. But now I knew that this was a lie, that power over this situation was within my will, if only I would use it. My heart would become Farinata's fiery tomb if I didn't do something about it.

The Terrace of Sloth forms an important bridge between the sins that came before and those that come after. The earlier terraces—those of pride, envy, and wrath—purge the more serious sins: those based on loving evil things, sins that destroy the bonds of community. Now Dante is entering the higher realms of purgation, where the sinful dispositions he confronts— avarice, prodigality, gluttony, and lust—have to do with loving good things in the wrong way and (mostly) harming the individual.

To conquer sloth, says Virgil to the pilgrim, you first have to under- stand that everything we do is motivated by desire, or love. If we desire the "primal good"—the will of God—above all and make our lesser desires subject to God's governance, we will be able to enjoy pleasures without sin. To order our desire, our power to love, rightly is to put the will of God first in our lives, and therefore to live virtuously. Virgil con- tinues:

> "But when it bends to evil, or pursues the good
> with more or less concern than needed,
> then the creature works against his Maker.

> "From this you surely understand that love
> must be the seed in you of every virtue
> and of every deed that merits punishment."

> [Purgatorio XVII:100–105]

This is the heart of the *Commedia*'s understanding of the human condition and how to overcome it: use faith and reason to train your will toward desiring the good. Loving God more than anything else, including yourself, is the first principle of ordering your desires.

Mastering the Mind: Ancient Wisdom and Modern Science

Disorganization has always been one of my greatest problems. That and a deep-seated tendency to be impulsive—to let my desire, or lack of desire, dictate my conduct. In high school and college I hated math and science and did poorly in my classes, not because I lacked the ability to succeed, but because I lacked the willpower. I have struggled off and on with my weight, not so much because I can't control what I eat, but because I despise exercise and lack the willpower to force myself to do what I don't want to do. And I am a world-class procrastinator, living by the rule "Don't do today what you can put off till tomorrow."

This slothful disposition put me at a disadvantage against pride, envy, and wrath. Somehow I had to strengthen my will. To this end, Father Matthew reminded me that Orthodox Christian spirituality has a wealth of methods and strategies for ordering the mind and the heart toward the will of God. He suggested that I read more deeply in our spiritual tradition.

The ancient teachings of Orthodox monasticism offer a surprisingly practical way of disciplining the will. These are not strategies reserved only for monks or spiritual athletes, nor are they practices and concepts that you have to be Orthodox to use.

You start by separating your thoughts and desires from your self. Your thoughts and desires are not the same thing as *you* and only define you if you let them. Thoughts and desires that assault us and tempt us to do the wrong thing are called, in Greek, *logismoi*.

They begin by attacking the mind. It is a potentially fatal error to begin a dialogue with the *logismos*, or bad thought. If your will does not turn the mind from the *logismos*, you may consent to do what the thought wants you to do. Do this often enough, and you fall captive to the *logismos*. Eventually it becomes part of your personality and grows like a spiritual cancer. All the damned in the inferno are souls whose *logismoi* conquered their souls and stole their eternal lives.

Learning how to deflect logismoi is crucial to the spiritual life. St. Theophan the Recluse, a nineteenth-century Russian monk, wrote that "the passions and desires rarely attack by themselves—they are most often born of thoughts. From this we can make a rule: cut off thoughts and you will cut off everything."

The secret is not to engage in direct combat with bad thoughts but rather to keep the mind focused on God and the good. Hieromonk Damascene, a contemporary monastic, writes, "In observing thoughts, we should not focus on them, but rather *defocus* from them. We should not try to analyze them, for analysis involves us in the very thing from which we are seeking to separate ourselves."

This was golden for me. My compulsively analytical nature kept my mind trained on the Starhill situation, as if it were a puzzle to be solved by thinking my way through it. Both Dante and the Church fathers were showing me that this is a snare. For me, finding freedom was a matter of turning away from those thoughts and from the false belief that intellection would deliver me from bondage.

The fathers teach that we must remain in a state of watchfulness against these thoughts and passions. This does not mean maintaining neurotic vigilance, it involves cultivating an internal spirit of calm, detached attention to the way we experience the external world. In this way, we can detect bad thoughts and disordered passions coming at us and serenely let them pass.

Finally, we must believe that it is not enough to gain control over our thoughts. Anyone can follow the same practices and hone their will in the service of evil. Those who would be free and whole must desire the good and communion with God—the Higher Power, the divine Source of all that is good—above all things. This you do mainly through regular prayer.

In time, you will have created a healthy version of what the ancients called a *habitus*: a way of seeing, thinking about, and moving through the world that makes it easier to live out the good in your daily life.

It turns out that those old monks, in teaching watchfulness and struggle against bad thoughts, were on to something profoundly true about human nature. As the research psychologist Roy Baumeister writes in his 2011 book, *Willpower*, scientists have demonstrated that exercising the will in a small, habitual way—say, forcing yourself to stop slouching and sit up straight—not only allows you to conquer the behavior that you wish to correct but also strengthens your overall self-control.

But there is a spiritual component to this as well. Baumeister and coauthor John Tierney, both confessed agnostics, write that the research data make it clear that religion offers powerful tools for self-control and for making the will obey reason. Leaving aside the possibility that there really is a Higher Power who responds to calls for help, religion magnifies willpower in two ways.

First, it builds within practitioners the habits of submitting impulsive desires to a higher standard. When you do things like make daily prayer a nonnegotiable part of your routine or you fast in accordance with the prescriptions of your religious tradition, over time you gain self-control.

Second, "religion also improves the monitoring of behavior, another of the central steps to self-control." That is, people who believe that God is watching them, or that they are accountable to their religious community, demonstrate measurably higher levels of willpower.

The thing is, it only really works if you have faith. "Psychologists have found that people who attend religious services for extrinsic reasons, like wanting to impress others or make social connections, don't have the same high level of self-control as the true believers," Baumeister writes. For those who have no religious faith, developing a strong commitment to some other ethical ideal independent of individual desire can serve the same purpose.

Orthodoxy, though, teaches that dedication to an ethical ideal is not enough. Given fallen human nature and the power of the ego, only steady communion with the spirit of God can effect this positive transformation.

I accept this as true, but it is hard for me to live by. I do not have a mind that is comfortable with stillness and that can sustain focus on a task. Often I start projects with zeal, but my enthusiasm peters out and I fall away from my goal because of my slothful disposition.

I knew from Dante that my healing depended on disciplining my thoughts. I thought of my prayer rule. For days and weeks, that hour had felt like I was sitting under a tin roof in a hailstorm. Stray thoughts—most of them benign but all of them unwanted—assaulted me constantly. The only way I got through my daily Jesus Prayers was by sheer force of will. I prayed like that because my priest told me to, not because I wanted to.

But I did it. And I saw results, especially after my experience on the Terrace of Wrath opened the door for healing graces. The habits of mind learned in saying the Jesus Prayer day in and day out made it easier to put into practice spiritual techniques for conquering pride, envy, and wrath.

Now, more than a year after I left chronic illness behind, there are days—too many of them—when my disordered zeal for writing or reading gets me to bedtime without having fulfilled my prayer rule. This is a hard habit to break. The things I love, I love intensely, so much so that it's hard for me to be aware of how lost inside myself I've become in satisfying those desires. What makes it especially difficult for me is that the things I love inordinately are good things, especially books and writing. Yet it is a sin to be insufficiently attentive to the things I am *supposed to be* zealous for.

The way out of the dark wood requires identifying the right things, then building your habitus so that you will find it easier to direct your will toward satisfying those desires.

"Time Watches From the Shadow"

As they near the end of the Terrace of Sloth, Dante and Virgil see a mob of penitents rushing toward them. They are purging themselves of sloth by running toward God, consumed now—as they were not in their earthly life—by desire for the good, for the things of heaven. The two shades leading the pack call out, urging the group on.

"Quickly, quickly, lest time be lost for lack of love,"
the others cried behind them. "Let our zeal
for doing good make grace grow green again."

[*Purgatorio* XVIII:103–105]

In his translation of this tercet, Mark Musa uses a less literal reading of Dante's original verse, but creates a phrase that haunts me still: *time is love.*

Time is love. Last year, my friend Jack died suddenly. He was only forty-one years old. He had been suffering from kidney problems, but no one, least of all Jack, knew how bad they were. His mother found his body; Jack had passed in his sleep.

Because Jack was a faithful member of our Orthodox mission parish, all the men of the church who were available—it turned out to be only Father Matthew and me—had to prepare Jack's body for burial, according to the Orthodox tradition. We went to a back room behind the funeral home, a cold, windowless chamber with a concrete floor where there were three embalmed bodies on gurneys, covered with sheets. There was a fourth in the center of the room.

Jack.

The funeral director pulled the sheet back, and there we saw our friend naked and pale, his eyes closed as if asleep. There was no pretense of modesty, no pretense of dignity. *This*, I thought, *is what it means to be dead.*

Father anointed Jack's body with an aromatic oil that miraculously streams from an icon. I was relieved for the sweet floral aroma to fill the room, temporarily driving out the antiseptic scent of embalming fluid. Father Matthew took a razor and shaved the stubble from Jack's face, with me cleaning behind him with a washcloth. Then we had to dress the naked body in its funeral attire: underwear, suit pants, a dress shirt, tie, and then a white baptismal gown. This took time and great effort. I had not realized that dead bodies are so heavy. I understood now what the Bible means when it calls our bodies "jars of clay." There was no clearer way to feel the absence of Jack's spirit than in my struggle with Father Matthew to clothe his body.

Father Matthew gave his white baptismal gown for Jack's burial. We could not get it on him, so, using scissors, we cut the garment up the sides, put it into place, then sewed it up with needle and thread. Father placed Jack's silver cross around his neck, and wound Jack's prayer rope, the one he was holding when he departed this life, around his right wrist.

Father Matthew stood at Jack's head and recited the prescribed psalms and prayers. Listening to Father pray, I found myself thinking, *Yes, this had been the right thing to do.* The strange ritual that I had dreaded had not been easy, but it had been holy. Standing there with my head bowed, having spent nearly two hours handling the body of my friend, I had felt underneath my fingers and palms the terrible chill of death, its weight, its finality. This is what Christ delivers us from. And yet because he sanctified the flesh by his incarnation, so too do we do the flesh honor by treating the body of our beloved dead with such tenderness and respect.

After final prayers, we were finished. The entire ritual took two hours.

At Jack's wake, his mother told me how much he had enjoyed spending time with his friends from Church. He had been in a lot of emotional and physical pain in the last year of his life and needed friends around him. It occurred to me later that the most time I had spent with Jack outside of the church in the last year was the Saturday morning I washed his body.

I was so ashamed. Many were the times when Jack had been so down about the end of his marriage that I'd thought, *I should invite him over for a beer. I bet he could use some company.* But I never had. *There would be time,* I had thought, *once I got this project out of the way, or once I finished this other thing.*

And then there was no more time. I had lost time with Jack because

I had failed to love him as I ought to have done. That memory is a bitter fruit of my slothfulness.

As I stood in Wednesday night vespers one night shortly after Jack's passing, praying for his soul, it occurred to me that my father was eighty years old and in poor health. He didn't have much time left. I loved him. What should I do?

It was not enough to be detached from bad thoughts and passions. I had to fill my soul with the good. True, I needed to be careful not to fall back into old patterns of thinking, but I could not allow slothfulness, which is a lack of love, to keep me from doing whatever reasonable thing was possible to bridge the gap between us, while there was still time.

HOW TO LOVE RIGHTLY

Practice actively cutting off thoughts that come between you and a desire for God and goodness. And practice thinking and doing good things by intention. Disciplining your mind is part of creating a habitus, or way of life, that makes it easier to progress in achieving wholeness.

Busyness is no indication that you are avoiding sloth. In fact, it can be a mask for slothfulness. The workaholic can be the laziest man around if he is using his work to avoid doing the things he is supposed to be doing. If you think of time as love, it becomes easier to stop wasting it.

24

GLUTTONY

I was wondering what makes them so famished,
since what had made them gaunt, with wretched,
scaling skin, was still unknown to me,

when out of the deep-set sockets in his head
a shade fixed me with his eyes and cried aloud:
"What grace is granted to me now!"

[*Purgatorio* XXIII:37–42]

Hunger and Thirst for Things That Cannot Satisfy

I love to cook and I love to eat. I freely admit that gluttony—the disordered enjoyment of food and drink—is one of my besetting sins. It's not the enjoyment that's the problem; it's the disorder.

Little gives me more pleasure than to spend an afternoon in the kitchen making roasts, stews, and casseroles. As a writer, I never know for sure if anything I've done is good. As an amateur cook, there's never any doubt. It is a pleasure to create something and know for certain whether or not I have hit the mark.

And little brings me greater joy than to make others happy with my cooking. In my house, and at my table, food really is love.

Sometimes it's too much. In Paris a few years back, I got carried away at an oyster bar—briny French oysters are my favorite food on earth—

and forced poor Hannah to listen to me hold forth on the sacramental theology of Gallic bivalves. It's a wonder she didn't toss a glass of Muscadet in my face and ask to be taken to McDonald's.

Because Orthodoxy is the one branch of Christianity that still takes weekly fasting seriously, learning to say no to my appetite for the sake of higher things has been spiritually beneficial to me. For a glutton like me, it is probably the hardest part of the Orthodox life. Avoiding meat and dairy for the forty days before Christmas, as the faith demands, is the Iron Man Triathlon of fasting, and I have yet to complete it cleanly. And still, as Julia Child, a secular saint in my book, said, "You must have discipline to have fun."

My sojourn with Dante and Virgil on the Terrace of Gluttony showed me that my disordered appetite for food applies to other things too. And it taught me that I needed to develop a more embracing attitude toward deprivation—an attitude that, in this age of instant gratification, could hardly be more countercultural.

Dante's description of the penitent gluttons brings to mind gruesome images from the German concentration camps.

Their eyes were dark and sunken,
Their faces pale, their flesh so wasted
That the skin took all its shape from bones.

[*Purgatorio* XXIII:22–24]

The pilgrim Dante marvels in horror at the physical torment of these poor souls, and at the visceral intensity of their craving for the fruit and water of a dewy, fruit-laden tree growing on this terrace. Suddenly one of the emaciated wretches looks at Dante and cries with joy: "What grace is granted to me now!"

Dante doesn't recognize the skeletal man at first, but then it hits him: this is his old friend Forese Donati, who grew up across the courtyard from him in Florence. His face has been utterly transformed by hunger. Forese explains that all on this terrace ate and drank with abandon in the mortal life but now, through punishing fasting, are purifying their souls. The fruit tree, glistening with dew, is the instrument of pain that makes them holy.

> *"All these people who weep while they are singing*
> *followed their appetites beyond all measure,*
> *and here regain, in thirst and hunger, holiness.*

> *"The fragrance coming from the fruit*
> *and from the water sprinkled on green boughs*
> *kindles our craving to eat and drink,*

> *"and not once only, circling in this space,*
> *is our pain renewed.*
> *I speak of pain but should say solace,*

> *"for the same desire leads us to the trees*
> *that led Christ to utter Eli with such bliss*
> *when with the blood from His own veins He made us free."*

> [*Purgatorio* XXIII:64–75]

Forese compares the wooden cross to the tree of life, a simile with an ancient pedigree in Christianity. And the blood of Christ is like the water of life. The message here: suffering is redemptive if it makes you humbler and brings you closer to God.

For me, these are among the most beautiful passages in the entire *Commedia*. Here is a man who is starving—starving!—yet he and his fellow penitents take comfort in their sufferings, knowing that they hasten their union with God.

If I believed with all my heart that my suffering could purify me, would I run from it with such vigor? This canto invited me to think about how the physical and spiritual struggles I had been through since coming home had at times brought me closer to God—and how my own bruised ego had, at other times, pushed him away.

I am a glutton for food and drink, no doubt, but I am also a glutton to feed my soul on other things that I cannot have. On this terrace, I grasped the nature of my hunger, my craving, for approval and acceptance by my family. I wanted it so much that I had made it more important than the hunger for God.

I had returned to Starhill expecting to find the fatted calf slain and prepared for a banquet. It wasn't there. I suffered this deprivation in sorrow and anger, regarding it as injustice, as my family giving me stones when I deserved bread. And I made myself sick over it.

In this canto, the poet revealed to me that the very thing that made me so sick and depressed was the thing that was the instrument of my salvation. Eating stones for two years had broken my teeth and starved me down to the spiritual bones. Yet as a prolonged drought dries up a lake and uncovers hidden structures long obscured by the water, that unslakable thirst and unsatisfiable hunger sharpened my inner vision and uncovered structures of sin deep within my heart—walls I never would have sought to tear down had I not moved home and been made to wait at the gate of Daddy's house.

In confession with Father Matthew—you don't purge wrath from your heart overnight—I told him that for all the emotional pain and physical affliction I had lived with, I did not regret for a second coming back.

"If I hadn't been starved for their love, I never would have discovered that I had been worshiping idols," I said. "I never would have read the *Commedia*. I never would have had this church. I never would have had the Jesus Prayer, and I never would have been given the gift of believing, for the first time in my life, that God the Father loves me."

The priest smiled. "God has a plan," he said.

I told him about Forese Donati and his joy amid his suffering. He knew that his pain was only temporary and a prelude to everlasting bliss. Forese knew that he deserved his penitential punishment, because he had made food and drink his idols. But he also knew that his imposed fasting, though extreme, was the only thing that would rightly order him toward God.

"I have to be that guy," I told Father Matthew. "I have to find joy in this situation, as hard as it is. I know that this is a severe mercy. I have had more spiritual growth in these past two years than at any time in my life. The two are connected."

"It hurts to take our medicine," my confessor said, "but it's the only way we're going to get healed."

Meeting with Mike the next week, I told him about the test of the gluttons' repentance. The pilgrim watches some penitent gluttons standing under another fruit tree dripping with water, jumping up and down like children begging for candy. Then, after hearing God's voice inside the tree speak to them, they go away, says Dante, "as if enlightened." They obey the authority of God's voice, not the commands of their cravings. They hunger more for righteousness than for food.

"This is where I need to be in this situation with my family," I said. "I'm so impatient. I want things to be fixed right now. I don't want to wait on God."

"God is teaching you patience," Mike said. "Learning to wait on him and let things play out according to his plan is part of your healing. Your role is to keep using those tools you have to keep yourself focused on the truth of things, and letting truth inform your emotions."

"And remembering that I am in control."

"Yes. And don't forget that this thing with your family might never be fixed," he continued. "The point is, you are being fixed, and you're being fixed by learning to satisfy that hunger within you by turning to God."

I mentioned to Mike that I had noticed in the past few days that I had been feeling stronger and no longer had to take a nap every afternoon. This encouraged me, but with Thanksgiving coming soon, I worried that a family event that in the past had triggered anxiety attacks and a physical shutdown was going to set me back.

"It doesn't have to," he said. "You are in control here. I want you to go there and to enjoy your family for who they are, not who you wish they were. Just try it and see what happens."

The previous Thanksgiving, I had taken Julie and the kids to New Orleans instead of to my mom and dad's place. We were all deeply at odds with each other, and I felt strongly that I could not bear to go to their house, sit at their table, and pretend that we were a family in which everybody got along and was happy to see each other.

When I was a teenager, my father had the authority to command me to sit on the couch and play the role of dutiful son in the scripted family drama. He no longer did—unless I gave it to him. That previous Thanksgiving, I had known that being at their table would tear me apart physically, and I had also known that I would be taking my family there not out of desire but out of guilt and fear of hurting my parents' feelings. Julie, the kids, and I had our Thanksgiving at a New Orleans restaurant as my exercise in self-preservation and autonomy.

This year we would go to my mother and father's. When Thanksgiving day came, I was nervous but prepared. I would impose a fast on my pride and self-pity for the sake of giving everyone a good time. I would resist the temptation to dwell on what I lacked in family solidarity, and instead focus on the good things I had. I would not expect more from them, or from this family meal, than they could deliver. And if things became stressful, I would remind myself that I was in control and had the power to deflect unwanted emotion.

It worked. Thanksgiving dinner went surprisingly well. It was no different from any other Thanksgiving there: good food, lots of diplomatically pleasant small talk, and all the cracks smoothed over with brown gravy and southern politeness. After dessert and coffee, Julie and I gathered up the kids, kissed everyone goodbye, and went back home.

I took a long, relaxing nap that afternoon, but not because of Epstein-Barr. It was a happy combination of the turkey and the relief that the worst of my long struggle might be over.

HOW NOT TO BE A PIG

Gluttony is not simply to be mastered by our passion for food. We can also be gluttons for anything: for sports, for fun, for the affection of others, and even for the approval of family. The man who will not restrain his appetite for food will likely not restrain his appetite for other things.

To be denied something your appetite craves can be a crucial aspect of breaking that passion's hold on your heart. Regular fasting trains the will in patience, and waiting on God. Learning to deny our desire to eat and to drink whenever we are hungry can be an important step in building the willpower to withstand the compulsion to fulfill other desires. Try a regular fasting discipline—for example, no meat or dairy on Wednesdays and Fridays—as a spiritual exercise in self-control. Don't forget, though, that avoiding food for its own sake is of no spiritual value. As Father Matthew says, even the demons do without food.

25

LUST

There is no going on, you blessèd souls,
without the fire's stinging bite. Enter,
and do not stop your ears against the distant song.

[*Purgatorio* XXVII:10–12]

Acquiring the Intelligence of Love

Only one level separates the pilgrim from the mountaintop now: the Terrace of Lust. The penitents there endure purgation inside a wall of flame. The pilgrim must pass through it before he can reach the Garden of Eden. The memory of seeing men burned at the stake, as was common in Florence, freezes Dante in place.

Trust me, says Virgil; *you will not be harmed.* Even though Dante believed him and wanted to move forward, he could not take a step.

When he saw me stay, unmoved and obstinate,
He said, somewhat disturbed: "Now look, my son,
This wall stands between Beatrice and you."

[*Purgatorio* XXVII:34–36]

That did it. Into the fire steps the pilgrim, who finds it so excruciatingly scorching that he says "I would have thrown myself straight into

253

molten glass to cool myself." But then he is through the wall and hears a voice inside a blinding light say, "Come, blessed of my Father."

The cantos on the Terrace of Lust, with only the promise of Beatrice giving Dante the courage to sacrifice his bodily desire to see her face, put me in mind of what I had once done to see the face of Julie, my own Beatrice.

My conversion to Catholicism led me to commit to chastity, and the gift of Tolkien's letters unmasked the false image of women that bound me to romantic love as an idol. My time in the desert of chastity lasted three years, which seemed a lifetime to a man in his mid-twenties. I did not know if there would be an end to this trial, nor could I be sure that there was a Beatrice on the other side of burning sands. But I was certain that if she was there, I could not see her face without having first had my passions refined by fire.

As I said earlier, it was a Friday night—October 11, 1996—that I stood in a bookstore in Austin and was introduced by a friend to Julie Harris, a journalism undergraduate. I remember taking her hand, seeing her smile, and thinking, *She's the one.*

Old couples love to embellish the story of their meeting to make it fit a romantic plot line, but in this case, it really did happen that way. Three days later, with me back home in south Florida, we were emailing and talking about the possibility of marriage. It was ridiculous, of course, but we had both been waylaid by love, and seized by a conviction that something we could know but not understand had us in its grip.

At the *Sun-Sentinel*, the newspaper where I worked as a film critic, we writers did not yet have email at our desks. I had to go to the newspaper's research library down the hall to check my email. I must have worn a groove in the carpet with my frequent trips from my desk to that Internet terminal. I also must have been half-drunk on infatuation, because the women in the library giggled sweetly at me every time I turned up.

Julie and I were both writers, and we took particular pleasure in seducing each other with our words on paper, as it were. We had a long phone call every night, but the greater part of our courtship—and certainly the most delicious aspect—was through letters.

She was a penniless college student and I was a newspaper journalist. We could not afford to see each other more than once every three weeks, usually with me flying to Austin. This made our words carry so much more weight. It was a lovely way to fall in love.

After four months of epistolary romance, punctuated by brief visits in person, I surprised Julie by turning up at her door one winter weekend. We drove out to the hill country, to an Orthodox monastery, to see an icon of the Virgin Mary.

That place was special to me, because it had been the first place Julie and I had gone together after our initial meeting. Though I was Catholic, I'd wanted to show my Orthodox writer friend Frederica that monastery and its icon. Julie, then a Presbyterian, came along. Being near her caused frissons of delight to run down my back and arms. No woman had ever made me feel that way, certainly not one I had known for less than twenty-four hours. When it was my turn to venerate the icon of the Virgin, I whispered a prayer to her. "If she's the one," I said, "please pray that it happens. Please help me not to mess it up." I kissed the image of Mary's face and moved on.

On that February day, Julie and I returned to the monastery. We kneeled before the icon and thanked God for bringing us together. Julie was not comfortable addressing Mary in prayer, but I thanked the Virgin for standing by me in my loneliness and for helping me find Julie, as I was certain she had.

And then I reached into my pocket, withdrew a diamond ring, and, my voice quivering, asked my true love to marry me. By New Year's Eve, we were husband and wife. Our two-week honeymoon to Portugal was the longest unbroken stretch we had spent together since we met.

That was seventeen years ago. When it's meant to be, it's meant to be.

What did I see in Julie? I can't guess what leaped in my heart the moment we met, and listing all the things that I adore about her—her love of books, cooking, and travel, her sense of humor, her kindness, her beauty—doesn't quite tell the story. Until I read the *Commedia*, I could not articulate what made me fall in love with her, and what makes me fall ever more deeply in love with her every day.

For years I explained it by saying, "She was the first woman I met that I couldn't see to the bottom of." After seventeen years of marriage, I know many more things about her but, happily, have yet to solve the mystery.

And then came Dante and Beatrice, who taught me that my Julie was and is an icon of divine love. I had dated beautiful women, women who were bright, funny, and bookish. But I had never met a woman who was all those things and who also put her love of God above everything else. She insisted, rightly, that I do the same.

We stood at the altar of Our Lady of the Rosary church in New Orleans, making our vows to each other. The priest introduced a custom he had learned in Bosnia into our ceremony. He had Julie and me clasp our hands together over a crucifix, and as we held it and each other, the priest said that as long as we hold on to Jesus, we will find the strength to hold on to each other.

That crucifix hangs over our bed today. The priest's promise is near the center of our life together. Because we both strive to love God above ourselves, we have found the strength to bear each other's burdens (including at times the daunting weight of the other's ego), to ask and to offer each other forgiveness, and to show care and compassion beyond what we think we can manage.

I freely confess that I have received far more of that care than I have ever given to my wife, never more than in the three years of my illness. I saw in Julie's weary but patient face a window into the infinity of God's love; in fact, I had seen it all along, though I did not understand what was in front of my eyes. I could not accept that the Father loved me, but I could believe that this girl from Texas did. Twenty years ago I prepared my heart for her, and then she, over the course of our marriage, prepared my heart for God. She held me up when my legs were too weak to stand and held our family together when my arms had no strength.

She was—she is—my Beatrice. It took the words and dreams of a medieval Tuscan poet to gentle my heart, and to open my eyes fully to the wonder of my wife and the unmerited grace of her love.

Eden: the Borderlands of Reason

Behind the fiery curtain that cleanses a soul of lust lies the Garden of Eden. Virgil has taken his charge as far toward wholeness and healing as reason and will unaided by grace can go. There is farther—much farther—to go on this pilgrimage, but Virgil cannot pass beyond this place. He has fulfilled his role of making the once-shattered pilgrim into a chalice capable of holding the love of God. Dante no longer needs a teacher; he needs a saint.

Freed now from the effects of Adam's curse, the pilgrim, Virgil declares, is at last sovereign over his body and intellect:

> "No longer wait for word or sign from me.
> Your will is free, upright, and sound.
> Not to act as it chooses is unworthy:
> Over yourself I crown and miter you."

[*Purgatorio* XXVII:139–142]

The pilgrim has been restored to his original innocence, perfected in virtue. From now on, all his desires will be just and right. He is an enlightened being who lives effortlessly by the natural law, or what the ancient Chinese would call the Tao, or the Way.

Soon Virgil will disappear, but not before walking a bit farther with the pilgrim through this new and verdant land. After the fire and foulness of hell and the punishing rigors of purgatory, this place feels like the promised land.

> A steady gentle breeze,
> no stronger than the softest wind,
> caressed and fanned my brow.

It made the trembling boughs
bend eagerly toward the shade
the holy mountain casts at dawn,

yet they were not so much bent down
that small birds in the highest branches
were not still practicing their every craft,

meeting the morning breeze
with songs of joy among the leaves,
which rustled such accompaniment to their rhymes.

[*Purgatorio* XXVIII:7–18]

There is a river, and on the other side of it is a woman named Matelda, who tells the travelers that they are in humankind's ancestral home.

"Those who in ancient times called up in verse
the age of gold and sang its happy state
dreamed on Parnassus of perhaps this very place.

"Here the root of humankind was innocent,
Here it is always spring, with every fruit in season.
This is the nectar of which the ancients tell."

[*Purgatorio* XXVIII:139–144]

She means that the age-old longing of the poets for Utopia is a recollection of Eden deep in the human race's collective memory. With Matelda's words, I saw the journey of my life, including my persistent longing for home, in a new light. I had spent all my adult life searching for a lost paradise, a home where I belonged, where I felt loved and protected and at one with everything and everyone around me.

I knew now, from reading Dante, that I suffered from what the

Welsh call *hiraeth* (pronounced "hear-wreth"), a boundless longing for a home from which you have been exiled, an unsatisfiable yearning for a home that may never have existed.

Pamela Petro, an American writer who fell in love with Wales, wrote about it in the *Paris Review*: "To feel *hiraeth* is to feel a deep incompleteness and recognize it as familiar."

So there is a word for this thing I feel, this desire that has defined the coming and going of my life, both on the map and in the landscape of my heart. Hiraeth was Loisie and Mossie's red leather sofa, and pecan cookies the size of a quarter, and the aroma of the sweet olive tree, and the musky smell of Daddy at the end of a workday as I snuggled in his lap with Ruthie, and the neat's-foot oil he taught me to rub into my baseball glove, and the bracing damp chill of a Louisiana winter's day, when the only sensible thing to do is make a chicken and sausage gumbo. These images, these sounds, these tastes and smells, whispered to me, saying, *You are safe, you are loved, everything is certain, and here we are together, at home.*

I was sick because that land did not exist, and maybe had never existed at all. I once believed, falsely, that I could find this sense of harmony, of completion, in the arms of a woman. Then I believed I could find it in a big city on the East Coast. Underneath it all, I believed that this paradise existed back in Starhill, and that if only I tried hard enough, I could cross the Mississippi and return to the land I had lost.

I had returned, and discovered that my most cherished images were an illusion. There was no Garden of Eden waiting for me, and never had been. Loisie and Mossie's cabin had long since fallen into ruin, pulled down into the damp ground by vines, then sold off by their heirs, bulldozed, and built over by strangers. My sister was dead, and the reunited family that all of us—Daddy, Mama, Ruthie, and I—had dreamed of and hoped for was now revealed as a vain hope.

I did not have paradise. I had Starhill. I had my wife and children. I had my church, I had my writing, and I had friends whom I loved and who loved me. They wanted me as I was, not as I existed in their imagination. That world was right here, right now, and until God sent me

Dante, Mike, and Father Matthew, I had been all but dead to it because of the hold the idealized past had on me.

Beatrice, Herald of Hope

I now see that in my lifelong brokenness, and in my eagerness to return to Eden, I came home expecting from my family what they, in their brokenness, could not or would not give. "To expect too much is to have a sentimental view of life and this is a softness that ends in bitterness," Flannery O'Connor wrote. It was true, and I had been so bitter for so long.

But now I saw hope.

In the Garden of Eden, the pilgrim watches an elaborate parade pass by. A chariot stops before him, and a veiled Beatrice descends from the chariot, then reveals her name, but Dante, filled with shame, cannot meet her gaze. He must do one more thing before he can be restored: confront the sin that caused him to leave the straight path.

For sixteen years on the earth, Beatrice tells the pilgrim and the gathered crowd, she tried to lead him by her presence to love the higher things, to seek after God. But after her death, she tells the throng in *Purgatorio*, "he took himself from me and gave himself to others."

> *"He set his steps upon an untrue way,*
> *pursuing those false images of good*
> *that bring no promise to fulfillment—"*

[*Purgatorio* XXX:130–132]

When Beatrice died, Dante lost her iconic image and became enthralled by false ones. Turning from things of the spirit toward the passions of the flesh, and allowing his animal nature, unrestrained by reason and grace, to flourish, he strayed from the straight path and stumbled into the dark wood.

So great was her love for Dante that Beatrice descended into the realm of the dead to arrange his rescue, in the same way that God became incarnate as a mortal man to save humanity. Why does the chariot contain Beatrice and not Jesus Christ? The answer, I think, has to do with the role art and beauty play in Dante's moral and spiritual imagination.

We have seen on the ascent up the holy mountain that Dante always has to turn away or shield his eyes from the intense brilliance of the angels. In his fallen state, he is incapable of looking directly upon holiness. Like all of us, he has to approach the glory of God indirectly, through created things. In the Middle Ages, people believed that the material world was a veil concealing the world of the spirit, of eternity.

The Chartres cathedral, for example, conveys the majesty of God through its symphony in glass and stone. The problem with this is that it is all too easy to worship the thing itself rather than to see the transcendent reality that lies behind the thing.

My father communicated paternal love to little Ruthie and me every night in his armchair through the warmth of his nightly embrace. We children could not possibly imagine what God was like, but the Bible told us he was our Father. We knew our daddy and how strong he was, and just, and tender. We knew he could do anything. He taught us right from wrong and would never lie to us. We feared him, meaning that we regarded him with utmost respect, but we were not afraid of him. Our happiness was in doing what Daddy asked, because we loved him and wanted to please him more than anything.

All the qualities they told us that God had, Daddy possessed. Because God the Father loved me so deeply through the love of my father, in my heart I confused my father with God, and did not grasp my error. And because I drank at my father's table from a cup of love mingled with disappointment and disapproval, I thought of God the Father as a compassionate but distant patriarch who loved me but was eternally disappointed in me, no matter what I did.

Ruthie never moved far from Daddy's will. She never fell from grace. I ran from Starhill, which I was raised to regard as an earthly paradise and have spent most of my life trying to crawl back up the mountain, go through the curtain of fire, and cross the river to home.

We are all born broken and in exile; it is the human condition. Dante taught me that I failed to heal my brokenness and that I deepened my sense of exile by making a fundamental error, the same one he made in his journey through life: I mistook gifts of God—family and land—for God. Nearly all the other sins and errors of my life, and the pain they have caused me, come from that one radical mistake.

My errors differ from your errors, and my sins are not your sins. But at bottom, they are the same.

God gives us work to provide for ourselves and our loved ones, and to express our desire to make and to create. But if we make our career into our god, then we turn what ought to be an icon into an idol. This was Brunetto's mistake, and Oderisi of Gubbio's.

God gives us worldly power and responsibility with which to do good, but if power becomes our god, it is an idol. This was the error of the bad popes, and of Pier della Vigne, who killed himself when he fell from the emperor's favor.

God gives us a craving for love, both physical and spiritual, so we can know the joy of intimate communion with another and create new life. But when we make satisfying sexual desire something we do for its own sake, it ceases to be an icon of God's creative love for us and becomes an idol. This was the fatal fault of Francesca and Paolo.

God gives us a desire to explore the world and to seek out new discoveries. But when we make satisfying our curiosity more important than obeying limits set by God, we are worshiping an idol. This was Ulysses's damnable fault—that, and the fact that he abused his gift of oratory and the trust of his faithful crew to trick them into serving his own glory.

God gives us the communion of others—in families, neighborhoods, towns, cities, and countries—to love and to serve, and in which to work out our salvation. But when they become ends in themselves, they become idols. This was the error of Farinata and Cavalcante, and my own.

Now, at the banks of the river Lethe, Beatrice tells the pilgrim that if he truly wants to leave the old life behind, he must reorder his imagination. Nothing in the earthly life lasts. Says Beatrice to Dante:

"And if the highest beauty failed you
in my death, what mortal thing
should then have drawn you to desire it?"

[*Purgatorio* XXXI:52–54]

Young Dante, infatuated with Beatrice, made her into a goddess. If she could be a goddess, then some other created thing could substitute, he figured. She is telling him now that what he responded to in her was the presence of God shining through her. If he had seen her rightly, after she died he would have dedicated himself to the pursuit of God, not of lesser goods. Only God is God; anything beneath God that we love as if it were God is an idol and could lead to our eternal destruction.

As Beatrice stands in Eden gazing at an iconographic representation of Christ, her dazzling beauty poleaxes the pilgrim, reducing him to profound contrition:

Even beneath her veil, even beyond the stream,
she seemed to surpass her former self in beauty
more than she had on earth surpassed all others.

The nettle of remorse so stung me then
that whatever else had lured me most to loving
had not become for me most hateful.

[Purgatorio XXXI:82–87]

This is what it means to be overawed by the holiness of beauty. If ever you are granted such a vision in this life, you will feel acutely the distance between yourself and perfection, and will long more than anything for unity with the source of such beauty. It can come from anywhere. I glimpsed that beauty in conventional ways: in a Gothic cathedral, in the face of my true love, and now, in the verses of Dante's epic poem. But the writer and Soviet spy Whittaker Chambers saw it while contemplating the ears of his baby daughter—"those intricate, perfect ears," he would later write. "I did not then know that, at that moment, the finger of God was first laid upon my forehead." His daughter's ears were the hook that caught Chambers, and drew him out of the service of Stalin and to light and freedom. They telegraphed to him that there is more to reality than he saw, and how very far he was from the unity of truth and beauty in God.

Dante crosses the waters of the Lethe and emerges on the other bank, purified of the memory of his evil acts. He is with Beatrice now. She leads him to his final earthly purification in the waters of the river Eunoe, which heightens in his mind memories of his good deeds—in Beatrice's words, to "revive the powers that are dead in him." His desire, his *eros*, has been joined to *caritas*, the selfless love of God and others. Dante leaves purgatory with these words:

From those most holy waters
I came away remade, as are new plants
renewed with new-sprung leaves,
pure and prepared to rise up to the stars.

[*Purgatorio* XXXIII:142–145]

Our pilgrim has come out of Egypt. He has crossed the desert of Sinai. Now he is ready to see the promised land.

If you stop here, you will have traveled far enough to grasp the secret of the *Commedia*, the holy grail itself: the meaning of life is found not in serving the self and things of the senses, but in serving the Higher Power that unites and orders and transcends all created things. We call this power God, and it is in God that we live and move and have our being.

For Christians like Dante Alighieri and me, that Higher Power has a name, Jesus Christ. He is the incarnation of love. He is the Way, the Truth, and the Life, and no one can reach unity with God, or *theosis*, except through him.

You can build a good life for yourself by following Dante through hell and up the holy mountain and doing as he has done. But a good life is not the same thing as eternal life, as the pilgrim discovers in the third and final stage of his journey.

HOW TO GENTLE YOUR HEART

In Dante's age, there was a tradition of courtly love in which the lady tested her lover to see if he had a "gentle heart," that is, to determine if his heart was dedicated to love rather than to lust. By renouncing lust, the lover gentles his heart, and makes it ready to receive the treasure of true love. If lasting romantic love eludes you, embrace chastity, fasting from sexual activity as an exercise in preparing your own heart, and the heart of your beloved, for strong and stable commitment.

Dante believed that finding a sense of completion in loving and being loved by another prepared our hearts for unity with God. More deeply, the heart's quest for happiness and fulfillment comes from an ancestral memory of a primal utopia, a sense of oneness with God and the cosmos. Stop searching; it doesn't exist this side of heaven. In truth, we are all wayfarers enduring permanent exile in this life. Any hope of creating heaven on earth—including the dream of everlasting happiness in the arms of your true love—will end in tears.

You cannot re-create Eden, but you can make an enclosed garden within your heart, a place of peace, love, and communion with God. If you follow the ascetic path laid out in *Purgatorio*, you clear the weeds of the passions and make the soil fertile for sowing the seeds of love.

Part IV

PARADISO, OR, HOW
THINGS OUGHT TO BE

26

INTO THE LIGHT

The glory of Him who moves all things
pervades the universe and shines
in one part more and in another less.

I was in that heaven which receives
more of His light. He who comes down from there
can neither know nor tell what he has seen,

for, drawing near to its desire,
so deeply is our intellect immersed
that memory cannot follow after it.

[*Paradiso* I:1–9]

Sailing Across the Ocean of Divine Love

*P*aradiso is a work of incandescent beauty and prodigious theological complexity. It charts the pilgrim's progress through the
vastness of space and across an ocean of light. His destination:
the mind of God.

It is not a place but a state of being; to reach God is to be completely
absorbed into him, which is *theosis*. It is to be utterly transformed by love
divine, to become one with Ultimate Reality. It is the desired end of life's
journey, the only safe harbor and our only true home.

Wise readers of Dante's *Paradiso* will heed the poet's warning at the beginning of this final stage of the journey:

O you, eager to hear more,
who have followed in your little bark
my ship that singing makes its way,

Turn back if you would see your shores again.
Do not set forth upon the deep,
for losing sight of me, you would be lost.

[*Paradiso* II:1–3]

The reference is to Ulysses, whose journey into the unexplored realms of the sea led his crew to their death. Dante promises death to us as well, but it is a death that will lead to life. If you follow him all the way to God, you will not see your shores again—or rather, you will see them with new eyes.

It is an apt caution for a more mundane reason: the metaphysically dense *Paradiso* is far more difficult to understand than *Inferno* and *Purgatorio*. It's easy to get lost in it. The poet expresses his account of love's transformative effects with enormous intricacy and profundity, certainly, but *Paradiso*, which takes place in a realm of pure light and being, is a more abstract tale than either of its robustly physical predecessors, *Inferno* and *Purgatorio*.

Readers seeking practical life-changing wisdom may find the mystical *Paradiso* less useful than the other two books. I sure did. Part of that had to do with the difficulty of the poem. Mostly, I think, it was because I was not (yet) able to receive its light. This is understandable for pilgrims not sufficiently advanced on the path of spiritual transformation. *Paradiso* shows us what our lives would be like if we lived completely free of our egos, transparent to God's love, with all our hearts, souls, and minds united to that divine love and through it. For people like me, so accustomed to speaking the language of egotism, *Paradiso*'s verses often sound like a foreign tongue (the art critic Titus Burckhardt calls them "inscrutable magic.")

That said, I have discovered on multiple readings of the *Commedia* that *Paradiso* is much my favorite, because of the gorgeousness of its language and the fathomlessness of its luminous mysteries. Despite its complexity, *Paradiso* is good training for the spiritually adventurous. Consider how Dante conveys the experience of theosis in these early lines from *Paradiso*:

> *Beatrice had fixed her eyes*
> *upon the eternal wheels and I now fixed*
> *my sight on her, withdrawing it from above.*
>
> *As I gazed on her, I was changed within,*
> *as Glaucus was on tasting of the grass*
> *that made him consort of the gods in the sea.*
>
> *To soar beyond the human cannot be described*
> *in words. Let the example be enough to one*
> *for whom grace holds this experience in store.*

> [***Paradiso*** I:64–72]

In Greek mythology, Glaucus was a fisherman who sampled a magic herb growing near the shore, and was turned into an immortal sea god. The verb Dante uses for "changed within" is, in Italian, "transhumanized"—to go beyond the human. The poet invented the word, stretching language further than it ever had been done for the sake of expressing what he concedes is inexpressible.

Dante tells his reader that to be saved is not to remain as you are now, only morally improved. He is saying that to be saved is to be utterly transformed, in a way that cannot be described in ordinary human experience. It is to be drawn into the very being of God himself.

This is a profundity that can be recognized, and can be experienced, but not comprehended abstractly. It can only be apprehended through the heart. You cannot think your way to theosis; ultimately we all must become mystics. This is what it means to be made whole. It requires the giving of nothing less than your entire self. Abandon hope you who seek only safety and comfort from the search for God. As a character in C.S. Lewis's *The Lion, the Witch, and the Wardrobe* said of Aslan, the god figure of Narnia, "Who said anything about safe? 'Course he isn't safe. But he's good."

Father Matthew encouraged the congregation one Sunday not to settle for easy comfort in our spiritual lives. We must dive into the murky depths of our hearts, find the wreckage on the bottom, bring it to the surface, and let God take it away.

"Go into the deep," he preached. "Go into the deep."

I smiled at that and thought, *This Orthodox priest doesn't know it, but Dante is his ally.* Indeed, Dante is the ally of every Christian and of every soul that seeks to be more serious about life and how to live it.

Finding The Peace that Passes All Understanding

The first blessed soul the pilgrim meets is Piccarda Donati, the sister of Forese Donati, the gaunt but joyful reformed glutton. In Florence, Piccarda was a nun kidnapped from her convent by her wicked brother Corso, who forced her to marry a man to seal a political alliance.

She is on the lowest level of paradise, a sphere reserved for those who failed to be entirely faithful to their vows. This doesn't sit right with Dante. To his way of thinking, Piccarda did not abandon her vows of her own free will; she was forced. How can she be happy with God's decision to assign her to heaven's farthest reaches?

Piccarda answers him "with so much gladness she seemed alight with love's first fire." She says:

> "Brother, the power of love subdues our will
> so that we long for only what we have
> and thirst for nothing else.

". . . And in His will is our peace."

[*Paradiso* III:70–72, 85]

Not only is love more important than justice, as Father Matthew once told me, but in heaven love *is* justice, and justice love. Accepting what you have been given with a grateful heart and not desiring anything else is the key to peace. According to the saintly Piccarda, it is not for us to question God's plan.

Says Dante in response:

Then it was clear to me that everywhere in heaven
is Paradise, even if the grace of the highest Good
does not rain down in equal measure.

[*Paradiso* III:88–90]

To be at peace is to cease to desire anything that God has not given. Heaven is a state of paradox in which everywhere is perfect, even though some places are at a higher degree of perfection than others. How can we speak of degrees of perfection? Because in heaven, we are perfected according to our own natures.

Piccarda, for example, bears as much divine light as her nature can accept. This reminded me of a teaching that Father Matthew gave in a sermon one Sunday: "God doesn't expect you to be St. Seraphim; he expects you to be the best version of the unique creation that is you."

We learn from Piccarda that in the Kingdom of God, perfection is not perfect *equality* but perfect *harmony*. If I loved as I should love, I would love my family—indeed, love all people—and expect nothing in return. Inner peace depends on practicing gratitude for what I have, not complaining about what I lack.

Dante the poet uses the figure of Piccarda to illustrate how pure love doesn't measure fairness and unfairness, doesn't meditate on past wrongs, is not bound by envy or any earthly passion. Piccarda is free. Moreover,

Piccarda is free in a way that I once was not. Now I can see that I was so knotted up by hurt over my family's broken bonds that I could not let go of my passion for what I considered to be justice.

I could not remain that fourteen-year-old boy weeping in a field over his shame, his weakness, and the wounds delivered by the mockery of his father and his sister. I was a middle-aged man now. Whatever their flaws, Daddy and Ruthie were not an excuse for me to shirk my responsibility to love. And it was easier to love them, because I no longer served the false image I created of them. Rather, I served the God who made us all, and who expects us to love others as he loves us.

What Dante Learned From St. Francis of Assisi

Francis of Assisi, one of the greatest saints of the Catholic Church, died four decades before Dante Alighieri was born. The spoiled-brat son of a silk merchant, Francis became disillusioned by material wealth, and in defiance of his father, took up a life of poverty in the service of God. Francis received a mystical call to rebuild the Roman church, which was falling into spiritual ruin because of its great wealth and earthly power. Francis's voluntary poverty, his willingness to renounce everything for the sake of God, renewed and transformed Western Christianity—and the heart and mind of Dante.

The pilgrim never speaks to St. Francis in *Paradiso*, but he hears the great Dominican theologian Thomas Aquinas sing the praises of the Franciscan founder in the Circle of the Sun. In Dante's time, the Dominicans and the Franciscans, the two major reform religious orders of the Middle Ages, were often bitter rivals. In *Paradiso*, the poet has Dominicans praise Franciscans, and vice versa, to show how if we loved as we ought, we would throw off the yokes of pride and envy, and work harmoniously.

The Dante scholars Bill Cook and Ron Herzman contend that St. Francis was a central figure in teaching the exiled poet how to survive his suffering and to redeem it. Francis is the anti-Farinata: where the Florentine noble took great pride in his wealth, position, and family background, Francis renounced his own, in the belief that riches and social position were snares for the soul. Cook and Herzman say it is precisely Francis's humility and acceptance of poverty that the proud Dante needs to internalize in order to survive his own impoverishment and ruin, and to allow them to become an instrument of God's peace.

"Dante, the poet of exile, must learn to do without. Franciscan poverty teaches Dante that it is possible to face the circumstances of his exile by embracing them," Cook and Herzman write. And Francis's humility, which taught him that the mercy of God is the only thing that saved him, gave the poet Dante, who was aware of his own extraordinary gifts, the grace to make public confession of his sin.

"Like the Francis who says that if great sinners had been given the same graces that he had, they would have responded to them better than he did," argue the scholars, "Dante asserts that his very salvation is more an act of mercy than of merit, and without that mercy he would be with the likes of Farinata, Pier delle Vigne, and Ulysses."

This is why Dante is not Ulysses, and not the writer Brunetto Latini encouraged him to be. He did not follow his own star to his destiny. Rather, the poet's humility taught him to prostrate himself before the wisdom of those who came before him and who charted a path to the glory of God. Like Socrates, Dante's greatness in part was knowing what he did not know.

The Humility of Refusing to Judge Others

In that same *Paradiso* encounter with Aquinas, the saint counsels the pilgrim Dante to rein in his judgment. Do not to be quick to assume any situation is as we take it to be, the saint says, because God's plan is not always clear to us. Francis, the Dominican recalls, went to the Sultan seeking martyrdom, but God had other plans for Francis's life. Aquinas continues:

> "For I have seen the briar first look dry and thorny
> right through all the winter's cold,
> then later wear the bloom of roses at its tip,

"and once I saw a ship, which had sailed straight
and swift upon the sea through all its voyage,
sinking at the end as it made its way to port."

[*Paradiso* XIII:133–138]

This passage cut deep. I am prone to high emotions. It's easy to look over my past and observe where my own passions led me to misinterpret certain situations. I didn't see the whole picture, and I did not have the patience to abide while the whole picture came into focus. The mistakes were in wanting clear answers *now*, instead of learning to trust the logic of love and letting the light of love make certain truths emerge from beneath the veil.

One weekend Julie took our teenage son Matt to a three-week stay at a summer camp. Lucas, his younger brother, was an emotional mess that evening. I asked him if he was upset that Matt was going away for almost a month.

"Yes," he muttered.

"That surprises me, Lucas," I said. "You and Matt argue so much that I thought you would have been happy to have him out of the house for a while."

"Well, I've always loved him," Lucas said in a quiet voice, looking down. "What if he gets sick, and we can't get to him fast enough? What if he gets thrown out of school for some reason, and we aren't there to get him?"

Suddenly I saw the boys' relationship in a different light. Lucas really did love his older brother more than his pride would let him disclose under normal circumstances. Appearances had been deceiving, even to the father of these boys, who ought to know them better than anybody.

As my mother told me after my sister died, Ruthie had said pretty much those exact words about me when I moved to the East Coast early in my career.

"I don't understand what he's doing," she told our parents. "He's way up there in the big city where we can't help him. What if he gets sick?" That's almost *exactly* what Lucas said.

Considering Lucas's admission in light of *Paradiso*'s counsel against hasty judgment, I wondered if beneath that layer of resentment Ruthie had against me was something purer and finer, a piercing love that became distorted when shining out through her own pride. Just like Lucas's feelings for his brother.

Maybe till now, I had been too blinded by my own pride to see that. Maybe I had been too blind to see a lot of things that were there all along. And maybe my blindness keeps me from seeing the hope for redemption that is always present in this life, when wills are free. If Manfred, who had been excommunicated, could win heaven by appealing to the mercy of God as he lay dying on the battlefield, there is never cause for despair.

The Salt of Another Man's Bread

For me, the final lesson Dante had to teach came from the pilgrim's meeting with his ancestor Cacciaguida, who had been a knight in one of the Crusades. Cacciaguida, presented by the poet as an exemplar of courage, prophesies the pilgrim's exile:

> "You shall leave behind all you most dearly love,
>   and that shall be the arrow
>   first loosed from exile's bow.

> "You shall learn how salt is the taste
>   of another man's bread and how hard is the way,
>   going down and then up another man's stairs."

> [*Paradiso* XVII:55–60]

In Florence, even to this day, they bake bread without salt. Every time he tastes his daily bread, Dante will know that he is not at home. Every time he descends from his bedroom at someone else's house, then returns at night, he will recall that he is not doing so in his own house.

Dante is never going to go home to Florence. This is his fate. Yet he must transcend it. How? He must stand outside of his pain and suffering, find meaning in it, and affirm the goodness of life despite its injustices. We know that he will create art from the experience and through it show the world the way to overcome the brokenness that led to his own exile and, metaphorically, to the sense we all have of being alienated from God, others, and ourselves.

Each one of us lives in exile from the life we would like to have, or that we think we deserve. Every time we feel disappointment or hurt, it is like tasting the salt of another man's bread. Every time we suffer, it is like going up another man's stairs. Exile is not just something that happens to refugees; exile is the human condition.

We are lost, we are searching, we are waiting for a sign to tell us the way home. The poet Dante had to have everything taken from him to discover how lost he truly was—and to find his way back. This is what the pilgrim Dante is learning on his journey through the afterlife, and this is what he, to fulfill his role as the hero, must go back and tell all the other wayfarers so they may save their own lives.

Dante Alighieri wrote a book explaining how to do this—a user's manual for the soul, you might call it—and cast it into the sea of time. There it remained, bobbing on the currents, until I came across it on a shelf I rarely browse in a bookstore I almost never visit. It was a message in a bottle. It was a sign. It was a gift and a source of grace that redeemed my exile and turned a tragedy that very nearly broke me into my own *divina commedia*—a story with a happy ending.

In the final moments of his epic quest, Dante raises his eyes to behold the Holy Trinity. As the pilgrim tries to comprehend what he's seeing, a bolt of lightning strikes his mind, and he can see no more.

Here my exalted vision lost its power.
But now my will and my desire, like wheels revolving

with an even motion, were turning with
the Love that moves the sun and all the other stars.

[*Paradiso* XXXIII:143–145]

Everything within Dante has been mystically and flawlessly joined to the will of God. He has reached the end of all his strivings. He has been perfected in Love. No longer subject to the highs and the lows of Fortune's wheel, the pilgrim now abides at the hub, the fixed point around which the universe turns.

Passing the Gift On

"I have seen a change in you," Father Matthew told me.

We were sitting at a table in the church rectory, talking about love.

"You are receiving something you weren't in a position to use before, or even to receive," he continued. "I think your investment in your spiritual growth within this mission is paying off. You have started to turn off your intellect to some degree, and are opening up your heart."

I was startled to hear that—and pleased. This was the fruit of following the Church's disciplines and living a more committed life in the Church than I ever had done before. This was the fruit of therapy with Mike Holmes. And this was the fruit of reading Dante. The Yale scholar Giuseppe Mazzotta says that Dante's pilgrimage is a journey of the mind, "but primarily a journey of the heart. You have to come to know God through the heart, or not at all."

"I appreciate your saying that," I answered. "I'll be honest with you, though. I couldn't do any of this without your help, and without this church. I came back to Louisiana looking for my family and my home. I found God and this church. This mission is the rock I've built my life here on."

The priest folded his hands and looked down at the table as he spoke.

"What you have here is nothing more than I received from Father Seraphim," he said, referring to his spiritual father. "He received it from

Mount Athos, living a life of asceticism, and living mystically in the Body of Christ."

"This life," he went on, "is all meant for one thing: to carry us successfully on the journey toward unity with God. Toward being consumed by love."

"You said from the start that you weren't here to be our friend, you were here to be our priest," I said, laughing. "I like that you take our spiritual lives that seriously."

"The Orthodox tradition is to hand on what we have received," Father Matthew said. "I'm just giving you what I received, is all."

Just like Dante. As Virgil explains to the pilgrim, the miraculous property of love is this: the more love you give, the more love there is to share.

"That infinite and ineffable Good,
   which dwells on high, speeds toward love
   as a ray of sunlight to a shining body.

"It returns the love it finds in equal measure,
   so that, if more of ardor is extended,
   eternal Goodness will augment Its own.

"And the more souls there are who love on high,
   the more there is to love, the more of loving,
   for like a mirror each returns it to the other."

[*Purgatorio* XV:67–75]

HOW TO KNOW PEACE

The only certain way to peace is to dwell within the will of God. Accept with a grateful heart all that you have been given. Desire nothing more than to please him. Regard suffering and adversity as something God, in his mysterious providence, allows to help us grow in love.

God does not expect you to be the same as everyone else. He only wants you to be perfected in the nature he gave you, and to find your place within the harmony of the cosmos. However small it may seem to us, each of us has a divinely appointed role to play in the destiny of others.

Because we are finite creatures who live in time, we cannot see things clearly. Be careful in judging others, because the truth of their character and their situation may be hidden from your eyes. Only God knows the whole truth—and only God knows the future. Don't expect all the answers now, but be patient and trusting, and seek to grow in love. Each act of love is one more step on the long journey to our true and only home: unity with God, in eternity.

27

DOWN BY THE RIVERSIDE

I, who had come to things divine from man's estate,
to eternity from time,
from Florence to a people just and sane,

with what amazement must I have been filled!
Indeed, between the wonder and my joy, I was content
neither to hear nor speak a word.

[Paradiso XXXI:37–42]

The Day I Finally Came Home

In the Orthodox Christian tradition, Theophany—from the Greek, meaning "appearance of God"—is the feast day commemorating the day that Jesus Christ was baptized in the river Jordan. When Jesus emerged from the water, the heavens opened and the Holy Spirit descended like a dove, alighting on the Christ. The voice of the Father said, "This is my beloved Son, in whom I am well pleased."

Our little flock gathered at the mission on a cold Sunday morning—January 19, in fact—to celebrate the liturgy. Father Athanasius, an old friend of Father Matthew's, was visiting from the Northwest, and gave the sermon. He dwelled for some time on the blessing God the Father spoke over his Son. I could have listened to that kind of talk all day.

This is my beloved Son, in whom I am well pleased. Here, in the middle of the journey of our life, for the first time ever, I was able to hear those words in church and believe that God meant them for me too.

I don't know when, exactly, in my healing process this change came over me. I had finished *Paradiso* over the Christmas break, but there had been no aha moment. I just noticed one day, a couple of weeks into the new year, that I felt pretty good. No chronic fatigue. No daily naps. Nothing. It was gone.

The night before Theophany, I mentioned to Julie that for the first time since arriving home, I felt at home. Settled. Stable. Healed. Free. Nothing had changed externally; the change was all within. But I saw the world with new eyes now.

Yes, the Epstein-Barr virus remains in my body and always will, and in periods of stress—which crop up every now and then—it takes me back down temporarily. But nothing like before. The change has been profound.

When Father Athanasius spoke of Jesus rising out of the river, I felt as though I had come not only out of a dark wood but also out of some turbulent waters, into a new life. After he finished his sermon, I thought, *Today is the day that I finally came home.* Theophany is the day I finally turned outside of myself and let God the Father embrace me and welcome me into his household.

After the liturgy, our congregation drove down to the Mississippi River landing in town for the traditional Theophany blessing of the river. We stood on the bank in the cold wind, listening to Father Matthew pray. As I gazed across the water, I smiled, recalling that it was on this spot in 1984 that I had left West Feliciana. When I boarded the ferry and it pulled away from the dock, my self-imposed exile had begun.

The river's edge, where my feet were planted, marked the borderland between my old life and my new life. And there I was on this sunny winter's morning, celebrating the blessing of the waters with my church family, and with one of the Virgils sent by God to bring me home. Really and truly home.

Here's what I saw on Theophany. If I had not felt called by God to return to my hometown after my sister's death, I would not have written

The Little Way of Ruthie Leming, a testimonial to her goodness and the goodness of my Louisiana family and their friends. It is a story that told the beautiful truth about them all, and that has been an inspiration for countless readers, some of whom come to Starhill to visit Ruthie's grave. Part of the money I made from the book allowed us to contribute significantly to the founding of St. John the Theologian Orthodox Mission in Starhill.

In a real sense, my sister, and the love she lived and shared with the world, offered us our church. She could not give me the love I wanted, nor could she receive the love I wanted to give. But because Ruthie lived and died radiant with love, she was able to give me priceless gifts.

She gave me the gift of homecoming. She gave me the gift of a church. And she (and others in the family) shattered my illusions and gave me the gift of exiling me into a dark wood.

It was indeed a gift. Through my fortunate fall, I had learned to pray more deeply than I ever had. I had made myself vulnerable to Father Matthew and Mike Holmes, mentors who led me to a place of light and grace. I had read the first three lines in the *Commedia*, and experienced the power of great art to change one's life. Most of all, I learned that suffering amid the brokenness of the world is not something merely to be endured with courage, but to be redeemed by love.

Without those things, I would still be in exile from God the Father, who was there all along, though I could not and would not let him see me.

"You came home expecting to find something else, but what you really found was God," Julie told me.

As I said repeatedly to Father Matthew as we walked side by side, heart to heart, on this journey, I never would have chosen this pilgrimage had I known how hard it would be. But I am so thankful for it, because it has taken me closer to God the Father than I have ever been. This brokenness has been a gift and a mercy.

In the autumn of 2014, I traveled with an old friend to Florence, to see Dante's hometown. I walked the streets of his old neighborhood. I saw what some believe was his house, just around the corner from where Beatrice lived, and across the alley from the Donatis. I prayed in the tiny church where legend has it that he and Beatrice met. I prayed in the old baptistery, where Dante was made a Christian and where he hoped in vain to return in glory.

I saw Cavalcante's house, and the bare space on the nearby Piazza Signoria where Farinata's mansion once stood before the Guelphs leveled it. I stood on the spot by the Ponte Vecchio where assassins ambushed and murdered Buondelmonte, sparking the Guelph-Ghibelline civil war. And I walked around the piazza where the riot took place that ultimately led to Dante's exile.

These were real people. This had been their world. They were now a part of me and always would be. They had changed my life. These saints, these villains, these extraordinary Florentines had come with Dante and rescued me.

My friend and I went on to Ravenna, a small city in northeastern Italy, where the exiled poet found his final refuge. Dante died there in 1321. You can visit his tomb next to the Franciscan cloister. It sits at the end of a quiet side street near the city center, under a stand of oaks in a garden. The sons of St. Francis have tended Dante's bones for seven hundred years.

On the day I visited, I approached the white stone mausoleum as a pilgrim. I waited for a German tourist to take his photo and leave, then I entered into the tiny chapel-like space all alone and stood before the marble tomb where lay the mortal remains of my master. An oil lamp burned at the side, and at the base of the grave was a bronze fixture: the poet's laurel that the exiled Florentine had longed for from his hometown but never received.

I prostrated myself on the floor, then after a moment rose and stepped forward to kiss the tomb. Then for a moment I simply stood still in the presence of the great man whose masterpiece had saved my life.

I thanked him for what he had done for me. And I thanked God for the life and trials of Dante Alighieri, who turned his own suffering to greater good and reached across the centuries to rescue me, as he, in his imagination, had been rescued by Virgil and Beatrice.

I asked for his prayers that I would write well of him, and in so doing reflect for the eyes of others the saving love God showed to him and which he passed on to me. Then I took *Paradiso* out of my leather bag, opened it, and began to recite, as if praying, Canto XXVI. Tears sprang to my eyes:

And I: "Both philosophic reasoning
and the authority that descends from here
made me receive the imprint of such love,

"for the good, by measure of its goodness, kindles
love as soon as it is known, and so much more
the more of goodness it contains."

I crossed myself, kissed his tomb once more, then went to sit in the garden.

The Open Road

Theophany may have been a decisive turning point, but the journey has not reached its conclusion, nor will it in this life. I'm still walking up the mountain of purgatory, still praying, still repenting, still reading Dante, still going to confession, still learning new things. There are times of darkness, when there is no progress to be made, only rest and reflection and preparation for the inevitable sunrise. And sometimes the sunshine pierces the darkness.

One sunny Saturday afternoon in late November, my son Lucas and I gathered and stacked firewood for my folks. We sat and talked with them on their front porch for a bit. They thanked us warmly, with gratitude and affection that were strong, clear, and genuine.

That night at vespers, I prayed for Mama and Daddy, and thought of how beautiful their faces had looked in the golden autumn sun, and how tender their voices sounded thanking us again as we kissed them goodbye. *These are such good, kind-hearted people,* I thought.

And then, in my mind's eye, I had a vision. I stood next to Mama and Daddy and Ruthie, and we stared into a white sun, so close we could almost reach out and touch it. Our eyes were wide open, we were looking upward, and all of us were grinning in wonder and delight. Ruthie and I were children again, and our parents were young, and we were all happy, so happy, staring at the sun together.

This, I knew, was paradise, and this was *Paradiso*: the world to come, the world where there are no more tears, and when all that separates us from God and one another has ceased to exist. This is the vision Dante gives us in the last and greatest of his three canticles. It is the home toward which we are all going, though some of us may not make it; the choice is ours.

I pulled my glasses off and wiped my tears away. After evening prayer ended, I was the first in line for confession. In the empty church, I stood with Father Matthew.

"During vespers, I was praying for my folks, and I had a kind of vision," I told Father Matthew. After telling him what I had seen in my mind's eye, I said, "I realized that I am so sick and tired of seeing my mom and dad and feeling disappointed over what might have been. I just want to enjoy them for who they are. They have given me so, so much.

"I accepted a long time ago that they aren't going to change," I told him. "But they have free will, and that means nothing is decided in advance.

In *Paradiso*, St. Thomas Aquinas cautions the pilgrim not to think he has the future figured out. Only God knows. Because of that hope, however, I feared falling back into the snare of believing that if only I give them this thing or do that thing, then they really will change.

"But I have to tell you that I don't want my heart to be an obstacle to the vision I saw coming true," I continued. "I know what we all want can only be fulfilled in God's presence, but if God wants to start it in this life, I don't want to stand in his way."

Father Matthew, his head bowed, kept listening.

"After this happened, I told God that I did not have it in my heart to get free of these expectations. If I could stick my hand in there and scrape them out, I would. But I can't. He can, though. I asked him to set me free. You keep telling me that love does not expect justice, and tonight I got it in a way I never had. So I'm laying all my expectations of justice at the foot of the Cross tonight. I'm asking God to forgive me, and to make me strong enough to love them for who they are, and only that."

Father Matthew surprised me once again by saying nothing. He just simply lifted his stole, and I knelt for absolution. He placed the sacred veil over my head and said the prayers, and a moment later I walked out of the church, lighter.

I will be back in that same spot every week or two, confessing to the same sins, and I will receive the same absolution. Again and again I will make that orbit from the confessional into the world and back again. By the grace of God, the particulars of my sins will change as I grow spiritually, but sin will always be there. If I stay faithful to my prayers and sacraments and keep a penitent watch over my soul, then I will create space for divine grace to work. The roundabout journey will spiral my heart upward, toward God.

As You Have Received, So Shall You Give

The next evening, Mama called to say Daddy had gone to bed with a severe fever. I drove over to check on him and found him under his covers, shivering. When I drew back the blankets to straighten them, his arms shook violently from the chills. His fever was 102.8 degrees and rising. He tried to get up to use the bathroom but was too weak to stand, even with Mama and me supporting him.

I phoned his doctor, who said to take him at once to the hospital. Off we went to Baton Rouge General, where we spent the entire night in the geriatric emergency room. He lay resting in a curtained bay, with doctors and nurses going in and out, testing, poking, and prodding. Throughout the long night, I would take walks in the ward. There were souls moaning behind the curtains and family members moving tensely along the hallways, some near tears.

It was almost daylight before we finally settled him in a room and I headed out for the long drive home to the country. I thought about how little time Daddy had left. Earlier in the evening, drawing his trembling hands together, he murmured matter-of-factly, "The windows on my life are closing to just a thin space."

There was no point in denying it. Though I had already decided I was not going to get the reconciliation with him that I wanted, I thought about what I wanted to say to him before he died.

Then it hit me: I needed to confess my sins to my father and ask for *his* forgiveness. What were my sins? Many were the times I had spoken in anger about him, especially since coming home and seeing everything fall apart. Many were the occasions when I had not gone to visit him because I was hurt and furious over the way he treated me. And many were the moments when I had withheld love because I hated the injustice.

The bottom line was that I had not loved him as I ought to have loved him.

God's will for me was to love this frail old fighter who was my father. That much was certain. *But the wrongs I have done to him aren't nearly as serious as the wrongs he has done to me*, I thought. *If I ask his forgiveness, he will think that he has won, when he hasn't.*

Won? Once and for all, I had to accept that this was not a court case. This was life. My father was losing it. And what was I doing putting our sins against each other in a balance? Love, as Father Matthew never tired of saying, doesn't expect justice.

Besides, God will not judge me for what my father did to me. He will judge me for what I did, period. There is no sin that my father committed against me that I have not committed also. If not for God's love, I would still be trapped in the inferno of my own passions. I received the gift of mercy from my father in heaven; I cannot hoard it, especially not from my earthly father.

Now I had the chance to allow the course of love to run in reverse, and to offer to my own dad the unconditional love I had craved from him.

Sitting at my kitchen table, I emailed Father Matthew, told him what I was thinking, and asked him to help me prepare for this conversation.

"I have been waiting for two years for you to see this," he wrote back. "I'll help you in any way that I can."

Forgive Me, Father, for I Have Sinned

Mama called early the next day to say that the hospital would be discharging Daddy later that morning. I finished my coffee and headed into the city, phoning Father Matthew as soon as I made it to Highway 61. We talked for a bit, and he said he would be praying for me.

When I joined my folks in the room, my mother excused herself to go have some breakfast.

Sitting knee to knee with my father, I began. "Daddy, I have something I need to say to you. I have sinned against you, and I'm asking for your forgiveness. I have been angry with you for a long time over the way you have treated me, especially since I came back home and things went to hell. I have let that anger get the best of me and harden my heart against you. I have not loved you as well as I should have. I'm sorry. Please forgive me."

His lower lip trembled. His left hand, resting in his lap, shook.

"I forgive you, darling," he said softly.

We talked for some time longer, and I told him that I had expected more from the family than they had given. The bad things, the painful things, that happened after I came home were all for the good, I told him, because they had made me face up to some sins in my own heart that I needed to repent of—and had brought me closer to God. I wanted him to know the truth: that as much as I had hated this struggle, it was a blessing.

"I . . . I just didn't know how to love you," my father said, raising his mottled arms. "You were not what I expected. The kind of man I was, I . . ." His voice trailed off. He did not have the words.

When he mentioned that forgiveness is important but that he had no one to ask it from, I felt my heart sink, but resisted the temptation to pity myself, to wallow in my wounded pride, to envy Daddy his untroubled conscience. *Lay that burden down*, I thought. *The day is coming, and coming soon, when you will miss these moments, however much they miss the mark.*

Love is not a contractual exchange; love is given with no expectation of return. Love does not keep a ledger. What mattered was that my dying father knew that I loved him, and his remaining days would not be burdened with the weight of my banked anger. What mattered was that I had done this not because of any goodness within myself but because God had given me the strength.

What mattered was that I had done this. Grace had moved my heart toward closer harmony with the love that moves the sun and all the other stars; grace turned my heart like a wheel, day by day carrying me a little bit further down the long road home. The path was straight. I was well. And I was free.

O plenitude of grace, by which I could presume
to fix my eyes upon eternal Light
until my sight was spent on it!

In its depth I saw contained,
by love into a single volume bound,
the pages scattered through the universe . . .

[Paradiso XXXIII:82–87]

HOW TO READ THE USER'S MANUAL OF YOUR SOUL

The persecuted Soviet-era writer Boris Pasternak wrote that his suffering under communism made him see the Bible "not so much as a book with a hard and fast text as the notebook of humanity and a key to everything that is eternal." The *Commedia* is not the Bible, of course, but for many of us, Dante's poem may have a similar effect that Scripture had on Pasternak. The *Commedia* reads you and teaches you how to read yourself, and the world.

You may read the *Commedia* and see it as a beautiful work of art and nothing more. That's worth something. But if you read it as I did, as a book that can save your life, you will find in its verses the key that unlocks the iron gates of the ego's prison and opens the door to a renewed sense of joy, purpose, and inner healing.

Like the Bible on which it depends, the *Commedia* is a book that is not a destination, but rather a map to the destination at the end of our life's pilgrimage. It is not an idol, but an icon—and it is not magic. It only works to save your life if you do what it tells you to do.

If you take up the *Commedia* and read, when you come to its end, you will understand its true message: *If you want to be healed, if you want to be free, then get up and walk—and don't stop till you get to the Promised Land.*

CONCLUSION

HOW TO MAKE YOUR OWN DANTE PILGRIMAGE

I f you have come this far and would like to experience the *Commedia* for yourself, here are the next steps:

Find a good modern translation. Don't buy the first one you see in the bookstore. No English translation of the *Commedia* can match the Italian, but some are clearly better than others. I prefer the Robert and Jean Hollander version, as well as Mark Musa's translation, both for clarity and beauty. Anthony Esolen's version is also quite good, and there are several others.

There are two important factors in deciding which translation to choose. The first is finding one whose sound and rhythm pleases you. The *Commedia* is a very long poem, and you are going to be spending a lot of time with the translator's voice. Some readers prefer the crispness of Allen Mandelbaum's translation, for example, but others find it too cerebral. John Ciardi's musical-sounding version has long been a popular favorite, but it is certainly not to everyone's taste. Compare the same passage from several different versions to see which one suits you best.

The second factor is choosing a version that has good notes, which you will need to understand historical, literary, and theological references. The Hollanders' notes are exhaustive and scholarly, but challenging for the first-time reader. Musa's notes are more accessible, but they

293

have been excised from the portable Dante version. Esolen also provides excellent notes.

Read slowly. A fast reader can get through the entire *Commedia* in a couple of weeks. But why would you want to do that? This is a book that needs to be taken slowly and savored. I spent six months with the *Commedia* the first time I read it. That's probably more than most people will care to do, but most of these cantos invite contemplation and self-reflection. There is no need to rush.

Consult other sources about Dante. One thing that slowed my reading was that I simultaneously read a number of books about Dante and the *Commedia*. This tremendously deepened my knowledge and appreciation of the work. It is not strictly necessary, but if you have the time and the interest, it's a great way to get more out of your Dante pilgrimage.

The best place for beginners to start is not with a book at all, but with the Great Courses audio lectures co-taught by Ronald Herzman and William Cook. Herzman and Cook are terrific teachers and superlative guides to Dante's text. I keep their course on my iPhone, and I listen to it repeatedly.

A must-read for Dante neophytes is Prue Shaw's *Reading Dante: From Here to Eternity*. Yale University published the notes from Giuseppe Mazzotta's popular undergraduate Dante course under the title, *Reading Dante*. It is not a polished work, but I found it remarkably helpful as a newcomer. A.N. Wilson's biography, *Dante in Love*, is a delight to read. I have listed more books I read or consulted in the bibliography.

Read Dante with others. The *Commedia* is a work of art that demands a serious commitment of time and thought. It's also a work that is so filled with luminous beauty and breathtaking insights that you want to share it with others. Why not go on a Dante pilgrimage with friends, your book club, or your class? As you have seen in this book, the *Commedia* connects powerfully with the real-life problems we all struggle with today. You don't have to be religious to love the *Commedia* and learn from it. You only have to have a curious mind and an adventurous spirit.

Fair warning: once you give yourself over to Dante, you might be forever changed. I know I will be reading the *Commedia* for the rest of my life. I am astonished by how much more I learn with each journey through its pages. It is an inexhaustible source of beauty, wisdom, and joy. May you discover in its pages the same hope, happiness, and peace that Dante gave to me.

ACKNOWLEDGMENTS

This book came together under unusual circumstances and would not exist at all if not for the indefatigable work of its editor, Alexis Gargagliano. Every writer should have the privilege of working with an editor of such skill and grace under pressure. And every writer should have the good fortune to work with a literary agent as devoted as Gary Morris at the David Black Agency, who has been a fantastic steward of my writing career.

The existence of this book would also not have been possible without my editor at *The American Conservative*, Daniel McCarthy, and my friends Howard and Roberta Ahmanson, who have been so supportive of my work these last few years. I also owe a huge debt of gratitude to Gary Rosen at *The Wall Street Journal*.

The readers of my blog at *TAC*'s website were a source of encouragement as this book took shape during 2014's Lenten season as they read and commented on my Dante blogging.

Ron Herzman, the eminent Dantist, was a helpful reader of the manuscript in various versions, and a valuable adviser. I owe Ron and his partner in *Commedia*, Prof. Bill Cook, a debt I can't possibly repay. Thanks also to Bo Bourne for introducing me to Herzman and Cook's work.

Thanks also to friends who read early versions of this manuscript and offered feedback, including Ryan Booth, Erin Manning, Frederica Mathewes-Green, Dewey and Michelle Scandurro, James Card, James K.A. Smith, and David Kern. Thanks to Bill Stephany for giving me a personal tour of Dante's Florence. I'm grateful for the friendship of Santo Vicenzino, and for his company (and for James Card's) on the pilgrimage to Florence, Ravenna, and Norcia. May we eat and drink forever in that great *salumeria* in the sky.

I thank as well my mother and father. With Ruthie's sickness and death, they have had to endure more pain in these past few years than any parents should have to suffer. I am sorry that I could not be a greater comfort to them. One day, God willing, we will all be together in paradise, where all tears will be wiped away, and all brokenness mended forever.

Dr. Tim Lindsey has taken good care of me in my struggle with the Epstein-Barr virus. The best thing he did for me was to refer me for therapy to Mike Holmes, without whose patience and direction I would not have found healing. Nor would I have found healing if not for the spiritual counsel and leadership of Father Matthew Harrington of St. John the Theologian Russian Orthodox Mission. Mike and Father Matthew were my Virgils. Let this book stand as a tribute to them as men of compassion, men of wisdom, and men of God.

If those men were my Virgils, then my wife, Julie, was and is my Beatrice. This book would not exist without her. Nothing I do would. She and our children, Matthew, Lucas, and Nora, have been infinitely patient with me during this writing of the book, and all that came before it. I am sorry that they had to deal with a husband and a father who was so sick for so long and whose vocation as a writer demands so much of them. But I am nothing without my wife and children. In them, God has given me a foretaste of heaven.

I say that, even though the last two revisions of this book were written with Lucas watching *Green Acres* in the next room. In my head, Beatrice sounds like Eva Gabor. Thanks, kid. I owe you.

BIBLIOGRAPHY

DANTE WORKS

The Divine Comedy, trans. Robert and Jean Hollander, New York, Anchor, 2002, 2004, 2008.

The Divine Comedy, trans. Mark Musa, collected as The Portable Dante, New York, Penguin USA, 1995.

The Divine Comedy, trans. John Ciardi, New York, New American Library, 2003.

Inferno, trans. Anthony Esolen, New York, Modern Library, 2003.

Vita Nova, trans. Andrew Frisardi, Evanston, Ill., Northwestern University Press, 2012.

OTHER WORKS CITED, CONSULTED, OR READ

Auerbach, Erich, *Dante: Poet of the Secular World*, New York, NYRB Classics, 2007.

Augustine, *The Confessions*, trans. Maria Boulding, Hyde Park, NY, New City Press, 2012.

Hawkins, Peter S., *Dante's Testaments: Essays in Scriptural Imagination*, Stanford, Calif., Stanford University Press, 1999.

Leithart, Peter J., *Ascent To Love*, Moscow, Idaho, Canon Press, 2001.

Markos, Louis, *Heaven and Hell: Visions of the Afterlife in the Western Poetic Tradition*, Eugene, Ore., Cascade Books, 2013.

Mazzotta, Giuseppe, *Reading Dante*, New Haven, Yale University Press, 2014.

Moevs, Christian, *The Metaphysics of Dante's Comedy*, New York and Oxford, Oxford University Press, 2005.

Nouwen, Henri J.M., *The Return of the Prodigal Son: A Story of Homecoming*, New York, Image Books, 1994.

O'Donnell, James J., *Augustine: A New Biography*, New York, HarperCollins, 2005.

Reynolds, Barbara, *Dante: The Poet, the Political Thinker, the Man*, London, I.B. Tauris, 2007.

Rubin, Harriet, *Dante in Love: The World's Greatest Poem and How It Made History*, New York, Simon & Schuster, 2004.

Shaw, Prue, *Reading Dante: From Here to Eternity*, New York, Liveright, 2014.

Smith, James K.A., "Imagining the Kingdom: How Worship Works," Grand Rapids, MI, Baker Academic, 2013.

The Dante Encyclopedia, ed. Richard Lansing, London and New York, Routledge, 2010.

Williams, Charles, *The Figure of Beatrice: A Study in Dante*, London, Faber & Faber, 1943.

Wilson, A.N., *Dante in Love*, New York, Farrar, Straus and Giroux, 2011.

ABOUT THE AUTHOR

Rod Dreher is a senior editor at *The American Conservative*. He has written and edited for the *New York Post*, *The Dallas Morning News*, *National Review*, and the *Washington Times* among others. Rod's commentary has been published in *The Wall Street Journal*, *Commentary*, and the *Weekly Standard*, among other publications, and he has appeared on NPR, ABC News, CNN, Fox News, MSNBC, and the BBC. He lives in St. Francisville, Louisiana, with his wife, Julie, and their three children. He has previously written two books, *The Little Way of Ruthie Leming* and *Crunchy Cons*.

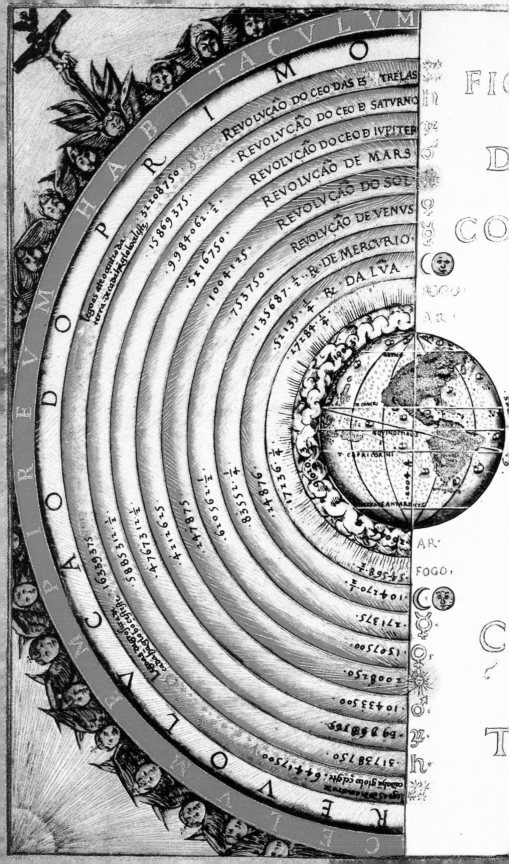